The Complete Idiot's Reference Card

Sarah's Top Ten Hints on Raising a Dog

1. **Selecting.** Research and find the right breed for you. Visit breeders and be sure to see both parents. Before picking out a puppy, use the Temperament Test to find a pup suited to you and your family.

2. **Housebreaking.** Housetraining requires consistency. Always bring your puppy to the same area to eliminate. Until the job's done, do not give your puppy unlimited access to your home. Use your Teaching Lead® to control your dog around the house and the crate or confined area when you're out of the house. Correct your puppy when he's *thinking* about peeing, *not* while he's doing it or after the fact. Praise all good elimination efforts.

3. **Doglish.** Your dog thinks you're a dog. He doesn't understand English. To train your dog properly, you must learn his language. Doglish is spoken through:

   - **Eye Contact.** You reinforce everything you look at!
   - **Body Language.** Use the peacock position to command your dog.
   - **Tone.** Dogs recognize three tones: A delighted tone, which is happy and praising; a directional tone, used to command your dog; and a disciplining tone, used when you disapprove of an action. Yelling is perceived as barking. Never yell.

4. **Negative Attention.** Your puppy/dog will repeat any behavior that is given attention, either positive (Good boy!), or negative (No! Get off! Bad boy!). Pay attention to the positive and that's what you'll get.

5. **Teaching Lead®.** Dogs learn best through structure and positive reinforcement, not chaos and corrections. Use the three applications of the Teaching Lead®: *Leading* will help you communicate leadership to your dog. He goes where *you* say! *Anchoring* teaches your dog to settle down at your feet. *Stationing* provides a special area in each room to which you can send your dog on command.

6. **Basic Training.** Training is a must! Learning the basic commands—"Heel," "Sit," "Stay," "Come," and "Down"—will help you control and communicate with your dog in all situations from going to the vet to cruising the town.

7. **Health Care.** Keep on top of your dog's health with a regular grooming schedule. You will need to care for your dog's coat, ears, nails, and teeth. Schedule the recommended series of puppy vaccinations, and follow up annually for a booster and a health check.

8. **Emergency!** Prevent emergencies by dog-proofing your home from dangerous plants and other poisonous items. In case of an accident, learn restraining techniques, CPR, appropriate transportation measures, and how to deal with life-threatening situations such as shock, choking, and bleeding.

9. **Life Changes.** Life changes can be stressful on a dog. She'll need your help adjusting. Be patient, and plan in advance to prepare for new meetings. Practice commands and encourage bonding.

10. **Grieving.** Losing your dog is horrible. When your dog dies, surround yourself with supportive people who will understand and listen. If you have a family, encourage everyone to talk about their feelings and memories.

alpha books

What To Do in Case of Poisoning

IV = Induce vomiting (if the dog swallowed the poison in the preceding 2 hours) by giving hydrogen peroxide (several teaspoons for a small dog or tablespoons for a large dog) or syrup of ipecac (1 teaspoon or 1 tablespoon, depending on dog's size).

L = Use a laxative (if it's been more than 2 hours since the poison was swallowed). Give mineral oil (1 teaspoon for dogs under 25 lbs., 1 tablespoon for 25-50 lbs., and 2 tablespoons for dogs 50 lbs. and up).

W = Wash off skin with water and vinegar.

M2M = Give Mouth-to-Muzzle resuscitation, as described in Chapter 21.

VI = Take dog to vet immediately.

VA = Schedule an appointment with the vet some time in the next week.

VO = Give a dose of vegetable oil and water to block absorption.

POISON	WHAT TO DO	POISON	WHAT TO DO
Acetone	IV, VI	Kerosene	IV, L, VO, VI
Ammonia	V, VO, VI	Lead	IV, L
Anti-freeze	IV, VI	Lime	W
Bleach	IV, VA	Insecticides	W, VI
Carbon Monoxide	M2M, VI	Paint Thinner	IV, W, VI
Charcoal Lighter Fluid	IV, L	Phenol Cleaners	W
Chocolate	IV	Rat Poison	IV, VI
Deodorants	IV, VI	Rubbing Alcohol	IV
Soap	IV, VA	Strychnine	IV, VI
Furniture Polish	IV, L, VI	Turpentine	IV, VO, VI
Gasoline	IV, VO, VI	Tylenol	IV, VA
Ibuprofen	IV, VI		

Quick Command List

Sit

Practice. As many times as you want—before a treat, dinner, petting, greeting, and playtime.

Do Not. Overcorrect your puppy for not sitting right away; by positioning and praising him, you will motivate him to want to learn!

Hand Signal. Sweep upwards from your dog's nose to your eyes with your index finger.

Down

Practice. Two to three times daily, four downs per session.

Do Not. Repeat the "Down" command more than once; command, then position. If your dog growls, seek professional help.

Hand Signal. Draw a line from your dog's nose to the floor.

Stay

Practice. Twice a day for a few minutes each time. Gradually increase the distance, duration, and distractions of your stays.

Do Not. Move more than six inches away from your dog to begin with. Remember, this is a hard one; be patient and stay calm when teaching this command.

Hand Signal. One quick flash of your flat palm in front of your dog's nose.

Come

Practice. Sparingly and never for negatives, for example to groom, crate, or discipline. Two times per day, about three downs per session. Blend in stays.

Do Not. Command come when you can't enforce it. For example, use a separate command to call your dog inside. Do not tell him to "Come," and then use treats to bribe him.

Hand Signal. A sweeping motion across your body.

Heel

Practice. Only in a counterclockwise circle to begin with, three circles, two times a day. Later, you can introduce turns and changes in pace.

Do Not. Watch your dog when you're heeling. Avoid physical contact with your dog if he gets too stimulated.

Signal. Your dog's signal is your left leg; when it moves, he moves; when it stops, so does he!

The COMPLETE IDIOT'S GUIDE TO

Choosing, Training, and Raising a Dog

by Sarah Hodgson

alpha books

A Division of Macmillan General Reference
A Simon & Schuster Macmillan Company
1633 Broadway, 7th Floor, New York, NY 10019-6705

To Christian and Laurel Eberle, my little elves.

©1996 Sarah Hodgson

International Standard Book Number: 0-02-861098-9
Library of Congress Catalog Card Number: 96-85455

98 97 96   8 7 6 5 4 3

Interpretation of the printing code: the rightmost number of the first series of numbers is the year of the book's printing; the rightmost number of the second series of numbers is the number of the book's printing. For example, a printing code of 96-1 shows that the first printing occurred in 1996.

Printed in the United States of America

Publisher
Theresa H. Murtha

Editor-in-Chief
Megan Newman

Director of Editorial Services
Brian Phair

Managing Editor
Michael Cunningham

Senior Editor
Dominique DeVito

Development Editor
Lisa Bucki

Production Editor
Noelle Gasco

Cover Designer
Dan Armstrong

Illustrators
Judd Winick
Jeff Yesh

Designer
Kim Scott

Indexer
Erika Millen

Production Team
Angela Calvert
Kim Cofer
Christine Tyner
Pamela Volk

Contents at a Glance

Contents

Foreword

I first met Sarah Hodgson a number of years ago during the Westminster Dog Show in the Press Room at Madison Square Garden. She was very young, just out of college, and was interning as an assistant to the Westminster press officer. It was hard not to notice how much running around she did from 7:30 a.m. until 12 a.m. without a pause, without one dip of energy, without one *faux pas*, unless you want to count not recognizing the president of the Westminster Kennel Club when he walked into the room. It exhausted me just to watch her as she constantly and madly dashed from the press room to the dog rings, from press room to various official booths, from the press room to japip and back again, sometimes with sandwiches for the boss, sometimes with show results clutched in her white knuckles (she was desperate to do a good job). It was something to behold. I have known only a few people in my lifetime with such great energy, and they have all enjoyed great success in their chosen fields. That is exactly what I predict for this dynamo of energy and imagination. I predict that the day is coming when people will say the name "Sarah" and everyone will know who they mean. Last name not required.

In a very short period of time, Sarah graduated from college, worked for the Westminster Kennel Club show, became a dog trainer, created her own dog training business, and wrote three books, the *third* of which you are now reading. It takes the breath away just trying to *say* the previous sentence, much less trying to comprehend it. How has she managed so much so soon? The truth is, Sarah is special.

There is a dynamic characteristic running throughout her books that draws me to them, each and every one. They are *fun* to read. And isn't that the essence of living with a dog? Sarah believes, as I do, that even training your dog can be fun. When I wrote my very first book, *Good Dog, Bad Dog*, it was highly praised and continues to be a bestseller all these years because it takes a lighthearted, somewhat humorous approach to dog training, which was until then, a very dry subject. The book was also based on what I wanted to know as a *pet owner*. This book, Sarah's book, not only offers solid, accurate information that the dog owner needs, but is highly imaginative and fun to surf through, even after you have read your fill about the essentials.

Sarah has fashioned and shaped this very clever dog book into a *kanine kaleidoscope* of basic, but very necessary, subjects for dog owners and is taking them into the 21st century with a smile and a warm feeling. Her writing style is refreshing to read and easily absorbed. Somehow, Sarah has mastered the art of the *quickpiece*, which is similar to the television sound bite. Her chapters offer bullets of important information that leap from the page. I think what I enjoyed best is her very personal writing style. It's almost as though she were talking to you rather than writing for you. Very stylish.

But the most important aspect of this book is what she has to say about dogs, people, and dogs and people. As an author of dog and cat books myself, I have a fair idea of what companion-animal people ought to know. Sarah comes through. This book addresses major dog-related issues from the cradle to the gravest of topics in a highly personal, friendly tone that is direct and enjoyable to read. *Mordecai Says*, "Look out dog people, here comes Sarah. Slide over and make room."

Mordecai Siegal

Mordecai Siegal is the President of the Dog Writers Association of America and lives in New York City. He is the author of 21 books about dogs, cats, and horses, among which are *The UC Davis Book of Dogs*, *The Cornell Book of Cats*, and *The UC Davis Book of Horses*. His work has appeared in many national magazines including *House Beautiful* where he was the monthly pet columnist for many years.

Introduction

Right off the bat, I just want to say that you're not an idiot. At least I don't think so. You may feel like one, but that's due more to a lack of appropriate information than stupidity. And that's the whole focus of this book: good information to guide you home.

Just so you know, I love dogs. Actually, "love them" is, perhaps, an understatement. I have this habit of sitting down on the ground whenever I see a dog to whisper lovingly into its ears and shower it with kisses. Yes—I even do this to strange dogs I've never met before, after I check to make sure they're safe, of course.

To me, there is nothing more appealing than a well-mannered, healthy dog. They're fun to have and be around. They're the ultimate stress-reduction solution. On the other hand, an untrained, sickly dog is a sorry sight. Why own a dog if you're not going to take care of and train it?

Now, I know most of you reading this book probably have an untrained dog, but there is a difference between you and the owners who need a shrink. You're admitting your shortcomings and doing something about them (buying and reading this book). Asking for help is the first step in solving the problem.

So let's not waste time. Whether you're starting off with a puppy or an older dog, this book covers it all. You can read it cover to cover, but you really don't have to. For example, one of the first chapters talks about purchasing a dog. If you've already done that, why read it? You might start off with a lot of regrets and I wouldn't want you to do that. No matter how many mistakes you've made so far, you probably haven't scarred your dog for life, so why be hard on yourself? The best way to approach this *read-a-book-and-train-a-dog* project is to read through the table of contents or flip through the index and find the best place to jump in.

What I Do All Day

I do have a real job in addition to writing this book for you. I am a dog teacher, or perhaps I should say a people teacher. I'm absolutely crazy about my work. Here's my typical day: I wake up at 5 a.m. to write. If I'm lucky, I get a half-hour nap around 8 a.m., then I get up, shower, and head out the door or to my office by 9:30 for my first appointment. This session can be anything from a puppy consultation to training an older dog to rehabilitating an aggressive dog.

Some days, I help people decide what breed to buy or to select a good family dog from a litter of pups. Every day is different. In addition to providing private help, I also teach groups—Puppy Kindergarten, Grade School, High School, and College—which is a whole different experience. The mix is quite exciting. Needless to say, I get a lot of experience coping with a wide array of dogs and an even greater array of people, the culmination of which is this book. In this book, I'm going to try to account for every lifestyle, dog personality, and problem that could arise in your day-to-day life. Together, we'll explore all sorts of "What should I do?" scenarios and "What if that doesn't work?" alternatives. Because every dog is different, many instructions will be presented for different personalities. And because you have different schedules and life commitments, I'll try to address those, too.

Dog school can be a fun, educational experience for all!

Decoding the Text

As this is a *Complete Idiot's Guide*, I assume that you know absolutely nothing about dogs. So if you're reading and you come across a "they have four legs and a hairy coat" description, please don't be offended. Seriously, some of what I write may seem redundant or basic to those of you in the "know," but please be forgiving to those of my readers who may be a little less informed. Raising a dog brings us together as a family, so be supportive.

Throughout the text, you'll notice a fair amount of acronyms, some of which are known in the dog world and others that just spill out of my head. Here are two examples:

AKC—The American Kennel Club

HIA—Hyper Isolation Anxiety

Can you guess which is which? AKC is known, while HIA is my own creation. To help you with jargon like this, I've included a glossary at the back of the book. If you bump into something you don't understand, check Appendix A, "Doglish Glossary" for a definition. If it isn't there, check the index in the back of the book and refer to the page provided if you need a broader explanation.

The AKC logo is recognized around the world.

Extras

One of the perks in reading (and writing) this book are the sidebar boxes that are sprinkled throughout the text. They're added to draw your attention to important information or just facts I think would be fun for you to know.

> ## Bet You Didn't Know
>
> These boxes offer insights or secrets I've picked up at work—stuff I wouldn't want you to miss.

> ## Sarah Says
> The Sarah Says tips simplify each process and clue you in to shortcuts. These tips may also highlight how to handle dogs with special temperaments.

> ## Grrr
> Don't forget to read the Grrr warning boxes! These will caution you about common errors and dangerous handling habits, such as holding the collar too tightly.

> ## Doglish
> Doglish boxes define key terms you'll need to know to come up to speed in the dog world.

Oh! One more thing before you read on. I've added a lot of stories to spruce up the text, all of which really happened. I have always found my clients—dogs and people—endearing and their individual journeys speak to us all. Again, we're one big family of Dog People.

Acknowledgments

My gosh! No project is ever the work of just one woman... This one is actually the joint effort of several women, all of whom colored this book with their charm and humor: Farah Mehta, a GREAT human being and my first reader. Thanks for being there and for pointing out all my "improper parallelisms." You're the best.

My editors...quite a team: Megan Newman, Lisa Bucki, Dominique DeVito, and Noelle Gasco. You cheered me on when my energy was low and frustrations were high. Laughter is always the spirit's best medicine.

And the others: friends and family—those with fur and without. I could not have made it this far without all of you. I would have collapsed at about Chapter 22.

Trademarks

All terms mentioned in this book that are known to be or are suspected of being trademarks or service marks have been appropriately capitalized. Alpha Books and Macmillan General Reference cannot attest to the accuracy of this information. Use of a term in this book should not be regarded as affecting the validity of any trademark or service mark.

Special Thanks from the Publisher to the Technical Reviewer

The Complete Idiot's Guide to Choosing, Training, and Raising a Dog was checked by an expert who reviewed the technical accuracy of what you'll find here. Special thanks are extended to:

Marion Lane is a writer and editor who specializes in dogs. She was employed for 10 years by The American Kennel Club, where she served as executive editor of *Pure-bred Dogs/American Kennel Gazette*. She has written hundreds of articles on a wide variety of canine subjects, and currently authors a monthly column for *Dog Fancy* magazine on living with a Staffordshire Bull Terrier. She has written one book, *Yorkshire Terriers: An Owner's Guide to a Happy, Healthy Pet*, published by Howell Book House in 1996, and is at work on another. Ms. Lane is a member of the Staffordshire Bull Terrier Club, and serves on the Board of Governors of the Dog Writer's Association of America and the Board of Directors of the American Dog Owners Association. She previously owned and operated a dog grooming shop.

Part 1
A Dog on Your Doorstep

Are you undecided about what type of dog would mesh with your lifestyle? A puppy or an older dog? A purebred or mixed breed? Small or large? High energy or couch potato? It would be divine if you could just close your eyes and wish a Lassie or Benji type to your doorstep, but (I hate to be the one to tell you) that just isn't going to happen. Even Lassie wasn't born trained!

But don't despair! That's what this part of the book is for. You'll be led through a description of the breeds and asked to consider your lifestyle in order to determine which breed or mixed breed would be best suited for you. The next few chapters will lead you step-by-step through the decision-making process for picking out your dog. From selecting a breed that will best meet the demands of your lifestyle, to finding a good breeder, to meeting your puppy's parents, or knowing what to look for in a pound puppy (or dog), these chapters cover it. Finally, before we plunge into the next part (Dog Psych 101), we'll go over what dog supplies you'll need and just how to get that puppy or dog home once and for all!

Chapter 1

A Breed-by-Breed Analysis

In This Chapter

➤ How breeding got started with domestication

➤ Breeds and the AKC

➤ Breed characteristics and mixed breeds

Before you find the dog that's right for you, let's get a better grip on the word *breed*. First, this chapter gives a little history of how the relationship between dogs and humans began. Then, the chapter takes a look at the characteristics of different breeds so you can begin developing an idea of what kind of canine companion may be right for you.

Humans have a long and intimate past with the canine. In ancient times, it wasn't even "dog" yet—it was wolf. The cave dweller and the wolf lived in a symbiotic relationship. One built fires and cooked meat; the other hung around the perimeters and ate scraps. It worked. The wolves got free food and the campsite was protected from other predators. Humans split up; some went into agriculture and some hunted. Some went north; others went south. Some took the high road...well, you get the picture. We diversified. And so did the wolf. An opportunist, he followed the fires. As human genes modified to meet the demands of the changing geography, so did the wolf's. Within each species, our size varied, our hair took on different textures, and our tolerance for climate adapted.

The Origin of Dog Breeds

Humans, always on the lookout for an opportunity, began to see the advantages of befriending the wolf. We knew from experience that wolves were excellent hunters with strong protective instincts and were loyal to their group. Though primitive at first, humans began a breeding program to produce puppies with similar instincts (for example, to herd or protect). Wolves became dogs and dogs became a species more varied and diverse in abilities and physical characteristics than any other on earth today. There are now dogs that weigh two pounds and dogs that weigh two *hundred* pounds, dogs with silky, flowing coats and dogs with no hair at all.

Bet You Didn't Know

Though it's not completely clear when the word "dog" found its way into our vocabulary, it has been estimated to occur between 15 and 25 centuries ago! The fancy name for dog is *Canis domesticus*. Wolves are called *Canis lupus*. Though dogs and wolves are considered two different species, based on their common ancestry, they can still interbreed.

From hunting, herding, and hauling to protection, pest patrol, and companionship, there's a breed to fit every function. There's even a hairless breed that was developed in Mexico to serve medicinal purposes as well as be a companion.

With some exceptions, a dog's skills are no longer necessary to our survival—but don't tell this to a dog! He still thinks his skills are very much in demand. And his breed drive won't let him slack off for lack of work. No sheep to herd? No problem. He'll herd people. No poachers to drive from the grazing lands? Then the mail carrier will have to stand in. No ducks to retrieve from the pond? That's okay. A tennis ball will do. Dogs love to work and can't be forced to make major career changes!

What's in a Breed?

If you're thinking about adding a dog to your family, it's important that you consider a suitable breed. Know what you and your family want and know what the breed was bred to do. The rest of this chapter describes the seven breed groups assigned by the American Kennel Club (AKC) and lists the breeds that fall into each breed group. These descriptions, along with Chapter 2, "Lifestyle and Litters," will help you find a breed to go with your personality and start off with a dog who can live up to your expectations!

The 142 breeds registered with the AKC are subdivided into seven groups: Sporting, Hound, Working, Herding, Non-Sporting, Terrier, and Toy. Each group shares common characteristics. To add another spin on this breed search, I have broken the groups into subgroups and listed which breeds fall under each description. Confused? Feeling dizzy? Read on; it's quite simple. Table 1.1 explains what I mean when I refer to various sizes of dogs.

Sarah Says
Please note that I refer only to the breeds recognized by the AKC. There are roughly 400 breeds recognized worldwide.

Table 1.1 Dog Size Chart

Category	Height	Weight
Small	Up to 5 inches	2–13 pounds
Medium	6–15 inches	14–45 pounds
Large	16–24 inches	46–90 pounds
Giant	25 inches +	91 + pounds

The Sporting Group

The dogs in this group were bred to aid man in hunting fowl (wild birds). Conditioned by nature to retrieve, these dogs can be trained to gather birds from the field or water or can simply stay at home and make excellent companions, fetching tennis balls, slippers, and the morning paper. There are four types of dogs in the Sporting group: pointers, retrievers, spaniels, and setters.

The Pointers

All pointers belong in the Sporting group. Tall, leggy dogs, bred to spend entire days running the fields looking for land fowl, these dogs are competitive, attentive, and *very* energetic. Without sufficient exercise, the pointing breeds have an abundance of nervous energy, which may result in destructive chewing, digging, jumping, and excessive barking. Given lots of exercise, however, you'll find them friendly, involved, and accepting of children. The pointers love an active lifestyle!

German Shorthaired Pointer

German Wirehaired Pointer

Pointer

Vizsla

Weimaraner

Wirehaired Pointing Griffon

German Short-
haired (top) and
German Wire-
haired Pointers
(bottom).

The Retrievers

Also in the Sporting group, retrievers were bred to stay close to their masters and retrieve water fowl (or nets in the case of the Portuguese version!). Well-built, large dogs, they're a bright, loyal, and active lot. Happy souls, they love to be involved in all family activities, take to training very well, and generally view all strangers as potential friends. Easy-going, retrievers make excellent family pets, but prolonged isolation upsets them. They may develop Hyper Isolation Anxiety, resulting in destructive chewing, digging, barking, and jumping.

Chesapeake Bay Retriever

Curly-Coated Retriever

Flat-Coated Retriever

Golden Retriever

Labrador Retriever

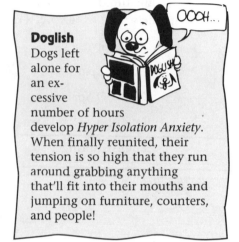

Doglish
Dogs left alone for an excessive number of hours develop *Hyper Isolation Anxiety*. When finally reunited, their tension is so high that they run around grabbing anything that'll fit into their mouths and jumping on furniture, counters, and people!

The Labrador Retriever.

The Spaniels

The low-riders of the Sporting group, spaniels were bred to find and flush birds. Trusting and friendly, spaniels fit in well with active families. Loyal, spaniels love family excursions and children, but don't like being left alone. If isolated or untrained, spaniels may become timid, whine a lot, or guard their food and other objects. As with all breeds, buy spaniels from experienced breeders only.

Water Spaniel

Cocker Spaniel

Clumber Spaniel

English Cocker Spaniel

English Springer Spaniel

Field Spaniel

Irish Water Spaniel

Sussex Spaniel

Welsh Springer Spaniel

The English Springer Spaniel.

The Setters

Majestic setters, bred to run the fields and point and flush fowl, also fall under the Sporting group. Highly intelligent, they are loyal, non-protective dogs who thrive on family interaction. As an added bonus, you'll look terrifically aristocratic as you stroll through town with a setter at the end of a leash. Exercise is a requirement for these large fellows; without it, they get high-strung and nervous.

Brittany

English Setter

Gordon Setter

Irish Setter

The Irish Setter.

Bet You Didn't Know

At first glance, the Brittany might look like a spaniel. In fact, this breed was once called the Brittany Spaniel, but the Spaniel was dropped because this dog hunts more like a setter.

The Hound Group

You ain't nothing but a hound dog. (Sorry, I just had to get that in.) These breeds like following fast-moving game and this penchant has won them over in the hunting circles. In addition to their keen noses or sharp eyesight, their easy-going and, at times, stoic personality has endeared them as family pets. There are three types of hounds: Sight, Scent, and Large Game hounds.

The Sighthounds

Relying on their eyesight to course fast-moving game, these sighthound breeds have been domesticated to make placid, gentle pets. The instinct to run after fast-moving targets, however, has never been bred out of the sighthounds—they'll need to be leashed when outdoors because you won't outrun them! In addition, they need to be socialized with common household critters at an early age so they won't confuse them for lunch as they race across your floor. Sighthounds are alert and mild and make wonderful pets in stable households.

Afghan Hound	Irish Wolfhound
Basenji	Pharaoh Hound
Borzoi	Saluki
Greyhound	Scottish Deerhound
Ibizan Hound	Whippet

The Greyhound is one of the sighthounds.

The Scent Hounds

Bred to follow scent, these hound breeds are active, lively, and rugged. That sensitive nose, however, makes them somewhat difficult to train; they'd rather trail a rabbit than hang around learning to Sit and Stay. A leash or enclosure is required when these dogs are outside—that nose again! Although a bit stubborn when it comes to training, scent hounds are happy breeds. Sweet, lively, and tolerant, they thrive on family involvement and accept children and strangers with ease.

Basset Hound	American Foxhound
Beagle	English Foxhound
Black and Tan Coonhound	Harrier
Bloodhound	Otterhound
Dachshund	Petit Basset Griffon Vendéen

The Basset Hound.

The Large Game Hounds

As you might guess, these hounds are large, powerful, and fearless when challenged as they were originally bred to hunt lions and elk. No longer used for their original purpose, the large game hounds now enjoy life as pets and watchdogs. All are strong-willed and independent and need training to enhance their sociability—and your control. These dogs are steady and calm and make devoted pets in the right home. But don't expect them to back down from an argument! Exercise and socialize these dogs to prevent destructive habits or territorial aggression.

Norwegian Elkhound

Rhodesian Ridgeback

The Rhodesian Ridgeback.

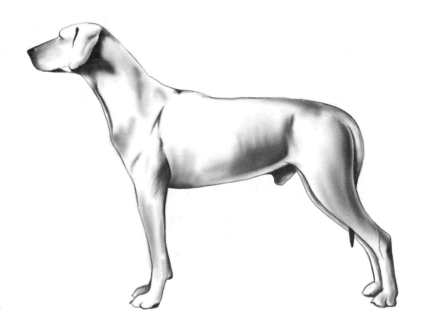

The Working Group

This classification needs little explanation. Though more varied in job description than the other groups, these breeds have one thing in common—throughout the centuries they have had a specific job to do and humans have been the beneficiaries. The sub-groups are Sled/Draft, Personal Protection, Rescue, and Estate Guarding.

The Sled/Draft Dogs

These working dogs, also referred to as Nordic breeds, love cold weather! Originally bred to pull sleds and live outside, sled dogs have thick, beautiful coats and a strong instinct to pull. Put one on the end of a leash and you'll see what I mean! Rugged and free-spirited, sled dogs need plenty of exercise and thrive outdoors. Don't try to coddle these dogs—they're not the cushion-by-the-fire type! Although strong-willed and hard to train, Nordic breeds make sweet, friendly pets if you work with them. They need exercise and attention to prevent destructive behavior. These fearless hunters will wander if given the opportunity.

Grrr
With their double coat, sledding breeds aren't much for really hot weather. If you live in a hot climate, consider another breed. These dogs would be miserable.

Sledding:

Alaskan Malamute

Samoyed

Siberian Husky

Draft:

Bernese Mountain Dog

Greater Swiss Mountain Dog

The Siberian Husky.

The Guard Dogs

Bred to protect territories and livestock without man's direction, the guard breeds are alert, intelligent, courageous, and independent. These dogs need structured training and a qualified leader. Please be sure you are up to the job—you must be the shepherd, not the sheep. Guard dogs living in a sheep's home may attack strangers who enter their territory. But in the right home (with the right owner), these dogs are calm, dignified, and devoted. Train and socialize them early to avoid later difficulties.

Akita	Komondor
Bullmastiff	Kuvasz
Great Dane	Mastiff
Great Pyrenees	Rottweiler

The Great Pyrenees.

The Personal Protection Dogs

These dogs were bred to work under the direction of man. Consequently, they are intelligent, strong-willed, and intensely loyal to one family unit. These dogs need a structured training program and early socialization to offset potential territorial aggression. For the determined and committed owner, these dogs make extraordinary companions. Without training and exercise, however, they may become aggressive, unruly, and destructive.

Doglish
What's the difference between *Standard* and *Giant*? About 6 inches and 40 pounds. It's a size thing.

OOOH...

Boxer

Doberman Pinscher

Giant Schnauzer

Standard Schnauzer

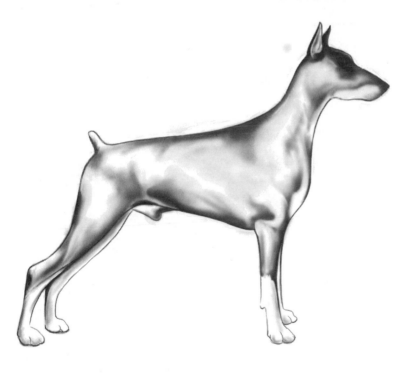

The Doberman Pinscher.

The Rescue/Water Dogs

The rescue breeds are large, low-key dogs with dense coats. They prefer cold weather to hot. Steady and intelligent, rescue breeds are exceptional around children when raised with them. Untrained and isolated, however, they than can develop Hyper Isolation Anxiety.

Newfoundland   Saint Bernard

Portuguese Water Dog

The Saint Bernard (top) and Portuguese Water Dog (bottom).

The Herding Group

The function of these breeds is as it sounds: to herd livestock. They're a hard-working crowd of dogs who, in most cases, work under the direction of a shepherd. This group can be broken down into two types: sheep herders and cattle herders.

The Sheep Herders

These herding dogs were not bred to guard the flock, but to move it. They are agile, alert, and very active. Easily trained, the sheep herders are devoted to their family, not prone to roaming, and tolerant of children. They can be protective of their property and suspicious of strangers, but they are not generally prone to serious aggression problems. These dogs love to exercise, work, and play. Always on the lookout for something to herd, they'll happily settle for children if sheep aren't available.

Australian Shepherd	Collie
Bearded Collie	German Shepherd Dog
Belgian Malinois	Old English Sheepdog
Belgian Sheepdog	Puli
Belgian Tervuren	Shetland Sheepdog
Border Collie	

The Collie is a sheep herder.

The Cattle/Sheep Driving Dogs

From the Herding group, these dogs were bred to drive sheep and move cattle long distances, often without man's direction. A hardy bunch, cattle/sheep driving dogs are more solidly built and stockier than the sheep herders. Athletic, dominant, and less predictable than their cousins, they need clear and consistent training. Generally reserved with strangers, they need early socialization to prevent aggression.

Australian Cattle Dog

Briard

Bouvier des Flandres

Cardigan Welsh Corgi

Pembroke Welsh Corgi

The Pembroke Welsh Corgi.

Terriers

Losing is not in a terrier's vocabulary. Own a terrier and one word will spring out at you immediately—determination! They take a bite out of life and won't let go! There are two types of terriers: vermin hunters and fighting breeds.

The Vermin Hunters

These self-assured, spirited breeds are a lively bunch. Originally bred to listen for and hunt vermin on the farm, they are always on the alert and feisty when set to a task. Agile and independent, they don't excel in off-leash training and need to be leashed when outdoors. If you're not a control freak and want a dog with spunk and good humor, take a good look at this list. Untrained or over-isolated, however, these dogs can become chronic barkers, chewers, or markers, and may develop aggression over objects and food.

Airedale Terrier

Australian Terrier

Bedlington Terrier

Border Terrier

Cairn Terrier

Dandie Dinmont Terrier

Fox Terrier (Smooth and Wirehaired)

Irish Terrier

Kerry Blue Terrier

Lakeland Terrier

Manchester Terrier

Miniature Schnauzer

Norfolk Terrier

Norwich Terrier

Scottish Terrier

Sealyham Terrier

Skye Terrier

Soft Coated Wheaten Terrier

Welsh Terrier

West Highland White Terrier

The West Highland White Terrier.

The Fighters

Originally bred to fight other dogs or to bait bulls, these breeds are cocky and courageous. Thankfully, they are no longer used for fighting and their combative instincts have been bred down. These dogs can make agreeable and entertaining pets. Early socialization and training are important—their pugnacious nature has been tamed, but not eliminated. Without this effort, fighting breeds can be dangerous around other animals, adults, and children.

American Staffordshire Terrier

Bull Terrier

Miniature Bull Terrier

Staffordshire Bull Terrier

Grrr
Some slightly deranged people still think it's cool to watch dogs rip each other limb from limb. Although it's illegal, it still happens, so be very careful when buying one of these puppies. Make sure your breeder is breeding for mild temperaments only.

The American Staffordshire Terrier.

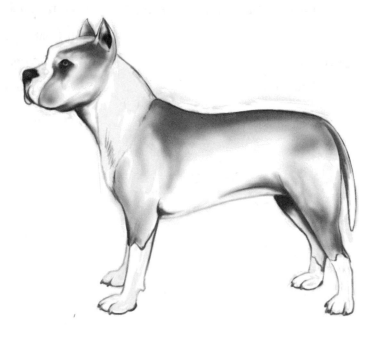

Non-Sporting Group

Many of these dogs were originally bred for specific work, but because dog work is hard to come by these days, they've become companions. Unlike other breed groups, there is little consistency in their personalities because they were all originally bred for different tasks. Before considering any of these breeds, consult breed-specific books and speak to a veterinarian to get a truer sense of what they are like.

American Eskimo Dog	Keeshond
Bichon Frise	Lhasa Apso
Boston Terrier	Poodle (Standard and Miniature)
Bulldog	Shiba Inu
Chinese Shar-Pei	Schipperke
Chow Chow	Standard Schnauzer
Dalmatian	Tibetan Spaniel
Finnish Spitz	Tibetan Terrier
French Bulldog	

The Finnish Spitz.

Toy Group

Many of these breeds are miniaturized versions of working or hunting dogs. Too small to work, they have perfected the art of being adorable. Needing little exercise (though they definitely need exercise), they are perfect for apartment dwellers and older people. Playful and devoted, they demand constant affection and attention. It's easy to neglect training for these little guys, but it's a big mistake. Although small, they can become quite tyrannical, ruling the house with constant barking and snapping. To get the most from these precious companions, train them!

Affenpinscher

Brussels Griffon

Cavalier King Charles Spaniel

Chihuahua

Chinese Crested

English Toy Spaniel

Italian Greyhound

Japanese Chin

Maltese

Miniature Pinscher

Papillon

Pekingese

Pomeranian

Pug

Shih Tzu

Silky Terrier

Toy Manchester Terrier

Toy Poodle

Yorkshire Terrier

A commonly seen member of the Toy group is the Toy Poodle.

Mixed Breeds

Many people contend that mixed breed dogs are better than purebred dogs. I've owned both and have loved them equally. Love and loyalty know no pedigree. The biggest difference between a mixed breed and a purebred is predictability. When you throw a ball into the water for a retriever, you can predict what's going to happen next. If you know or can guess something about a puppy's background, you may be able to gain some insight into his personality. Like any other dog, a mixed breed needs attention, exercise, and training.

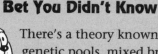

Bet You Didn't Know

There's a theory known as Hybrid Vigor. It contends that due to their larger genetic pools, mixed breed dogs are superior in health and temperament to purebred dogs. What do I think? The theory sounds good. There are a lot of health discrepancies among breeds, such as hip dysplasia. Regarding temperament, I've met as many purebred dogs as mixed with good personalities. The choice is up to you.

A friendly, garden-variety mixed breed dog.

The Least You Need To Know

➤ Now it's time to find a breed best suited for your function, which is your lifestyle. Owning *any* dog will demand a commitment of time; all require that you feed them, pet them, and take them out—even on rainy days. Certain breeds, however, will need more of your time and attention for specific activities.

➤ Breeders have created well over the 142 different breeds currently recognized by the American Kennel Club. The AKC has organized the breeds into seven groups: Sporting, Hound, Working, Herding, Terrier, Non-Sporting, and Toy.

➤ Dogs have the same gene pool, so theoretically a Chihuahua could mate with a Great Dane. Though that isn't too realistic, many dogs of different breeds mate to create mixed breed puppies.

Lifestyle and Litters

"A dog is a dog is a dog." A less true saying was never spoken! Sure, most like dog biscuits and a scratch on the special spot above their tails, but the similarity ends there. All dogs face the world in different ways. Some dogs thrive on human interaction; others prefer an independent lifestyle. Some love the general mayhem created by small children; others find it less than thrilling. Some see all house guests as long-lost friends; others see them as enemies. Some cherish quiet, solitary times; others will eat your house if you come home too late. What sounds good to you?

In this chapter, we'll consider the many aspects of dog ownership. As you read, consider *your* lifestyle. What breed personality best suits you? If you abhor the thought of exercise, you'd better stay away from very active breeds. A great-looking dog loses her appeal when she's climbing your walls. Similarly, if you're the outdoorsy type, bent on strenuous dog/owner hikes through driving snow and scorching sun, don't set your heart on a tiny companion dog. She just won't be up for it. You'll hike alone. And if your house functions as the local basketball/swimming/video game/bridge club headquarters, a protective breed might develop career stress trying to keep track of all the comings and goings.

The rest of this chapter helps you take an honest look at your schedule and lifestyle so you can make the right choice when selecting your new best friend.

Do You Know How Busy I Am?

You can see how important it is to think about your life and your personality before choosing a breed. There's lots to think about and many breeds to choose from, so let's start looking at the considerations.

Some Lifestyles Are Not Suited for Dogs

I think of one lovely woman who brought her German Shorthaired Pointer to me. At 10 months old, this dog was wild. Granted, this is a high-energy breed, but that wasn't the least of it. I found out this dog was kept in a crate in a basement 12 hours a day while everyone worked and an additional 8 while everyone slept. The husband refused to let the dog into the house because he jumped and chewed. Though this woman loved her dog, I helped her see that the dog was miserable and the most unselfish act of love would be to find this dog a new home. Fortunately, she agreed.

If you're a busy person who's out of the house the majority of the time, the kindest thing you can do is wait until your life frees up some to get a dog.

Sarah Says
A tip for potential puppy purchasers: If your schedule is unpredictable, changing from week to week, you'll need to plan ahead for your new pup. New puppies need regular feedings and lots of outings when being house-broken. Older puppies can adapt to a more flexible schedule, as long as you don't forget a feeding.

Schedules and Commitments

Are you a person with a busy social or work calendar? Dogs need lots of attention, especially when you're breaking them in or if they're pups. Just how much attention will be relative to the breed and the age, but all dogs need two to four exercise periods, two square meals, and a good block of love and attention every day. Certain breeds will need more interaction than others. Unlike guinea pigs or gerbils, dogs don't accept social isolation very well. You can't expect them to enjoy sitting in a room all day with newspapers and a bowl of water. But busy people need dog love, too! If you're an always-on-the-go type, choose an independent breed with a medium-to-low energy level *and make time in that schedule for your dog!*

If you're a work-at-home type, you (and your future dog) are in luck. Although your schedule can be complicated and hectic, you probably have the flexibility to pay lots of attention to the new arrival.

APPOINTMENT SCHEDULE	
Early Morning	*Meet Jamie for coffe at Cafe Ole*
8	*Dentist annual checkup*
9	*Group meeting*
10	
11	*New client presentation*
12	*Lunch with new clients*
1	
2	*Planning session for Smith project*
3	
4	
5	*Review session with boss*
6	*Pick up proofs from photographer*
7	
8	*Meet Chris for dinner at El Greco's*
Late Evening	

If your typical daily calendar looks like this, you should reconsider getting a dog. Four-legged friends need time and attention, too!

Fun and Leisure

What do you do for fun? Can a dog be included? Dogs don't like to be left out. And they're not choosy! Attending a soccer game, running in the park, sitting on your lap (small dogs only!) during a Garden Club meeting—it's all in a day's fun for your dog. It's lonely to be left at home. Some dogs can be very destructive if they feel deserted.

Living Quarters

Do you live in a big house or small apartment? Dogs need stretching room; the more energetic the dog, the more room required. Little dogs fit fine in big houses, but the opposite may not be true. The following table lists what living conditions are ideal for various breeds.

Also consider your neighbors. Some neighbors are less tolerant than others; if yours are the type who complain, you may run into trouble if you get a barker. Yes, they're a pain in the neck, but they're within their rights. The following table lists various breeds and how much they tend to bark.

Breed	Big House	Small Apt.	Bark Proneness
Pointers	✓	no	high
Retrievers	✓	no	medium
Spaniels	✓	with exercise	medium
Setters	✓	no	medium
Sight Hound	✓	with exercise	low
Scent Hounds	✓	with exercise	high
Large Game Hunters	✓	with exercise	low
Sled/Draft	✓	no	medium
Guarding	✓	with exercise	medium
Personal Protection	✓	with exercise	medium
Rescue	✓	with exercise	low
Sheep Herders	✓	with exercise	high
Cattle/Sheep Driving	✓	no	high
Terriers	✓	with exercise	high
Fighting Breeds	✓	with exercise	medium
Non-Sporting	✓	with exercise	varies
Toy Group	✓	yes	varies

Of course, there are always exceptions to the rule. The preceding table considers the average dog in the group. Some are worse; some are better.

Travel

Are you always flying off somewhere? Some breeds can't handle excessive kenneling. Jet-setters should find a breed that can. A few weeks here and there won't hurt. And don't forget that some hotels accept pets (hint, hint)!

Expenses

If money's a little tight right now, avoid high-maintenance dogs, such as those with pushed-in noses or skin flaps who are naturally prone to health problems. Consult a veterinarian about the breeds you're considering before you settle on one.

Your Lifestyle Situation

In addition to your activity level, you need to consider the other people and commitments in your life, too. Are you single? Do you have kids? Are you retired? These things should influence your breed decision. Listed below are six *general* lifestyle situations. You might not fit perfectly into any one category—just read them over and keep that thinking cap on!

Single People

Single. Free. No commitments. Few responsibilities. Except one—a new puppy. You'll need to adjust your schedule around her. You'll need to socialize with her, take her out to meet your friends. If you work outside the home, consider a calm breed who won't need a five-mile run twice a day to be happy. Think ahead…a long way ahead. Where will you be in five years? Ten? No pressure here, but do you think you'll have kids? Think about a kid-friendly breed and take the time to familiarize her with kids while she's a puppy.

Couples

Do you both work? Can one be home enough to care for the new four-legged baby? The more attention she gets, the better. Puppies hate to be alone! You'll need lots of patience, tolerance, and perseverance. If you plan to have kids, puppies are great practice! You'll need to plan and share responsibilities. Someone needs to walk her, feed her, and social-ize her. If you're considering a family, avoid protective, guard, and fighting breeds unless you're committed to early training and socialization with children and adults. If you both work all day, consider a more independent breed. You'll still be missed, but it won't be totally traumatic.

Families with Children Younger Than Five

You already have puppies! Kids this small see puppies as playthings, so get a breed that can tolerate rough handling. I probably don't have to tell you that it's hard to teach a three-year-old not to pull and poke the puppy; it's important to find an accepting breed. You might want to consider an older puppy between four and twelve months old. If properly raised and socialized, an older pup will be calmer and less mouthy. Unless you're an experienced owner, avoid guard, protection, and fighting breeds. They are less tolerant of visitors and children.

Families with Children Older Than Five

Kids over five can participate in a lot of puppy activities. Though you can't expect them to do all the work, they can learn a lot about responsibility through feeding, basic health care, and walking. If your kids are pretty rough-and-tumble, you'll need a breed that tolerates this. If your kids are past the rough-and-tumble stage (leaving for college, perhaps), you can consider many breeds. Again I caution you against protection, guard, and fighting breeds unless you're experienced and can make time in your schedule for extensive training. With doors flying open and kids running in and out, you want a kid-tested breed who can take it all in stride.

Retired

You made it! Congratulations. This is a great time to add a dog to your family! Your schedule is probably a bit more flexible and you can be very attentive to your new pup. But remember, a puppy can be as demanding as a baby, so if you already did the diaper changing/4:00 a.m. feeding thing and don't care to repeat it, consider an older pup (between four and twelve months) who will have a head start on house training. If your retirement plans call for quiet walks and introspection, investigate the calmer breeds. If you intend to spend your retirement hiking and cross-country skiing, choose a breed that will complement your energy level.

Households with Other Pets

Do you fit into one of the categories previously presented, but you already have other pets? That will change the dynamics, especially if your other pet is a dog. Having a well-mannered dog to teach your new addition the ropes will make your life a lot easier. On the other hand, if your resident dog is a nut case, perhaps you should consider a little training before bringing another dog into your home.

When To Consider an Older Dog

Though we'll address the issue of choosing a young pup versus an older dog more in the next chapter, there are some major differences to note while you're considering your lifestyle. Young pups often demand more time for training. They're also more active and rambunctious than most grown dogs. Some dogs, however, act like oversized pups, so if you do decide to get an adult, make sure you get one who's matured a bit!

Ask Yourself...A Questionnaire

Now for the exciting part, picking your breed! I wish I could be there to help you in person, but since I can't, here's the next best thing: the questionnaire I give to clients who hire me to help them select the right breed. Don't worry—it's fun!

Interpreting Your Questionnaire

Once you've completed this little form, look it over and cross reference your decisions to other sections of the book. For example, in Chapter 18, you'll find an exercise chart that can help you determine the energy level of various breeds. Chapter 1 goes over breed size and purpose to help you determine whether your living environment, family situation, and activity levels will coincide.

What Next?

Are you wondering what to do with this masterpiece you've just created? You have some choices:

➤ Bring it to a dog professional (trainer or veterinarian) in your area.

➤ Mail it to me. I have a service where I read these forms and suggest which breeds are best suited to your lifestyle. For $30.00, you will receive a read-out of two or three breeds and the parent club contact to locate reputable breeders in your area.

Choosing a Breed: A Questionnaire

1) **Your name:** _____

2) **Number of adults in family:** _2_____

3) **Number and ages of children (under age 18):** _____

4) **Your daily schedule (hours at home):** _____

5) **Your leisure activities:**

_____

movies _____

driving trips _____

6) **Will you include the dog in these activities?**

❏ Yes ❏ No

7) **I have other pets.**

❏ Yes ❏ No

8) **If yes, what kind?**

_____ Age _____

_____ Age _____

9) **I've owned a dog before.**

❏ Yes ❏ No

10) **I've had success training a dog.**

❏ Yes ❏ No

11) **I live in a(n)**

❏ Large house ❏ Small house ❏ Apartment

12) **I have**

❏ A large yard ❏ A small yard ❏ No yard

Please enter one of the three following responses to the activities listed below.

Ⓐ**Very little**   Ⓑ**Moderate amounts of**   Ⓒ**Extensive**

13) I have time for a dog that needs _____ grooming.

14) I have time for a dog that needs _____ training.

15) I have time for a dog that needs _____ attention.

16) I have time for a dog that needs _____ exercise.

Please check the appropriate response:

17) **I'm getting a dog to be**
   ❏ A family member   ❏ A watchdog   ❏ Used for work (type of work: _____)

18) **I'd like a dog who is _____ of children.**
   ❏ Very accepting   ❏ Tolerant, but aloof

19) **I'd like a dog who needs _____ affection.**
   ❏ Very little   ❏ Moderate amounts of   ☑ Much

20) **I'd like a dog who _____.**
   ❏ Is naturally active   ❏ Enjoys quiet walks   ☑ Doesn't need extensive exercise

21) **I'd like a dog who is _____.**
   ☑ Eager to please   ❏ Independent   ❏ Strong willed

22) **I'd like a dog who is _____ with guests.**
   ❏ Enthusiastic   ☑ Calm   ❏ Reserved
   ❏ On Guard   ❏ Indifferent

23) **I'd like a dog who is _____ strangers.**
   ❏ Naturally protective around   ❏ Accepting of   ❏ Aloof toward

24) **When we go on trips, the dog would be _____.**
   ❏ Taken along   ❏ Kenneled   ❏ Left with friends or family   *It depends*

25) **I'd prefer a dog who sheds _____.**
   ❏ Very little   ❏ A couple of times per year   ❏ Shedding doesn't matter

26) **I'd like a dog whose coat is _____.**
   ❏ Long   ❏ Short   ❏ Thick   ❏ Feathery
   ❏ Curly   ❏ Wiry   ❏ Any of the above

The Least You Need To Know

➤ Think about breed or mixed-breed personalities and what would suit you best.

➤ Take a good hard look at yourself. What do you like to do for fun? Get a breed or mixed breed who can share your interests.

➤ How much space and time do you have for your dog? Get a breed or mixed breed who can cope with your lifestyle.

➤ What's your lifestyle situation? If you have children or other pets, choose a happy-go-lucky breed that cohabitates well with others. It makes a big difference!

Chapter 3

Somewhere, Out There, a Dog Waits for Me

In This Chapter

➤ When you should bring your dog home

➤ Finding a breeder versus going to the shelter or pet store

➤ How to pick your puppy out of a litter

➤ A temperament test to take with you

➤ Selecting an older dog

Dogs are a major responsibility! If you're reading this chapter, you're off to a good start. Though getting a dog is definitely one of life's most exciting moments, please read these pages carefully before you jump in head first. There are a few things, including a puppy temperament test, you should become familiar with ahead of time.

Grrr

If you're getting a puppy older than 10 weeks, make sure the breeder has "socialized" it by introducing it to everyday situations: people, sounds, and so on. An unsocialized pup may go to pieces around strange new things like vacuums, cars, or new people and grow up to become a nervous dog.

Sarah Says

If you get a dog who misbehaves, be understanding. Bad habits result from not knowing what was expected from him in his last home. This dog will need a lot of patience and training. Remember, harsh discipline only creates more problems.

OOOH...

Doglish

Hyper Isolation Anxiety (HIA) is anxiety, canine style, that occurs when you leave your dog alone. It usually starts within minutes of separation and may (in severe cases) continue until you come home. HIA may cause destructive behavior like chewing, barking, or housesoiling.

What's the Best Age To Bring Home a Dog or Puppy?

The best age to get a dog or puppy depends on one thing: whether you're getting a dog or puppy. If you're getting a puppy, the best age is between 8 and 12 weeks. If you're getting a dog, you may have a few surprises in store; old habits might need some correcting. So unless you're sure you've picked out a perfect peach, the younger, the better.

Getting a Puppy

Many experts will tell you to bring a puppy home when it's between 6 and 8 weeks old, but I hold my "8 to 12 week" ground. Six-week-old pups nip and play in an early attempt to define a hierarchy. They even use mom as a biting bag, but she puts them in their place and teaches them respect. Respect is a good lesson for them to have learned before you bring them home. They're also just developing bladder control; waiting for a little more of that has benefits far beyond my casual explanation.

Getting a Dog

If you're getting a dog, you may have a few bad habits to deal with. This isn't a bad thing, but, at the same time, I don't want to leave you thinking all older dogs act like Lassie. Dogs are more set in their ways, like people. If "their way" jives with your lifestyle, then you're all set; if not, you may have some initial problems. For example, if you work all day and find an older dog who's accustomed to being left alone, you'll be set. If, however, you get a dog that has Hyper Isolation Anxiety or one who learned bad manners in his last home, you may have some *big-time* regrets when you come through the door of your home.

Here are some questions you should ask before bringing your dog home:

➤ How old is this dog?

➤ Has he had any training?

➤ How many homes has he had? If more than one, why?

➤ Do you know of any bad habits I may encounter: barking, housesoiling, aggression, chewing?

I'm not arguing against love at first sight. Just know the cards you're dealt beforehand.

Finding a Reputable Breeder

If you're getting a purebred puppy, do me a *big* favor—find a reputable dog breeder. How? Ask your veterinarian. Call the American Kennel Club and ask them for the parent club.

They'll recommend good breeders in your area. Use good sense when visiting a kennel. Is it clean? How about the smell? What about the dogs; are they perky and friendly? A good breeder will have as many questions for you as you will for him. Don't be offended. Concern is a good sign. If the breeder is sloppy, the kennels are a mess, and the dogs are listless and poorly kept, you won't be able to trust anything he might tell you—from the pups' pedigree to their immunizations. Be sure to question the breeder's knowledge of genetic health conditions for your specific breed. A common example is hip dysplasia, affecting dogs ranging from 15 to 200 pounds, which affects the proper development of the hip joint. Dogs prone to this condition should be OFA certified before they're bred. Insist that your breeder provides you with certification slips before you consider buying a puppy.

Here are some questions you can ask a breeder from whom you're considering buying a pup:

➤ How long have you been breeding dogs?

➤ Are the puppies socialized to unfamiliar sounds and people?

➤ Can I meet both parents?

➤ Is the purchase of the puppy guaranteed against health or behavioral defects?

Doglish
OFA, *the Orthopedic Foundation for Animals*, rates dogs' hips as excellent, good, fair, borderline, or dysplastic (mild to severe) when they're two years of age. Make sure your puppy's parents have been certified and are over two years of age.

Sarah Says
You can get a list of breeders in your area by contacting the AKC and asking for the parent club of a specific breed. This information is available from the AKC's North Carolina office. Contact them at 5580 Centerview Dr., Raleigh, NC 27606, (919) 233-3600.

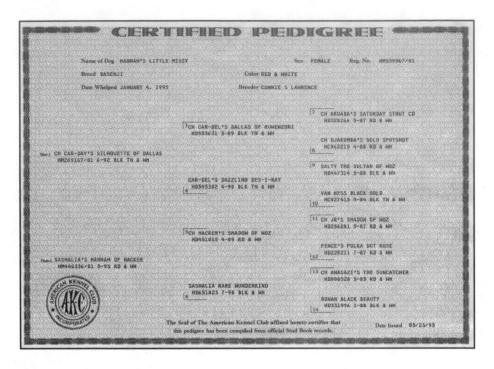

CERTIFIED PEDIGREE

Name of Dog HANNAH'S LITTLE MISSY   Sex FEMALE   Reg. No. HM559967/01

Breed BASENJI   Color RED & WHITE

Date Whelped JANUARY 4, 1995   Breeder CONNIE S LAWRENCE

Sire CH CAR-DAY'S SILHOUETTE OF DALLAS
HM269167/01 6-92 BLK TN & WH

    3 CH CAR-DEL'S DALLAS OF RUWENZORI
HD553651 5-89 BLK TN & WH

    CAR-DEL'S DAZZLING DES-I-RAY
4 HD595302 4-90 BLK TN & WH

    7 CH AKUABA'S SATURDAY STRUT CD
HD328266 5-87 RD & WH

    CH DJAKOMBA'S SOLO SPOTSHOT
8 HC962215 4-88 RD & WH

    9 SALTY THE SULTAN OF WOZ
HD447314 5-88 BLK & WH

    VAN NESS BLACK GOLD
10 HC927415 5-86 BLK TN & WH

Dam SASHALIA'S HANNAH OF HACKER
HM440356/01 5-95 RD & WH

    5 CH HACKER'S SHADOW OF WOZ
HD451015 4-89 RD & WH

    SASHALIA RARE WUNDERKIND
6 HD651823 7-90 BLK & WH

    11 CH JR'S SHADOW OF WOZ
HD256281 5-87 RD & WH

    PENCE'S POLKA DOT ROSE
12 HD228211 7-87 RD & WH

    13 CH ANASAZI'S THE SUNCATCHER
HD008528 5-85 RD & WH

    RONAN BLACK BEAUTY
14 HD331996 1-88 BLK & WH

The Seal of The American Kennel Club affixed hereto certifies that
this pedigree has been compiled from official Stud Book records.   Date Issued 05/23/95

Check out your puppy's background (pedigree)!

Sarah Says

Temperament is the key word while you're out there searching for your puppy. Purebred puppies cost money. How much will depend on the breed and your location. Ask a breeder if she stresses conformation or temperament in her breeding lines. Does she socialize the puppies? A well-bred and socialized pup will be more relaxed, less of a chewer, and more acceptable of everyday occurrences. Cost can range from $300–1,000.

➤ Have the parents been certified clear of genetic defects inherent to the breed? (You can ask your veterinarian what to look for.)

➤ Do you temperament test the litter? If not, do you mind if I do so before selecting my puppy?

The ideal situation would be to find a breeder who is dedicated to the good temperament of the breed as well as the dog's *conformation* (the dog's physical characteristics compared to the ideals for the breed), who guarantees the puppy's health, and who is willing to let you temperament test the puppies (if he or she hasn't done it) to ensure that you're ending up with a healthy puppy whose personality matches your lifestyle. When you visit the breeder, insist on meeting the mother dog and, if possible, the father dog. Their personalities leave their mark.

Pet Store Puppies

It's unbelievably cute, it's desperate, it looks so lonely, and it just went on sale—I'll take that doggy in the window!

Is this happening to you? If you're deliberating over a pet store pup, let me fill you in on the facts and then you can make your own decision. First, you have to know about puppy mills. Not every pet store gets their pups from *puppy mills*, but some do, so it's best to be informed. Puppy mills are farms that breed dogs for profit, like chickens. If you haven't seen the pictures, let me tell you, they'd break your heart—cage on top of cage, row upon row, dogs getting little human contact and poor care...a pupomatic factory. Somewhere down the line, there is a price to pay for this neglect and it usually lands in the lap of the puppy buyer. Stress takes its toll on these little creatures; they often grow up to be nervous or distrustful. If you have a choice—pet store or breeder—you know where I'd place my vote.

If you find a pet store you'd like to buy a pup from, insist that the store prove that the puppy came from a breeder. Then call that breeder and ask the same questions for breeders listed in the previous section.

> **Sarah Says**
> Avoid buying any puppy who looks sickly, acts nervous or afraid, or who can't calm down after a half hour of interaction.

A Trip to the Shelter

Going to the shelter or checking the classifieds to find a dog can be depressing. These are faces you may see in your soup for a while, so prepare yourself. You may see some dogs with limp tails and soulful expressions. There is a lot of love at animal shelters, so it's not the worst-case scenario, but it's still no fun for a dog who would much rather be curled up at someone's feet. No matter what, though, resist the temptation to take them all with you. Most dogs coming into a new home suffer from *shelter shock* and will need all your love and understanding to pull through.

Don't let all this talk scare you from your decision to rescue a dog from a shelter. It's the noblest of acts. I found the sweetest dog I've known at a shelter in Michigan and have never regretted it. But it is important you go to the shelter prepared. Here are some things to keep in mind:

> **Doglish**
> Abandonment isn't fun; abandoned dogs typically experience *shelter shock*. Sometimes it's for the best that the dog has a chance to find new owners, especially if he suffered from abuse or neglect, but a stay in the shelter is still hard on a dog's spirit.

1. What physical and personality traits are you looking for? Small or big? Pup or dog? Calm or energetic? Make a list before you go and check with the kennel workers, who can be quite helpful and can guide you to puppies or dogs that fit your criteria.

Sarah Says
If you adopt a dog from a shelter, count on having a behavior problem or two to iron out. Dogs who have spent any time at the shelter may need a refresher in the house manners department! The staff can give you an idea what to expect, but as the dog adjusts to you, more of his personality will emerge.

2. Try to find out each candidate's history. Most dogs end up at the shelter with an excuse that their owners were "moving" or have "allergies," but there's usually more to it than that. If a dog has been neglected or abused in any way, it may have behavioral problems you'll need to be prepared to cope with.

3. If you have children (or plan to have them), determine whether a dog likes them before bringing him home. Either bring your kids with you to the shelter to meet the dog or borrow some!

4. If you have other pets at home, try to determine whether or not your candidate will be accepting of them. Ask the shelter personnel if the dog was in a home with other pets or if he has had any exposure to other animals at the shelter.

5. Has the dog's health been checked? Are there any conditions (such as epilepsy or hip dysplasia) you should know about?

Sarah Says
If you find a dog, please check for tags, notify the police, and call all local shelters to make sure she isn't lost. You'd want someone else to do it for you.

6. Walk the dog. Commune with him. Look into his eyes. Does it click? Is it love at first sight? I do believe in fairy "tails" (where dogs are concerned anyway)!

When Your Dog Finds You

A day may come when a dog finds you. If it happens, it will feel like a gift from above. It'll strike you like lightning. I know; though it was a cat who found me, the experience is similar (I'm nuts about cats, too!). Life, responsibilities, and time commitments are all temporarily non-existent. "Temporarily" is the key word, however. Suddenly, you're faced with a big decision: "What do I do with this dog/puppy?" First, you must take him to the veterinarian and check his health. If he's sick or has some contagious illness, take care of it immediately. Next you need to sit down and have a heart-to-heart with yourself; can you really take on the responsibility of caring for a dog? It's the closest thing to having a baby without the diapers.

If you tally up your schedule in the dog's favor, then great! You have a new member of the family. It's time to pick a name and begin training. Most dogs who find you are going to have some baggage (bad habits) and probably suffer from isolation anxiety, so you'll have a little work to do.

If you tally up your schedule and as much as it breaks your heart, it's not consistent enough for a dog, don't feel guilty. Nothing is worse than keeping a dog cooped up all day. Use all your energy and love to find a good home for your new friend. It's far better to be part of a solution and happy ending than to create another problem—an anxiety-ridden dog. Remember, dogs need more than love to survive.

Grrr
Beware of bugs. Not to freak you out, but street dogs often play host to a whole array of parasites, both internal and external. Do the dog and your home a big favor: get to a veterinarian immediately!

Picking Out Your Puppy

You're on your way to see the puppies. You haven't seen the litter yet. I'm warning you, they're going to be unbelievably cute. This is the time to take a very firm stand: I am only taking one. Repeat this command as often as necessary until the urge to pile them all into the car passes. For more information on a multi-puppy household, please see the "Double Header" section near the end of this chapter.

So now you're peering into a box full of wriggling puppies. Chances are, one or two will capture your fancy right away. Maybe you'll like the biggest pup, the smallest pup, or the one with the most soulful expression. First impressions can be very persuasive, but you do need to look at the puppy behind the pretty face before you make your decision. You can't jump into a long-lasting relationship without asking a few questions!

Each puppy has a character all his own. Each will have his own way of approaching other puppies, interacting with you, and exploring his environment. You need to measure these qualities so you can see how the puppy's personality will complement your own.

Doglish
Littermates are siblings, canine style!

Litter Language

By seven weeks of age, puppies have begun to develop a world-view. Each has a special way of relating to littermates, mom, and the world beyond. There's a pecking order in litterland, the beginnings of a *dog pack hierarchy*. Every puppy has a place and behaves accordingly. Bright, energetic, and bossy types are highest. Those puppies with a more *laissez-faire* attitude occupy the middle ground, preferring leisure over leading. More timid types rank lower. These puppies like peace and quiet; sitting on the sidelines is just fine with them.

Doglish

Dogs live in a world that's defined by a hierarchy, not a democracy. There's order in that world—it's just different from ours. If you want to impress your dog, think leader, Top Dog, alpha— whatever!

There's a place in the world for all of these puppies, but which is right for you? You'll need persistence to convince a high-ranking puppy of your authority, patience to train the relaxed middle-grounders, and time to build up a shy puppy's self-esteem. The payback is always worth double the effort, but only *you* know what you're capable of doing.

Let's look at the range of personalities in a hypothetical litter of five puppies. You may see litters of more or less than five, but generally, each pup's personality will fall into one of these categories.

Litter Line-up

Our hypothetical litter is composed of three males and two females. I'll list each one's rank, approach to play, exploratory behavior, and greeting behavior. Then I'll describe who the right owner would be.

These pups know who's #1. Make sure you do, too!

Puppy 1: The Leader of the Pack

With Littermates: "Challenge and Win" is this puppy's motto. She loves to play and wrestle, mainly because she always wins. She thinks she's hot stuff and her behavior shows it. This is the puppy who is mock-fighting with the squeak toys and relentlessly attempting to break down the barricade.

With You: You'll probably meet her first. She'll charge forward, leap in the air, and wag her tail furiously. Don't get a swelled head—she's like that with everyone! This gal will mouth excessively, jump, and maybe even climb on top of you to show off her confident flare.

The Right Owner: Many people fall for this girl's fancy greeting act. It's so flattering! But she's not trying to flatter you—she just wants to be *first*. Very intelligent and funny, she needs an owner with the time and perseverance to train her. Without a serious commitment to training, she'll become a tyrant and will make a difficult family pet.

Puppy 2: The Next in Line

With Littermates: This puppy loves a good wrestle, too, and spends a lot of time fending off the Top Dog. When he's not under assault, he spends his time mock-fighting with lower-ranking pups and exploring his surroundings.

With You: Confident and happy, he's just not as pushy as the leader. He may mouth you and jump just to show you that he's a pretty outgoing puppy, too!

The Right Owner: Although not as cocky as #1, this puppy is energetic and boisterous and needs an owner with similar qualities. He'll keep a close eye on you and may take advantage when your back is turned. He's great with older children and a family dedicated to an assertive training regimen.

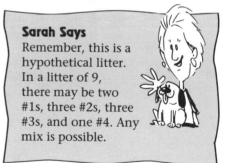

Sarah Says
Remember, this is a hypothetical litter. In a litter of 9, there may be two #1s, three #2s, three #3s, and one #4. Any mix is possible.

Puppy 3: The Middleman   *Perfecto!*

With Littermates: I call this puppy the explorer. She'll defend herself in a wrestling match, but competition is not really her cup of tea. She'd rather explore her surroundings and pursue more peaceful activities with littermates.

With You: What a relaxing change from the other two! She'll sit calmly, maybe getting up to follow you as you walk around the room. She might mouth or climb on your chest, but it will be moderate compared to you-know-who and her cohort.

The Right Owner: This dog is often ideal for laid-back families. She'll have a high tolerance for noise and confusion. Though she'll need training, occasional lapses won't result in a battle for control.

Puppy 4: The Passive Pup

With Littermates: This puppy is shy with his littermates. He submits passively to the other puppies who always know a softie when they see one. He interacts with lower-ranking siblings and enjoys quiet exploration and play.

With You: The passive puppy is calm and quiet. He might mouth you, but it will be pretty tentative. When you walk around the room, he may be more content to watch.

The Right Owner: This calm, considerate temperament needs an owner with the same qualities. Older children may enjoy this dog, but everyone must be aware of his sensitivity and use the gentlest handling techniques. This puppy needs training to enhance his self image, but it must done with much patience, very little discipline, and a lot of positive reinforcement.

Puppy 5: The Shy Pup

With Littermates: Your heart will go out to this little creature. She'll show fear when approached by her dominant littermates. She may play with puppy #4, but will usually play by herself. This pup will be the one playing with a chew toy in the corner or exploring by herself while the other puppies are wrestling.

With You: You'll feel sorry for this puppy. She'll be happiest curled in your lap and may show fear if you make sudden movements or walk across the room. She won't like loud noises at all.

The Right Owner: The shy puppy is not good with children because loud noises and chaos send her into a state of shock. She'll need a very special owner who is patient and supportive. Gentle training methods will help to develop her self-esteem.

Puppy Tryouts

Now, that you've taken a look at different puppy personalities, it's time to select your pup! The rest of this section presents seven exercises that you'll use to assess each puppy's personality. Perform each exercise with each puppy, and then rate each puppy's performance on the following Puppy Tryouts Score Card. (You can copy the card and take it with you as you visit various puppies.)

Puppy Tryouts Score Card

Rate each puppy using the following scale:

A—Active (Top Dog and Next in Line)

N—Neutral (Middleman)

P—Passive (Passive and Shy)

Name/ Number of Pup	1. Observe	2. Uplift	3. Flip-Flop	4. Gentle Caress	5. Wacky Walk	6. What's That?	7. Crash Test

By now, you should know which type of puppy you'd like to bring home with you. Active puppies are a lot of work, but they're also lots of fun. Spirited and intelligent, they are well-appreciated by those who have the time and determination needed to train them. Neutral puppies are relaxed and undemanding—sort of the "regular guys" of the dog world. Passive and shy puppies appreciate love and support, but are fearful of change. They'll do best in a consistent environment.

Test each puppy while he's awake and active. Perform each of the following activities with each puppy:

1. **Observe.** As they play with each other, observe the puppies and rate each one according to its rank in the litter. (It may help to refer to the preceding "Litter Line-up" section.)

2. **Uplift.** After observing, take each puppy aside one at a time. Cradle him mid-body and suspend him four inches off the ground. If he squirms wildly and reaches out to mouth you, give him an A. If he squirms a bit but then relaxes, give him an N. If he shudders in fear or pins his ears back and tucks his tail, give him a P.

The uplift test.

3. **Flip-Flop.** Next, lift the puppy up and cradle her upside-down like a baby. Does she squirm and try to grab at you with her mouth? Give her an A. If she wiggles a bit and then settles happily, she gets an N. If she whimpers or pulls her mouth back in tension (a submissive grin), she gets a P.

4. **Gentle Caress.** Okay! Back to Earth. Sit next to the puppy and pet him. Gently stroke him at least 15 times to judge his willingness to be handled. Does he immediately jump toward your face or scamper away toward a more stimulating distraction? Give him an A. Does he relax and sit quietly or climb in your lap? Give him an N. Does he cower, tuck his tail, pin his ears, or pull his mouth back in tension? Give him a P.

The flip-flop test.

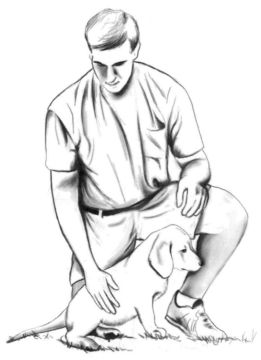

The gentle caress test.

5. **Wacky Walk.** Stand up, shake your legs, clap your hands, and encourage the pup to follow you. Bend down like a monkey if you must, just do what it takes to get her attention. Does she attack your legs or get distracted by a more interesting stimulation? Give her an A. Does she follow enthusiastically, looking up to your face for reinforcement? Give her an N. Does she sit and watch you quietly or withdraw in fear? Give her a P.

6. **What's That?** You'll need two spoons for this exercise. When the puppy is distracted, tap the spoons together above his head. If he jumps up and tries to wrestle the spoons, give him an A. If he ignores the sound or sniffs the spoons calmly, give him an N. If he cowers in fear or runs away, give him a P.

7. **Crash Test.** Walk at least six paces away from the puppy. Suddenly drop to the floor like you've fallen and hurt your knee. Don't get carried away, but make it look fairly realistic. Does the puppy take this as an invitation to play? Give her an A. Does she walk over and act curious? Give her an N. Does she run away or cower? Give her a P.

The crash test.

Letting Kids Help with the Puppy Testing

Young children can help out on the Gentle Caress and Crash Test exercises. In fact, it's a good way to see how your future puppy might get along with your current, less hairy "puppies." Older kids can do all of the tests, but only one test per puppy, please. If everyone in your family starts crashing to the floor, even the bravest puppy will head for the hills.

Tallying the Score

Now for a little score analysis. Count up your As, Ns, and Ps. Got it? If you're all As, I don't want to tell you what you're dealing with: a Leader type; one who'll want to take control if no one else steps up for the part! All Ns and you have a Middleman on your hands. Ns and Ps mean your dog is likely to be a passive and easy going. All Ps mean your dog may turn out to be shy without appropriate socialization. Identifying your pup's personality from the start will help you mold a training program that will be good for everyone.

Two Puppies: Twice the Fun or Double the Trouble?

Unfortunately, two puppies usually mean more trouble than fun. They'll pay more attention to each other than they will to you because they're dogs and you're not (nah, nah!). A single puppy will figure out ways to bridge the species gap; two puppies won't bother. This impedes training, housebreaking, chewing, and overall polite behavior. Your rules are just not as compelling as what the other puppy is doing. If one starts to tear a pillow apart, the other will join in. If one wants to obey but sees the other ignoring you, you'll be forgotten.

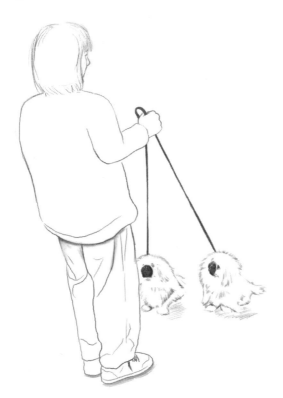

Two puppies will often pay more attention to each other than to you. You'll have to work hard to keep the training on track.

As they grow up, one will be more bossy, while the other will be a willing follower. The head honcho will want to take control in all situations, while the follower may show excessive submission and poor coping skills. Both will suffer when separated, often barking, peeing, or chewing until reunited.

At puberty, same-sex pups (especially males) often fight for Top Dog position. There may be competition for attention, food, or toys. Without behavioral conditioning, their differences could be irreconcilable.

But having two dogs can be a lot of fun for you and for them. So what to do? I suggest training *one* puppy for the first year, and then getting a second. The first puppy will form a bond with you and teach the newcomer house rules and behavior etiquette.

Selecting an Older Dog

Selecting an older dog of any age can be a lot easier. The cute factor has lost its shine. You're usually testing one dog at a time, instead of twelve. But if you have a bleeding heart like mine, a dog's individual story can suck you in even though the dog may be unsuited for your lifestyle.

So, to help you keep your head on straight, I've written some guidelines and a few tests you can set up if you're strong enough to let your head lead your heart. Nothing is sadder than rescuing a dog and having to return it because the dog couldn't cope with your life. Be strong—find out ahead of time by taking the following steps:

Sarah Says
Sometimes people get purebreds from a breeder or even from a shelter. If you get a dog from a breeder, ask her to transfer your new dog's registration to your name. If you get a purebred dog from a shelter, you can take pictures of your dog and send them to the American Kennel Club. If they agree, they will offer your dog purebred status and provide you with a registration number. Although you won't be permitted to show in conformation, this number allows you to show your dog in obedience trials.

➤ Do you have kids? Make sure you introduce them to the dog before you bring your dog home.

➤ Startle the dog. Toss your keys on the floor. Does the dog fall to pieces or attack them? These are not good signs.

➤ If you have an animal menagerie at home, make sure the dog can cope with creature chaos.

➤ Ask one of the staff (or the previous owner) to lift the dog. What happens?

➤ Bring a soft brush and try to groom the dog while feeding her treats.

Bear in mind, dogs are less accepting of strangers and strange situations than puppies, so allow some room for edginess. But if you see anything more extreme, back off, especially if it's aggression. Unless you want a major training project, look for a dog who is accepting in each test and shows patience with kids or other animals if they're a factor.

The Least You Need To Know

➤ The best age to bring a puppy home is when he is between 8 and 12 weeks old.

➤ Buy your puppy from a reputable breeder. If the breeder has more questions for you than you have for him, don't take it personally! It means he cares.

➤ Rescuing a dog or bringing one in off the streets is a truly respectable gesture—just make sure the dog's personality matches your lifestyle.

➤ How a puppy relates to littermates is how she will relate to you!

➤ Take time to check out every puppy. Doing little puppy tryouts, like those described in this chapter, will give you insight into their personalities.

➤ Resist the urge to get two puppies. They'll bond less to you, focus more on each other, and get into twice as much trouble.

➤ If you're getting an older dog, make sure you "dig up" as much information as you can and put the dog through some test situations to determine whether his personality will mesh with your lifestyle.

Chapter 4

Rolling Out Your Welcome Mat

In This Chapter

➤ Charge it!

➤ Home sweet home

➤ Surviving those first days

The day to bring home your new dog has finally arrived and your life will never be quite the same again! If you've planned ahead, rung up some goodies on the plastic, and thought through the day's events from the car ride home to the first 24 hours, you'll be off to a good start. The day may toss a screw ball or two in your direction, but if you've thought it through, there won't be anything you can't handle!

Mom's right, again—first impressions really count. To make this homecoming as smooth as possible, please read the suggestions in this chapter and resist the urge to spoil your dog or puppy before you've even brought him home. This is a pretty tall order, I know!

Doggie Decor

The day is arriving—it's time to pull out your plastic and do a little shopping for your new arrival! Though temptation may strike to buy every gimmick—from the latest toy to that designer doggy raincoat—I suggest you bring a list and stick to it. This chapter includes a sample list; the most important items are discussed next.

Shopping List for My New Dog:

❏ Crate

❏ Baby gates

❏ Fold-out pen

❏ Dog bed

❏ Collar

❏ Three bowls
(two for water and one for food)

❏ Puppy or dog food

❏ Leash

❏ Dog toys

❏ Expandable lead

❏ Soft grooming brush

❏ Nail clippers

❏ Identification tag

➤ **Crates.** The crate should be large enough to accommodate your dog when he's fully grown. Because some puppies may soil an oversized crate, buy one that has a divider available in case you need it. Ideally, the crate should be placed in a bedroom because both puppies and dogs hate being alone at night. If this is out of the question, place the crate in a well trafficked room like the kitchen or family room.

Sarah Says
You don't have to break the bank on bedding! Most dogs are happiest curled up in an old sweatshirt or a towel. Some even prefer cool tile over soft and snuggly bedding. Feel free to improvise for this item.

There are two types of crates you should consider: metal or plastic. The metal crates are sturdier and allow better ventilation—definitely a must in hot environments. The travel kennels are made from a durable plastic and serve the same purpose. If you plan to air travel frequently with your dog, I'd suggest plastic.

If the idea of a crate turns your stomach or you're home all day, *there is* another way to get through the early stages without it. I'll discuss "how to" in the training section. No dog should be left in the crate longer than six hours.

➤ **Baby Gates.** Gates are a must to close off a play room (ideally the kitchen) and to block off forbidden or dangerous areas.

➤ **Leashes.** We'll discuss training leashes more in Chapter 7. For now, purchase a lightweight nylon leash and an expandable lead, which you'll use for outdoor playtime and advanced training.

➤ **Bowls and Beds.** If you're a decorator at heart, you'll have fun shopping for these things. Look hard enough and you'll find bedding to match every room and bowls to match the tiles in your kitchen!

Stainless steel metal bowls are best for food and water. They're completely hypoallergenic, they wear well, and are easy to clean. I suggest two bowls for water: one as a staple and one to keep by the toilet bowl to discourage bowl sipping. Have the bowls and bedding ready and in position before you bring your dog home. Put water in one dish and some treats in the other dish and in the bedding. What a cool surprise!

➤ **Food.** Decide on a nutritional plan ahead of time. Dry food is best in the long run, though it may not be suitable for puppy's first few months with you. Consult your breeder or ask your veterinarian or local pet store about your dog or puppy's nutritional needs.

➤ **Collar and tag.** Have a buckle collar and tag waiting for your new arrival. If you're getting a puppy, purchase a lightweight nylon collar and a small tag. Don't worry if you haven't picked out a name. A good tag should give your phone number with a short message, such as "Please return me to 666-555-4444."

When fit properly, you should be able to comfortably slip two fingers under the collar. Check it often if you have a puppy—they grow faster than you'd think.

If you're getting a dog or puppy over 4 months, invest in a training collar. Please refer to Chapter 7 for choices and sizing.

Grrr
A tag with your dog's name and your address may endear him to dognappers or let thieves know your dog's not home to protect you. No, I'm not paranoid—just cautious.

➤ **Toys.** Be sensible. Resist the temptation to buy one of everything; too many toys will be confusing. Your dog will think that everything mouthable is fair game. And please avoid designating old shoes, socks, or other household objects as toys! You'll be sorry.

Hard bones are the best. If your plan is to use plastic or gum bones, don't give your dog edible toys. He won't settle for anything less. White, knotted rawhide can expand in the stomach, so I don't recommend it. Puppy pacifiers, gumma bones, hooves, or pig ears are safe.

Sarah Says
Call your local animal shelter and ask for more information regarding tattooing or ID chips. These quick and painless procedures are another insurance should your dog get lost or stolen.

The Trip Home

You've selected your one and only. The moment's arrived to bring him home! Unless it's a neighborhood litter, I'll assume you came by car. Now depending on the situation, the car ride can be quite an experience, so let me prepare you. Worst case scenario: your new dog gets car sick. It's a sorry sight, although there are a few precautions you can take:

> ➤ Have paper towels ready.

> ➤ Spread a sheet across the seat area prepared for your dog and bring a few clean ones just in case you need a change.

> ➤ Bring along a box for the puppy as you ride home. Boxes add a feeling of security. Place a towel on the bottom and bring extras in case your puppy gets sick.

> ➤ Bring someone along to sit with the dog, encouraging him to talk softly should the pup get nervous.

> ➤ Secure a light collar with an identification phone number (you can write it on the collar itself) in case you have an emergency or accident.

> ➤ Bring along a few chewies to divert the dog's attention.

> ➤ Drive slowly, taking each curve with care.

> ➤ Play some classical music and speak softly.

You may butt heads with some other nervous behaviors, such as whining, barking at passing objects, or eliminating. Stay calm. Don't correct your dog; it's a bad start and will only make him more anxious and homesick. Expect the worst, so no matter what happens, you'll be prepared.

Home Sweet Home

You've made it, somehow! All the anticipation has come to this very moment. The excitement level is probably up there, so take a few deep breaths. Too much tension can startle an older dog and may frighten a young puppy. I know you want to rush in and give your newest member the full tour, but hold your huskies! Remember dogs don't see their environment, they sniff it. Sniffing out an entire home might take hours and would be overwhelming. It's better to pick one room ahead of time, clean it, decorate it with dishes and bedding, and take the new pup or dog there initially. Share his curiosity as he checks out the room and speak to him sweetly. If your dog has an accident or grabs something inappropriate, don't correct him. He's too disoriented to retain anything so soon and you'll just frighten him. Relax! You're doing fine. This is just the beginning!

Are some of you wondering what you should do with the rest of your household? If you have some anticipating eyes waiting for you at home, the next few suggestions can help.

The Two-Legged Puppies

Talk about excitement. This day may be on a future "fondest memories of my childhood" list. However, it's your job to keep the kids calm. Too much squealing and loving in the first five minutes can be somewhat overwhelming for a pup. Explain the situation ahead of time and ask your children to help you make the dog or puppy feel comfortable. The rule is that they can follow quietly and speak gently, but all roughhousing, shouting, and fighting amongst themselves is forbidden. This may be your last peaceful moment for a while, so enjoy it!

Have a pow-wow! Gather everyone together and create a large circle by spreading your legs so your feet touch. Place the dog in the center of the circle and let him approach each person on his own. Discourage all unfair attention-getting ploys!

Sarah Says
Don't over-stimulate your new pal with 300 toys and millions of people.
If he is enthusiastic and wants to explore everything, go with him. If he wants to sit in a corner all day, just mill around the room, petting him as a reward for venturing out. Don't pet him if he's cowering in a corner—you'll reinforce that behavior. If you pay attention to a timid dog, you'll have a timid dog.

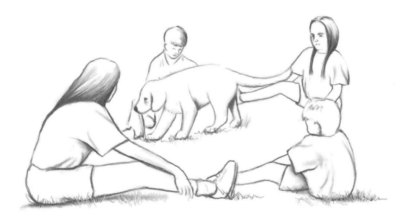

Have a pow-wow; place your puppy in the middle of a circle of family members to get acquainted.

Friends

Your friends will be the hardest creatures to control. They'll all have ideas on the best way to raise a pup. First this suggestion: don't follow your friends' advice. No offense, but what works for one person and his dog probably won't work for you and if you follow everyone's suggestions, you may aggravate your puppy. If you need help, seek out a professional.

Now for those guests—encourage company to get on the floor or sit in a low chair once your dog has calmed down. Bring your new arrival over and cradle him in a sitting position. If he's too excited, offer him a special bone to help him calm down. By ignoring him when he's excited and petting him when he's calm, you're getting a head start on encouraging good manners.

People with Special Needs

Let your common sense take over. If your dog is going to be around someone who's physically challenged, don't start off introductions by lifting the dog up to the person's face or putting a young puppy in his lap. Oh sure, your puppy may be small now, but what will happen when he grows into a 130-pound Great Dane and *still* wants to sit in Grandma's lap? Better teach that puppy to sit down next to the person and chew a special toy, one he only gets when visiting this person.

Other Pets

Don't expect your resident pets to be wearing party hats when you pull into the driveway. In all likelihood, they won't share your enthusiasm for the new family member.

Don't expect an older dog to jump with joy at the prospect of sharing his space with your new arrival. The concept may take some getting used to. It's best to make the first introductions on neutral ground before bringing them together in your home. You'll probably see a lot of *bluffing* when the two first meet.

Don't interfere unless you see an unusually aggressive response—glaring eyes, withdrawn lips, and a growl that starts in the throat or belly. Some older dogs will growl or paw at a new puppy—this is a good sign. Big dog is showing little dog who's boss. Sometimes new dogs shriek if the resident dog even comes near; again, don't interfere! If you comfort the new dog, it may alienate your resident dog and make the relationship between them rocky. To keep the hierarchy harmonious, pay more attention to your resident dog, greeting and feeding him first. As long as he feels like he's still number one in your heart, he should cope just fine. It's hard not to meddle and feel protective of your newcomer, but remember, these are dog pack rules!

Cats have mixed feelings about new dogs. Some cats head for the highest object in the house and stare at you reproachfully. Some wait confidently for the curious dog to get close enough for a good, solid bat on the nose. In either case, keep your response low-key. Overreacting will make both of them nervous. If your cat can't come to grips with the idea, keep them in separate areas and bring them together when your dog is experienced with the Teaching Lead®, which is described in Chapter 7.

Doglish
Bluffing, canine-style, can be recognized by showing of the teeth, raised hackles, and shoulder pawing. It all looks pretty scary, but rarely surfaces to a fight, so stay calm and don't interfere.

If there are other caged animals in the house, like ferrets or guinea pigs, don't bring them out immediately. Let the dog get used to you and then show him the cages when he's in a sleepy mood.

Cats and dogs can get along.

The First 24 Hours

The first day your new dog is home with you can be a little odd. After all the anticipation and preparation, your dog is home. Some dogs jump right into the swing of things; others prefer a more reserved approach. Don't compare your dog to others you've known and don't worry if he seems too rambunctious, too cautious, or too anything! This is all very new; he's trying to figure out what's going on. If he wants to sleep, let him sleep; put him in his crate (or sleep area) with the door open. At mealtime, put his food in or near his crate and leave him alone for 15 minutes. If he doesn't touch his food, that's okay. It's probably just his nerves! After the meal, give him some water and then walk him outside or to the newspapers (see Chapter 9, "Housebreaking," for more about this kind of training).

Ideally, your dog should sleep near you at night, in a large open-topped box or crate by your bedside (one he can't climb out of). He may whine the first few nights, but he'll feel a lot safer here than if he's alone in another room. If he whines, lay your hand in the box or on the crate. He (and you) may need to get up one to three times during the night to eliminate. Quietly take him to his spot and then back to his enclosure. Don't start playing games with the dog at 3:00 in the morning unless you like the habit. This topic is covered in more detail in the "Housebreaking" chapter.

If a bedroom is out of the question, crate him or enclose him in a small area, like a bathroom or kitchen. Turn off the lights, turn on some classical music, and be ready to walk him if he cries. Ahhh, the joys of doggy parenthood!

Your puppy can start out sleeping in an open-topped box by your bed so he can be close to you, but under control.

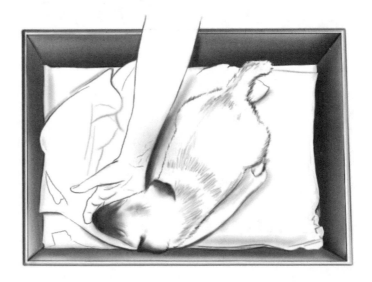

The Least You Need To Know

➤ First of all, clean up! If you bring your dog into confusion and chaos, he may act accordingly. Prepare the introductory room so when you bring your dog home, he'll have a place to go to meet the rest of the household.

➤ Do some shopping. Get bowls, a collar, leash and tag, some dog food, and bedding.

➤ Prepare for the worse possible car ride home in the history of mankind! Most dogs are fine in the car, but some get a little anxious. If your dog messes or cries, avoid disciplining him; it'll freak him out.

➤ Make a pitch to all house members to stay calm when you first come home. If you get too excited, so will your dog. Designate responsibilities and make some rules regarding "people behavior" before you bring the dog home.

➤ Your dog won't feel at home for a couple of weeks. Your dog may be fidgety, hyper, or just too disoriented to follow your plan. Avoid all discipline and try to put yourself in his paws; be patient, understanding, and attentive to his needs. Does this sound like a baby? Now you have the right idea!

Part 2
Dog Psych 101

Want to know the ultimate training tip? Your dog thinks you're a dog. Your family and friends—all dogs. Children are little dogs, other puppies perhaps, but they are factored into the equation, too. The coolest thing, if you sit down and think about it, is that dogs are the only species on the planet that will trust another species as their own. You should be honored.

What's the bottom line? To train your dog well and to solve any and all difficulties, you must start thinking and acting like a dog. Dogs can't understand what it is to be human. Sure, a dog may look afraid when someone starts yelling, but fear isn't understanding. My friends would cower too if I yelled at them, but they wouldn't like me too much.

In this part, you'll get a crash course in dog psyche, which is fascinating stuff. Not only will you know how your dog thinks, but you'll also learn how you must think if you want to be a successful teacher. You'll learn about Doglish (your dog's native language) and how to speak it and decode all of your dog's messages to you. For those of you with kids, I'll teach you how to help them avoid being typecast as puppies. Whew, there's a lot to cover! The fun awaits… your destiny is calling. It's time to start acting like a dog!

You Can Be a Good Dog Trainer, Too!

Being able to talk to animals was my lofty aspiration at the age of two. In reality, there are lots of people who have a way with animals. You'll know them in a heartbeat. They can walk into your house and have your dog behaving in seconds and looking to them as their long-lost leader. When I did this with one particular dog, it was enough to bring one of my clients (the dog's owner) to tears, "Why doesn't Alice look at me that way?" she asked.

Alice eventually did look at her owner that way, but first I taught the owner what I knew by instinct and experience—a new thought pattern, which began with a respect for her dog and an understanding of how she had played a role in creating the problem with her dog. In this chapter, you'll learn what I taught her.

A lot goes into being a good dog trainer and most of it's a mental thing. Even big dogs—dogs that weigh more than their owners—can be muscled or scared into good behavior. Dogs have spirits, just like the rest of us, that must be understood and encouraged in ways that make "dog sense." Your dog has bestowed upon you the highest honor, one you'd never receive from a human: a lifetime commitment to respect your judgment and abide by your rules. You need only to show her how.

Your First Lesson

The point of this section is to help you become a good dog trainer before you begin working with your dog. I'll go over stuff I'd teach you if I were working with you personally, stuff that will help you understand and train your dog better. There are five *key* things to remember.

A good dog trainer:

➤ Never blames the dog

➤ Recognizes the dog's unique personality

➤ Accepts and modifies his own personality

➤ Understands his role in the training process

➤ Learns from the dog

Let's go through them one at a time!

Never Blame the Dog

Believe it or not, dogs don't react out of spite. Their behavior is directly related to their owner's reactions. My mantra?

A dog will repeat whatever gets attention.

Whatever! And they don't care whether the attention is negative or positive! So if anyone is out there saying, "I tell her she's bad, but she just ignores me!" I have something to tell you: Your dog interprets your discipline as interaction and will repeat the unwanted behavior again and again. Now I probably have you wondering how to handle unruly situations. Good. I'm whetting your appetite. The first step to becoming a good dog trainer is to stop blaming the dog!

Recognize the Dog's Unique Personality

Yes, dogs have personalities, too! If you've had more than one dog, I'm sure you know exactly what I'm talking about. So many of my clients have started their sob stories with "My last dog was so easy…" "But," I respond with a smile, "this isn't your last dog. This dog is unique. And to train him, you must begin by understanding his personality."

Dogs Have Personalities, Too

Based on my experience over the years working with countless numbers of dogs, I've noticed that most dogs fit into one of six character types. Identify your dog's character type and remember it as you work through the training chapters later in this book.

➤ **Eager Beaver.** These creatures will do whatever it takes to make you happy, though they can be difficult and manic if their training is ignored. They want to please so much they stick to whatever gets attention. If you like to toss the ball, they'll bring it back 500 times. If you encourage them to jump, they'll jump on you, and everyone else, whenever excitement builds. If you encourage them to sit and settle down on command, that's what they'll do. With this dog, all you have to do is decide what you want. There is no need to use harsh training techniques.

➤ **Joe Cool.** Laid back and relaxed, they have control of every situation and seem to be less focused on you than their image. Give these fellows a command and they'll look at you as if to say, "in a minute," and then they'll forget. Organize a lesson and they'll fall asleep. Though they're quite funny and easy to live with, training is essential. Without it, they may not respond to you off lead. They may also be unmanageable in social situations. Diligent and patient training techniques are necessary.

➤ **The Jokester.** I've owned a little comedian. A quick minded perfectionist, Calvin taught me more about dog training than a lot of books I read. The reason? Comedians are revved up Wonder Dogs who'll get into a lot of trouble if they're not directed. Dancing on the edge of good behavior, they're biggest accolade is laughter and they must be firmly persuaded to cooperate. Laughter, after all, is attention—trust me, it's hard not to laugh at a dog prancing around with an oversized gourd in his mouth. Given clear, consistent, and stern instruction, comedians take to training well. Their puppyhood will test your patience, but they make wonderful dogs if trained.

➤ **The Bully.** These dogs take themselves far too seriously. In a group of dogs, these dogs would have been destined to lead, and your home is no different. Unless you're experienced, dogs of this nature can be difficult to train. Aggression, physical leaning, and mounting are common. Training must be consistent and firm and should begin in puppyhood. If this is your dog, you must lay down the law now. Professional training may be needed. Do not proceed with training if your dog threatens you.

➤ **Sweetie Pie.** Docile and mild, these dogs like to observe situations rather than control them. They adore the people they love and must be trained under a soft hand. If you yell at them, or even at one another, they'll crumble. There is little to say against these dear dogs. It's easy to skip over training for these dogs, but it's essential for their safety.

➤ **Scaredy Cat.** These dogs like to view the world from behind your legs. Soothe this behavior and you'll make it worse. Unlike children, who might feel relieved, soothing actually reinforces the dog's fear and makes it worse. You must act confident and relaxed in new and startling situations. Step away if the dog ducks behind you and only reinforce her if she calms down. Training is essential to help them feel more secure. These dogs respond best to a gentle hand.

What To Do about Psychotic Dogs

It's very rare that I come across a psychotic dog, but because they do exist, it would be irresponsible if I didn't address this issue. Some puppies have been bred very poorly and suffer brain damage as a result. These dogs can become very vicious and are a danger even as very young puppies. This problem is identified by erratic or fearful aggression responses in very atypical situations. There are two categories:

Erratic Viciousness. At unpredictable intervals, dogs with erratic viciousness will growl fiercely from the belly. It may happen when his owner passes his food bowl, approaches when he's chewing a toy, or even walks by him. At other times, the dog is perfectly sweet—a "Jekyll and Hyde" personality.

Fear Biters. These dogs show dramatic fear in or a startled bite response to non-threatening situations, like turning a page of the newspaper or moving an arm. They can act extremely confused or threatened when strangers approach. Please note that many well-educated dog people use this term incorrectly. There is a big difference in a dog that bites out of fear and a fear biter. Don't automatically assume the worst if someone labels your dog with this term.

Please don't panic if your dog occasionally growls at you or barks at the mailman. A lot of puppies growl when protecting a food dish or toy and the guarding instinct is strong in many breeds. These are behavioral problems that can be cured or controlled with proper training. Even many biters can be rehabilitated. The situations I'm speaking of involve *severe* aggression—bared teeth, hard eyes, a growl that begins in their belly, and a bite response you'd expect from a trained police dog. These personality disturbances are seen very early, usually by four months of age.

It's both frightening and tragic because nothing can be done to alter their development. Their fate has been sealed by irresponsible, greedy people. If you suspect that your dog might have either of these abnormalities, speak to your breeder and veterinarian immediately and call a specialist to analyze the situation. These puppies must be euthanized. In my career, I've seen only six; five were purchased from unknown or suspect breeders and the sixth was a mixed breed.

Recognize Your Own Personality

Now it is time to analyze yourself. What kind of person are you? Demanding? Sweet? Forgiving? Compulsive? Be honest now…Take out a pen and paper and write down three adjectives to describe your personality. Now compare them with your dog's character (identified from the list of six presented in the last section). Are you demanding, but your dog is a sweetie? Someone is going to have to change. Making too many demands on a sweet dog will frighten him. He'll shut down or run away when training begins. If you're compulsive and you have a laid back dog, you'll be laughed at. Have you ever seen a dog laugh at his owner? It's quite embarrassing. For you to be a good dog trainer, you must modify your personality to suit your dog's.

Understand Your Role in the Training Process

One of my clients called me in jubilation one day. After weeks of group training, she had figured it out. "Training is about making the dogs *want* to work with you!"

In class, I repeat the same concept many different ways. However, I understand that hearing the words and feeling their meaning rarely happens simultaneously. Though this student had listened to me, until this point, she had been training her dog by dictating her commands and muscling through all corrections. Additionally, she carried out my suggestions to the extreme: If I said to enunciate commands, she'd shout them. When I encouraged people to tap their foot lightly to end a heel, she'd stamp it.

She loves her dog tremendously, but when she started training, she was more obsessed with the mechanics than the process itself. "Remember," I would tell her, "Dog training involves two spirits: yours and your dog's. One affects the other." To understand your role in the training process, keep these things in mind:

➤ Training is about making your dog want to work with you!

➤ Your dog isn't a machine; he's a spiritual being.

➤ You are your dog's leader.

➤ Every dog learns at different rates. Frustration is catchy, so stay calm.

➤ Your mom's right again—patience is a virtue.

Learn from Your Dog

But isn't dog training about controlling the dog? No. That's not the whole story. Any dog trainer worth his weight in dog biscuits knows that learning is never a one-way street. A few years ago, I took in a rescue dog named Calvin (whom I mentioned earlier in this chapter). Here is his story:

"But Calvin, You're the Dog Trainer's Dog!"

In May of 1992, I went to Massachusetts with a friend to help her pick out a Labrador Retriever puppy. The pups were adorable, but we were continually interrupted by relentless, frantic barking coming from the other end of the barn. Occasionally, the owner would march over and spray a dog crate with a garden hose, an unkind and completely ineffective correction. I learned that this barking machine was Calvin, a seven-month-old chocolate Lab who was looking for a home. He had already driven several previous owners to distraction. My friend insisted that we take a look at this poor homeless fellow and finally I agreed. The crate opened and out popped Calvin. He was brown. He was cute. He was out of his mind!!!

We tried to ignore this leaping, licking, barking bundle of misdirected energy, but it was impossible. Suddenly, his temporary owner produced a riding crop, and I knew I had to help this confused creature. My intention was only to evaluate his personality to better help her place him. This is the first thing I do with every dog I meet. I believe that no matter how badly behaved a dog may be, there is a spirit beneath the confusion that can emerge with proper understanding and training. I saw the spirit in this dog immediately and found myself uttering the fateful words, "I'll take this dog."

I'd like to say that the rest of the story was just a perfect canine fairy tale, but it wasn't. Our first night, he grabbed a sandwich right out of my hand and swallowed it whole. The next morning, he tore the molding off of my car door and urinated all over the house. For several months, I thought I had lost my mind. He was a case study in behavior problems: housebreaking, chewing, jumping, nipping, barking, and leash pulling. He ran in the opposite direction when I called him. I enrolled him in a dog class and had to quit because he whined and agitated the other dogs.

I cried at night. I wrote poetry to keep my spirits up. Petting his head, I kept pleading with him, "But Calvin, you're the dog trainer's dog!"

Twice, I nearly gave up. Although I felt that my life had become a dog training nightmare, I realize now that Calvin taught me more than any book or lecture could. He frustrated and aggravated me and made me feel like a fool. But he also taught me patience, understanding, and commitment. And his most valuable lesson? I learned what it feels like to be one of my clients.

Somehow, we got through it. And we did it without electronic collars, riding crops, or garden hoses. Negative corrections like these create fear and confusion, not love and trust. Dogs seek out attention of any kind. In his previous homes, Calvin got negative attention for acting up. In his mind, negative attention was better than no attention. I was determined to show him a new way of doing things. I taught him that good behavior gets attention, but bad behavior does not. He learned to bring things rather than steal, to fetch a toy for guests rather than knocking them over, and to lick my hand instead of nipping it. I didn't break his spirit; I just helped him focus all that energy.

In the end, Calvin taught me a lot. In fact, here's the poem Calvin helped me write.

Our Reward

Treat me with respect, teach me your rules, and train me with patience.

Let me know what pleases you, for if you don't, my unbridled enthusiasm may place unnecessary and stressful demands on you.

There is not an animal on the planet that can offer you the same unconditional devotion that I can, if you show me the path to your heart.

Through my puppyhood I may test you, but only because I'm a puppy. Persist, for I will remember your structure as I grow into doghood.

Do not take advantage of me.
Though I have many needs, I cannot speak.

Be my leader, my keeper, my friend, and my voice.
Your efforts will be our reward.

    Sarah Hodgson

The Least You Need To Know

➤ Like snowflakes and babies' feet, no two dogs' personalities are alike. Recognize your dog's personality before you begin training.

➤ A dog can behave in various ways. How she acts is determined by your attention. Whether that attention is negative or positive makes no difference to your dog.

Understand your role in creating problems, and trust that your dog can and wants to be good.

➤ To train your dog properly, you may need to modify your personality traits. If you have a passive personality and a strong-willed dog, own up and act tough. If you're a nervous hysteric and you have a sweet pea, ease off a bit.

➤ The best dog trainers are the ones who are open to lessons only a dog can teach: patience and faith that you can develop a rewarding relationship.

Chapter 6

Not English, Doglish!

In This Chapter

➤ English to Doglish translations

➤ The irony of negative attention

➤ Positive attention rules

➤ How to be a Doglish interpreter

There is more to your little fur ball than blinking eyes and four paws! A fascinating creature in his own right, he needs you to understand where he's coming from before he'll give you his full cooperation. No matter how many stars you wish on, he'll never understand what it is to be human. Before you learn specific training techniques, you need to explore your dog's individual personality and learn his language.

Until you can think *with* and *not against* your dog, you can't really train him properly. It's impossible for your dog to be human, no matter how much you work together. So how do you think like a dog? It's quite an adventure.

The Leadership Principle

Dogs have a lot of team spirit. This is often referred to this as their "pack" instinct, but I like to think of it in "team" terms. Team consciousness and the canine psyche have a lot in common. Teams focus on winning; each player works for it, wants it, thinks about it, and strives for it. There are also some other, less obvious factors that determine a team's success. Three come to mind immediately: cooperation, structure, and mutual respect. Without these, even a group of phenomenal players would be pure chaos. A good team is organized so everyone knows who's in charge and what's expected from them. And should someone get in trouble or become hurt, he can trust that another teammate will help out.

Grrr
If you don't organize the team hierarchy, your dog will, and that can be a real nightmare. If your dog has the personality to lead, you'll be living in a very expensive doghouse under dog rule. If your dog doesn't have what it takes but feels he must lead because no one else has applied for the job, your house will be one big headache; dogs in this state are very hyper and confused.

Dogs live their entire lives, their every waking moment, by team structure. Instead of winning, however, their mantra is survival. And to personalize it one step further, you and your family are their team. For your dog to feel secure and safe, he *must* know who's in charge. It's your job to teach him what you expect from him in your home. Do you have more than one person in your household? In dogland, teams are organized in a hierarchy, so you must teach your four-legged friend that two-legged dogs are the ones in charge. This will take some cooperation on everyone's part, but it's very do-able.

So how do you organize your team and teach your dog the rules? The first step is understanding what motivates your dog's behavior. Then you need to master his communication skills. It might sound like hard work, but it's quite fascinating. Your dog will respond to you more willingly if you make the effort to understand and learn his language.

With an ounce of effort, a little time, and some structure, you'll earn your dog's respect, cooperation, and trust. Plus, you'll have a teammate who'll be at your side when the cards are down. You can't beat that bargain!

The Attention Factor

Dogs are motivated by attention. They live for it, love it, and will do anything to keep the spotlight focused on them. Does this remind you of a three year old? Well, add to this similarity the fact that they don't care whether the attention is negative or positive.

The Irony of Negative Attention

Though I'll go in depth on specific problems in chapters 9 and 10, I want to give you something to chew now to whet your appetite! Picture a very excited jumping dog. You're trying to read the paper calmly, but he wants your attention. What if you tried to correct the dog by pushing him down and screaming "Off!"? In all likelihood, the dog will jump again. Do you know why? Because you just gave him attention. Attention in a dog's mind includes anything from dramatic body contact to a simple glance. Yes, even looking at your dog will reinforce his behavior.

Does this blow your mind? Though it may sound far-fetched at first, it's actually pretty elementary. Dogs think of us as other dogs. If they get excited and then we get excited, we're following their lead. The fact that you might be upset with their behavior just doesn't register. Being upset is a human emotion. Excitement and body contact is a dog thing. Even if you push your dog so hard that he stops and slinks away, the only thing you've accomplished is scaring your dog. And who wants to train a dog through fear? Trust me, there's a better way.

Let me give you another example. What happens if a dog grabs a sock and everyone in the household stops to chase him. Dog party? You bet. Because the puppy views everybody as a dog, he's thinking, "What fun!" as he's diving behind the couch and under the table. Chasing doesn't come across as discipline; it comes across as prize envy—"Whatever I have must be really good because everyone wants it!"

Now you're wondering how to resolve these problems. We'll get there, I promise, but for now keep in mind that out-of-control negative attention reinforces the very behavior you're trying to change. I know it's frustrating. But read on and be patient.

Power of Positive Attention

When I ask my clients what they do when they catch their dog resting or chewing a bone quietly, most say, "Nothing. It's a moment of peace." I appreciate such honesty; however, that's when they ought to be showering their dog with attention. Not wild, twist-and-shout, hoot-and-holler attention, just calm, soothing, loving attention that makes them smile inside. A soft whispering praise is best mixed with a massage-like pat. Remember my mantra?

Your dog will repeat whatever you pay attention to.

So you decide. What would you rather have? A dog that stays by your side with a chew bone or a frantic sock stealer that races around the house like a maniac? If you like the sock stealer, close the book. But if the bone-chewer image appeals to you, stick with me—we're going places!

Doglish

One more thing before we jump into the how-to's of training: I have to teach you the dog's language. To be the best teacher, you need to be fluent in *Doglish*. Give your family or friends a lesson too and encourage consistency.

Doglish consist of three elements:

➤ Eye contact

➤ Body language

➤ Tone

Words, feelings, and lengthy explanations don't count anymore. Complex reasoning is impossible for your dog to follow. Dogs are so innocent in their simplicity, it's beautiful.

Eye Contact

If you're constantly looking to your dog in stressful situations (someone's at the door or the dog's stealing the dish rag) and are having trouble encouraging your dog to pay attention to you, guess what? Your dog thinks you are depending on him to be the leader. He thinks you want him to make all the judgment calls. I know you're wondering how to handle these situations. In just a few moments, I'll tell you. But for now, understand that to train your dog, you must encourage him to look to you for direction. To leave you with an off-shoot of my attention statement:

You reinforce whatever you look at.

Look at a well-behaved dog and guess what you'll have?

Body Language

Body language is a funny thing. Imagine this…your dog becomes excited and hyper when company arrives at the front door. Desperate to save face, you start shouting and pushing your dog as the company is fending the two of you off with their coats. You try every possible command—"Sit Boomer! Down! Off! Bad dog!"—but to no avail. The whole arrival scene is one big fiasco.

If your dog becomes excited and then you become excited, who's leading whom?

What's happening dear readers? Who has copied whom? Whose body language has mimicked the other's? Are you feeling silly yet? Body language is an integral part of Doglish. Play, tension, relaxation, they all have different postures. Going on the knowledge that your dog thinks you're a dog and doesn't quite grasp the *"I'm pushing you frantically because I'm unhappy with your greeting manners"* concept, what do you think you're communicating to your dog? You're the one who copied his body language. As you blaze the training trail, remember these three things:

➤ Stand upright and relax when directing your dog. I call this the *peacock position*.

➤ Don't face off or chase your dog when you're mad. To your dog, you'll look like you're playing.

➤ When trying to quiet or direct your dog, stand in front of him and stay calm.

Always remember, you set the example.

Sarah Says
Imagine a peacock—beautiful and proud, chest out, confident, and in control. When giving your dog direction or a command, throw your shoulders back and stand tall just like a peacock. Tell your family and friends about this *peacock position* and start strutting your stuff!

I hear two questions ringing throughout the pages already:

How on earth can this be done?

Can't I ever get down and play or cuddle with my dog?

We are getting there, and certainly you can get down and cuddle or play; that's one of the biggest perks in having a dog. But don't do it when your dog's in a mischievous mood or you'll be asking for trouble.

Stand up straight, relax your shoulders, and make eye contact. Peacocks rule!

Tone

If your dog thinks of you as another dog and you start yelling, what does he hear? Yes, he hears barking. And would barking calm excitement or increase it? Right again, it would increase it. Now some of you may have a dog that backs off from a situation when you yell, though he'll probably repeat the same behavior later. That's because yelling frightened him. He backed off because he was afraid of you, not because he understood. Yelling at any angle is just no good. So what works? Well, we'll get there in just a few moments, but before we begin, there are three tones you should commit to memory. I call them the three Ds:

➤ **Delighted Tone**. Your praise tone should soothe your dog, not excite him. Find a tone that makes him feel warm and proud inside.

➤ **Directive Tone**. Use this tone for your commands. It should be clear and authoritative, not harsh or sweet. Give your commands once from the peacock position.

➤ **Discipline Tone**. I'm not much of a disciplinarian. My approach encourages more structure than strictness, but you should have a few tones that tell your dog to back off or move on. I use "Ep-Ep" a lot. I'll go into more detail later, but the word doesn't matter as much as the tone. The tone should be shameful or disapproving, like "How could you" or "You better not touch that..." Discipline has more to do with timing and tone than your dog's transgressions.

Grrr
If you bend over when giving your dog a command, don't be surprised if he doesn't listen. You're doing the doggy equivalent of a *play bow* (a posture that invites a game). To put it in human terms, if you asked me to have a seat while you were hunched over looking at the floor, I'd think less of where to sit and wonder what on earth you were looking at. Stand tall and proud like a peacock when giving your dog directions.

Sarah Says
Do you have kids? Since they'll copy you, over-enunciate all of your commands so they'll learn to pronounce them properly. For example, instead of saying, "Sit," say "SIIIT." When your kids copy your intonations, the control will transfer from you to them!

As you can see, Doglish is quite different from English. Many people assume that their dog understands them when, in fact, he's often picking up the opposite message. If you chase your table snatcher, your English is saying, "How dare you," but your Doglish is saying, "PARTY!" Remember, every interaction you have with your dog gets translated into Doglish. From now on, you're being watched from a canine's eyes, so you had better start acting like one!

Grrr
Don't repeat your commands. Dogs don't understand words as words; they learn to respond to specific tones and syllables. If you say "Sit, sit, sit, Boomer sit!" that's what Boomer will learn. If you want your dog to listen when you give the first command, make sure you give it only once and reinforce your expectations by positioning your dog.

The Least You Need To Know

➤ Dogs view humans as other dogs. They relate to you, your family, and close friends as their team.

➤ Each member of the team is ranked according to leadership and organizational ability. Two-legged dogs should lead four-legged ones!

➤ Dogs don't care whether attention is negative or positive. If an action gets a reaction, a dog will repeat it. If you pay attention to a calm, well-mannered creature, then that's what you'll get. Unfortunately, the opposite is also true.

➤ Dogs don't understand English. They have their own unique language, called Doglish. To be a good teacher, you must learn their language and speak it as you train them.

Part 3
Surviving Those First Few Months

Now that the early excitement is waning, a few things may be dawning on you. For one thing, you didn't bring home a stuffed animal. Oh sure, your dog's a darling, but when she starts peeing on the rug, jumping all over the house guests, and chewing the furniture, her charm may wear off quickly. It's time to lay a good foundation for proper behavior. If you let your dog know what you expect early on, you'll run into far less trouble down the road.

If you're picking up this book and you already have a delinquent dog chewing your shoelace, it's time to start anew! Make an oath to create some structure for your dog immediately and stop all negative patterns that may have communicated a mixed message in the past. You owe it to your dog and you owe it to yourself!

This section covers everything from selecting the right equipment to finding a good diet, to laying the proper training foundation and communicating household structure—couches aren't for chewing, socks belong in the laundry basket, garbage isn't something to play with, and so on. In the end, I'll teach you some games you should be playing with your dog. After all, training doesn't have to be all structure and regime—you can have some fun, too!

Chapter 7

Collars, Leashes, and Crates, Oh My!

In This Chapter

➤ Walking you through the pet store

➤ The training collar that's right for your dog

➤ Is there an alternative to crate training?

You've come to a pivotal point in your dog training journey. If you don't start out with the right equipment and make some effort to organize your home—I repeat, *your home*—you'll have a hard time earning your dog's respect. An untrained dog running free through the house, grabbing everything in sight, and pulling you all over the neighborhood is not a pretty sight. There's a better way.

It doesn't take too much to teach your dog the necessary skills for your mutual survival: a good collar, a few leashes, and a realistic enclosure system, both inside and out. Though you may feel the restrictions of such a structured lifestyle temporarily, you'll both be a lot happier in the long run.

The Right Training Collar

You can't simply ask for a training collar. You need to be more specific. There are many different types of collars available and finding the one for your situation is a must! An ineffective training collar can hurt your dog and/or hinder the training process.

Training collar options.

Self-correcting collar

Training collar

Halter

There are quite a few collars to choose from! Since I can't be there to help you determine which is most appropriate, you'll have to question a knowledgeable source if you're confused. Other trainers, veterinarians, or groomers may be helpful. Some dog people, however, are one-collar oriented; they'll tell you only one type will work. Shy away from that advice; every situation is different. What may work wonders for you could be someone else's nightmare. Choose a collar that works for you from those described next (try them all out if you have to).

The Original Training Collar

I call this the "original" because it has been around the longest. It has some other names too, like a chain or choke collar, though when used properly, it should never choke your dog. Choking and restraining only aggravate problems. It is the sound of the collar, *not* the restraint, that teaches. To be effective, you must put on the collar properly and master the zipper snap.

If put on backward, this collar will catch in a vise hold around your dog's neck and do what the collar is not suppose to do—choke! Take these steps to ensure this doesn't happen:

To put a training collar on, create the letter "P" with the chain, slide your hand through, and hold your dog's muzzle as you slide it over his head.

1. Decide which side you want your dog to walk on. You must be consistent; dogs are easily confused. Because left is traditional, I'll use *left* as my reference.

2. Take one loop of the collar and slide the chain slack through it.

3. Create the letter "P" with the chain.

4. Holding it out, stand in front of your dog. Show him the chain.

5. Give him a treat as you praise him and slide it over his head.

Master the zipper snap. It's the sound of the collar, not the restraint, that teaches! Used properly, a quick snap (which sounds like a zipper) will correct your dog's impulse to disobey or lead. Try this without your dog: Stand up straight and relax your shoulders, letting your arms hang loosely at your side. Place your hand just behind your thigh and snap your elbow back so that you're swinging at the air behind you. Pretend my hand is there and you're trying to hit it. Now find your dog. Place your hand over the leash and snap back as he starts to lead forward. Touché!

Grrr
Do not use a training collar on a puppy younger than 16 weeks. Training collars should be used for teaching purposes only. Remove the collar when you leave your dog unattended because it can be deadly if snagged. Put your dog's tags on a buckle collar.

Doglish
Adjustable collars made of cotton, nylon, or leather are called *buckle collars*. They do not slide or choke. Their purpose is to carry your dog's tags.

If you find yourself in a constant pull battle with your dog that's only broken by occasional hacking, you might want to investigate other collar options, especially the self-correcting collar or chin lead.

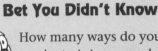

Bet You Didn't Know

How many ways do you think you can hold the leash? Just one way when you're training your dog! If you hold the lead improperly, you'll pull your dog off the ground, which will choke him. To hold the lead correctly, wrap your thumb around the bottom of the lead and your fingers over the top. Keep your arm straight as you lead your dog and snap straight back.

The Nylon Training Collar

For the right situations, these collars are a must. The rolled nylon collars work best on fine-haired dogs, whereas the flat style can work with any type of coat. These collars are a must for breeds with sensitive throats and can also be used with slow, cooperative dogs. Count your blessings if your dog falls into one of these categories.

Grrr

If you decide to try this option, let me warn you: occasionally, these collars pop off. To prevent a possible emergency, purchase an oversized training collar and attach your leash to both when walking in an unconfined area. Use this collar only when working with your dog on a leash. Left on indefinitely, these collars can cause nerve damage.

The "Self-Correcting" Collar

Yes, I know, it looks torturous, like a choke collar with large prongs. But it is perfectly humane (I promise), especially if you fall into the *I-can't-stop-choking-my-dog* category using an original training collar (choke chain). This collar works on the quick external pinch-pain principle, which is less damaging than the constant choke of the chain collar.

Developed by the Germans for many of their bull-necked breeds, it works wonders for dogs who are insensitive to pain or too powerful to be persuaded with simpler devices. Though it's officially termed a *Prong Collar*, I refer to it as *self-correcting* because it requires little strength to use. By simply locking your arm into place, even the rowdiest of dogs will feel a pinch and slow down. It's no small miracle.

The "Chin" Lead

Once again, I have given an existing product a more descriptive name. Actually, this product comes in two forms. The pet stores sell a version known as a Halti®. The other brand is called a Promise Collar® and is sold exclusively through veterinarians. What's the difference? Price, color, and a fancy video, which is available when you buy the Promise Collar®.

Some of you may think this collar looks like a muzzle when you first see it. Trust me—it's not a muzzle; dogs can eat, chew, and play happily while sporting their chin lead. If I can take that a step further, it's probably the most humane way to walk a dog. It eliminates internal or external pressure around the neck, similar to a horse on a halter.

So how does this wonder collar work? It works on the "mommy" principle. When your dog was a pup, his mom would correct him by grasping his muzzle and shaking it. This communicated, "Hey, wild one, settle down!" The chin lead has the same effect. Left on during play, the pressure on the nose discourages rowdiness and mouthing. By placing a short lead on your dog when you're expecting company, you can effectively curb jumping habits. Barking frenzies are drastically reduced and training is made simple as you guide your dog from one exercise to the next.

For those of you who can look beyond its muzzle-like appearance, the chin lead is a safe, effective, humane training tool that will give you a leg up in correcting negative behavior patterns. Another plus is that leading by the chin demands minimal physical strength, so nearly everyone can use it—kids too! Here are a few more notes:

➤ **Wearing time.** How often you should leave the chin lead on is a question best answered by your dog! If yours is relatively well-behaved, you can use it exclusively during training times. If he's the mouthing, jumping, or barking type, leave it on whenever you're around. Remove it at night or when you're out.

➤ **Sizing your chin lead.** Chin leads have a sizing scale. The chin lead must fit properly around your dog's neck. If it is too loose, your dog will pull it off and perhaps chew it. You want it to fit snugly about his ears, with enough room to fit two fingers under his neck. You may need to tie a knot with the remaining slack once you've fitted it to prevent it from loosening.

➤ **Observe how your dog reacts.** Initially, dogs don't love the idea of a head collar. Their reaction reminds me of the first day my mother dressed me in lace—I hated it. But after an hour or so, I hardly noticed it at all. I learned to tolerate it. So will your dog. When you see him flopping about like a flounder, take a breath. Once he realizes he can't get it off, he'll forget about it. Some take an hour and some take a day or two. If you want to give this collar a try, you may have to tolerate some resistance. Be patient.

Sarah Says
If a chin lead irritates your dog's nose, buy Dr. Scholl's moleskin at the drug store and wrap it around the nose piece. It's softer and will feel more comfortable. If that's ineffective, remove the chin lead and contact your veterinarian for ointment.

No-Pull Harnesses and Other Gadgets

There is nothing wrong with no-pull harnesses, though I don't recommend them professionally. They will prevent any pulling and give you a more pleasurable walk with your dog. However, prevent is the key word. They won't train your dog to walk next to you and may actually encourage more pulling when they're removed; for sled dog wanna-be's, when the leg contraption comes off, it's like being released from a shoot—see ya!

Regular harnesses encourage pulling because they force your dog in front of you. With the exception of tiny breeds, I don't recommend them to anyone who has his heart set on a well-trained dog.

Gates, Crates, and Other Enclosures

You'll need to designate an area for your mischievous dog to stay while you're not home and to cool off if things get out of hand. I like to think of the area as a cubby because it should be small, quiet, and cozy. Don't worry, dogs like cubbies—it reminds them of their wolfish den roots. You can create a cubby by gating them into a small area or buying a crate.

Gates

Gates can be used to cubby your dog in a small area, such as a bathroom. Pick an area with linoleum or a tiled floor in case of accidents and be sure it's dog-proofed. Gates can also be used to enclose a play area. Kitchens make an ideal play area because they don't confine your puppy from you.

Use your gate to discourage your dog from entering off-limit rooms and to block off dangerous stairways and ledges.

Grrr
Do not use the crate if you're gone for long 8–12 hour days. It will drive your dog nuts. Isolated all day in a kennel, he'll learn to sleep during the day and keep you up all night. You'll create a nocturnal nightmare with the energy of six stallions, which is not good for either of you.

Crates

There are several different types of crates. Sizing is important. Crates come in two varieties: wire or mesh crates, some of which fold down nicely, or portable travel kennels made from polypropylene. Both do the job. If you're an airline traveler who wants to bring your pet along, I'd opt for the travel kennel. If you're a car traveler and want a crate that's easy to transport, mesh or wire crates are your best bet.

Crates are comforting for dogs who don't know how to handle open spaces and are especially useful for those pups having toilet training troubles. The size of the crate is important when you're housebreaking a dog or pup. If the crate is too large, the puppy may eliminate in one end and sleep in the other. If you have a growing puppy, buy an adult size crate with a crate divider. Divide it so your puppy can lie comfortably and turn around only. Do the same if you have a big dog and a bigger crate. If no manufactured dividers are available, create one out of a safe, non-toxic material.

Bet You Didn't Know

Dogs love to pee on absorbent surfaces! If you're still having housebreaking problems, consider the bedding. Is it thick and plush? Maybe it's too plush—change it if needed.

Crates can be a handy training tool.

Crates can be an invaluable training tool, but they can also be emotionally destructive to your dog if overused. Crates are good in the following situations:

➤ When your dog must be left unattended for less than six hours

➤ During sleeping hours for young, unhousebroken, or mischievous puppies

➤ As a feeding station for distractible dogs

➤ As a time-out area for over-excitable pups

There are drawbacks to using crates. True, your dog can't get into trouble there, but it won't teach him how to behave in your home. Isolation provides little training and has other drawbacks too:

➤ It doesn't communicate leadership.

➤ It separates you from your dog when you're at home.

➤ It can't communicate how to behave in the house.

Canine Playpens

Do you work all day? Consider the TIP Canine Playpen for your dog. This encloses your dog to prevent destruction while giving him plenty of room to stretch and move about. You can open it during work hours and fold it down when you're home.

When you leave your dog, go quietly, dim the lights, close the curtains, and turn on some classical music to encourage peaceful rest while you're out.

Leash Essentials

Ideally, your dog should be with you when you're home. But perhaps that concept has some of you shaking in your shoes. With all that unsupervised running around and destruction, your house will be trashed, your dog will be wild, and you'll be really sorry. Obviously, there's a better way: Keep your dog on a lead. Don't worry about keeping your dog on a lead in the house; it's only temporary.

You'll need to keep your dog secured for other reasons, too. The car comes to mind quickly. Keep your dog secured for his safety as well as your own peace of mind while you're driving. Romps too. If you're not in a confined area, it's unwise to let your dog run free. Let's take a look at leads, which are another training essential.

The Teaching Lead®

The *Teaching Lead*® is a leash, but not just your garden variety. It's a sturdy leather leash with lots of holes that's designed to teach your dog good manners passively. You'll use it to limit household freedom and structure situations so you can train your dog through positive reinforcement. Sound like a dream? Too good to be true? It's not. But before you take off, you need to learn and understand its three applications, which are explained more in the next chapter. For now, let me whet your appetite:

➤ **Leading.** You'll secure your dog to your waist and lead him around using specific commands. Eventually, you'll be able to use these commands off lead. *Leading* also helps you control your dog in stressful situations and allows you to make quick corrections when necessary.

My patented teaching lead in action.

➤ **Anchoring.** *Anchoring* is the process of sliding the leash around to your backside so you'll be able to calm your dog when talking on the phone or to company or waiting for your turn at the veterinarian's.

➤ **Stationing.** Select special areas in each room for your dog that you frequent. Decorate each area with a bed and toy. Initially, you'll need to secure your dog on a lead in a special area, but eventually you'll be able to send your dog there with a command like "Settle down."

The Seat Belt Safety Lead (SBSL)™

Driving is a job in itself! Avoid being preoccupied with your dog while driving because it's a safety hazard for both of you, not to mention other motorists. Letting your dog ride in your lap or hang his body half way out the window may seem like a good idea, but it's really not. Maybe I've witnessed too many accidents, but to me, cars aren't toys and your dog is too precious to lose in a fender bender. Here's my safety rule: confine your dog while driving. There are car gates, crates, harness belts, and my invention, the *Seat Belt Safety Lead (SBSL)*™.

Car gates confine dogs to a back area in a vehicle. I find them bothersome in my station wagon because it limits what I can transport. But if you buy one, buy the best quality gate you can find. When I was in college at Michigan State University, I bought a cheap gate to confine my husky-mix, Kyia, in my station wagon. We were on our way home to New York when the gate collapsed. Poor Kyia. Being a sweet pea, he was sure he had caused the crash and was remorseful the rest of the trip home. Moral of the story? If you're going to buy a gate, buy the best!

Crates are cumbersome, but can also be used to secure your dog. Another alternative is a harness-type seat belt. This is a great concept, but is difficult to use. Dogs aren't thrilled about sitting still as you clip them in and, let's face it, who has the time?

There is, however, a great alternative that I invented. It's called the Seat Belt Safety Lead (SBSL)™. Here's what it looks like and here's how it works:

1. The handle of the SBSL™ fastens onto a seat belt. It can be left in the car permanently.

2. Now your dog has a car station. Decorate it with a blanket and a toy!

3. Bring him to the car and say "Go to your spot" as you point to the area. Offer a treat for cooperation.

4. Hook him up on a buckle collar (not a training collar). Ignore all initial protests. Praise him when he's calm.

The SBSL™ protects dogs like a seat belt protects people. It's quick, easy, and your dog will feel more secure and calm knowing his place. You're both ensured a safe arrival. My SBSL™ can be purchased by sending in the order form found in the back of this book.

*My SBSL™ will help
your dog travel
safely.*

The Short Lead

Short is relative to the size of your dog. A short lead should not be more than eight inches; for small dogs, one inch will do. My SBSL™ doubles nicely for bigger dogs. If you have a half-pint, buy a key chain and use that. Use this handy little device for two things: encouraging manners and off-leash training. Here's the theory behind both:

➤ **Encouraging good manners.** A lot of clients complain that their dogs behave like a saint on the Teaching Lead®, but when they take it off, the old derelict emerges. A short leash can serve as a nice transition from being on the Teaching Lead® to full-fledged freedom. Wearing it reminds the dog that you're still watching him and having it on gives you something to grasp for correction purposes if things get out of hand.

➤ **Off-lead training.** When we progress into off-leash work (yes, we *are* going to get there), the short lead again serves as a reminder. In addition, it gives you something to grab graciously if your dog slips up.

The Flexi-Leash®

Flexi-Leashes® are fun, period. The longer, the better. Initially, they're great for exercising. Your dog can run like mad while you stand there reading the morning newspaper. If you feel like exercising too, all the better. You can quadruple your dog's workout. When we progress to off-leash work, the Flexi is a staple. Its tidy design works like a fishing reel, letting length in and out. Although it takes some coordination, once you've mastered it, you won't be able to live without it.

Initially, do not use it near roads or heavily populated areas. Its high-tech design takes some getting used to. Practice in isolated areas until you have the system down pat! If you're out with other people, watch their legs. Most dogs get a little nutty when finally given some freedom to run. If a person gets sandwiched between you and your dashing dog, he's in for a wicked rope burn! It's best to keep play times private.

Some dogs love to chew their Flexi. After all, the exercise and freedom are so exciting! Soaking the cord in Bitter Apple® liquid (purchased from the pet store) overnight can be a good deterrent. If this is ineffective, try snapping the cord into your dog's mouth. If the worst happens and the cord is severed, get a Phillips head screw driver, open up the box, and sew the cord back together. It takes ten minutes and is cheaper than buying a new one.

> **Sarah Says**
> Are you a good knots-person? If so, you can create your lines. If not, it's better to buy canvas leads to prevent a catastrophe.

Long Lines

I'll explain how to use long lines in later sections of the book. I don't want to overwhelm you now with the details, but if you're really organized and optimistic, you can create your own long lines out of a durable dog clip and rope (all of which you can purchase at a local hardware store) and put them aside for later. There are three:

➤ **The Tree Line.** You'll tie this line onto a tree to work on long-distance focus. Buy, or create a 30-foot line.

➤ **The Drag Line.** Create or buy a 25-foot line.

➤ **The House Line.** Create or buy a 10-foot line.

Outdoor Enclosures

Dogs need to be safely enclosed when allowed to run free outside. As I tell all my clients, "If you can't fence them, leash them." It's your responsibility to provide for your dog's well-being in the world, so think it through, talk to some educated folks, and make the right decision.

If you're lucky enough to have a yard, you should think seriously about enclosing at least a portion of it. Many people ask my advice about confining their pets using pens, tie outs, runs, or electrical fences; isn't it possible to just train a dog to stay on your property?

The kind of enclosure you need differs in every situation. What kind of dog do you have? What's the dog's personality like? How do you want to use the fencing system; are you planning to leave your dog confined when you're not home or just when you're out with him? What kind of confinement would his temperament allow? How much property do you own? These are all very important considerations!

Grrr

Property training is not impossible, but it is not a safe idea. It takes a certain canine temperament and consistent training procedures over a long period of time. A dog that is property trained should not be allowed outside unsupervised.

Pens and Tie Outs

Pens and *chain link runner lines (RLs)* designed to leave the dog out of doors unattended often create what I term *Hyper Isolation Anxiety (HIA)*. Being social animals, dogs get anxious when left alone. This anxiety manifests itself in excessive barking, digging, destructive chewing, or frenetic activity when reunited with the owner. Runner lines are only beneficial if the owner remains with the dog and focuses him on exercise games. Keep in mind that the dog must be leashed when taking him to his confinement area; otherwise, he may bolt.

Full Yard Fences

Enclosing your entire property is a great option for many dogs. This enclosure enables them to enjoy their freedom and accompany you on your outdoor tasks. You can install a doggy door so your dog can monitor his own comings and goings between the house and yard. Unfortunately, full yard fences have their drawbacks, too. If the dog is left alone for prolonged periods of time, this enclosure also can create HIA. Given close access to the house, some dogs may chew the base boards around the entrance door or the welcome mat. Dogs prone to digging can also escape quite easily. Hounds, Nordic, Sporting breeds, and Terriers are just a few breeds famed for their acrobatic escapes! It only takes one escape to lose your dog to a tragic occurrence.

Electrical Fences

Grrr
Collars that transmit the stimulus are battery run. You'll need to check the battery and replace it approximately every six weeks.

One option growing in popularity is the *electrical fencing system*. This seemingly magical creation keeps dogs enclosed by an underground wire that creates a shock when a dog wearing a battery-powered collar approaches. It is the ideal system for the above mentioned dogs who habitually dig and love to run, as long as the dog is otherwise properly trained.

Dogs can get through this fence. The best guarantee is proper and patient training.

The Least You Need To Know

➤ Your first mission is to find a good training collar. Seek professional advice if you need help choosing one.

➤ If you're dealing with a young or delinquent dog, you'll need to devise an indoor enclosure system. Crates, gates, or the Teaching Lead® can all be used to monitor your dog's activities until you can trust his freedom.

➤ Securing your dog in the car is a must, for his own safety as well as yours and other drivers. Here again, you have options: a crate, harness, or Seat Belt Safety Lead (SBSL)™.

➤ Even the most well-behaved dog can be tempted outdoors. I highly recommend an outdoor enclosure system or the use of a Flexi-Leash® if your home doesn't have a yard.

Chapter 8

Bricks and Mortar: Getting Started with the Teaching Lead®

In This Chapter

➤ Using the Teaching Lead® in place of the crate

➤ Encouraging good household manners

➤ Teaching your dog to "settle down"

➤ Laying a proper foundation for training

The first thing you must accept is that your dog really doesn't know too much. She's willing to learn, but until you follow a good training regimen, she probably won't respect your rules. The complexity of the human household—the furnishings, the walls, the counters, the garbage pail—doesn't mean too much to your dog. Don't worry, though. She'll understand soon enough!

Teaching involves communication. You must convey your expectations in a way that gets through to your dog. Remember, dogs aren't human. Lengthy explanations aren't going to impress her. You'll have to be a little more inventive. Need help? Let me share with you a little invention of mine called the Teaching Lead®.

I invented the Teaching Lead® concept when training one of my own dogs, Kyia. Coming from the shelter, she was nervous, peed frequently in the house, and chewed things. Because the crate terrified her, I tied her to me and clipped her to things around the house. Soon she caught on...and the Teaching Lead® training method was born.

Working with the Teaching Lead® (or a Reasonable Facsimile)

The Teaching Lead® is a leash designed to communicate control and condition appropriate household manners without discipline or force. Have I peaked your interest? Here's what else the Teaching Lead® can do:

➤ Take the place of the crate when you're home

➤ Help you house train your dog

➤ Eliminate excessive jumping and counter sniffing

➤ Encourage appropriate chewing habits

➤ Discourage nipping

➤ Calm your dog around company

The Teaching Lead® unveiled!

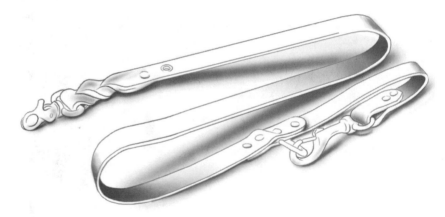

Sarah Says
Leather leashes provide better leverage while training your dog. I've always insisted on leather for my Teaching Lead® and have been complimented on its sturdiness. If you have a chewer, protect your leash with Bitter Apple® (available from pet stores) or Tabasco sauce.

And this is just the tip of the iceberg. There are many hidden benefits to using the Teaching Lead®. The best thing about it is that it's completely dog-tested, veterinarian-approved, and user-friendly!

The Teaching Lead® can't be bought in stores, but I've patented it and made it available through the order form in the back of this book. Its attractive and innovative design enables you to quickly clip the dog from your waist to immovable objects without fuss.

You can make your own by buying a sturdy leather lead and tying it around your waist. Though it's more cumbersome, it is equally effective.

It's a solution that allows you to keep your dog with you and hang onto your sanity…are you ready for more? The Teaching Lead® has three applications: leading, securing, and stationing. I'll describe each of these next.

Leading with the Teaching Lead®

This is the most humane training technique out there and it's not as hard as it sounds. *Leading* involves securing your dog to your side and leading her around the house using specific commands. (Once she understands this, you can extend your control outside.) Eventually, she'll respond to you off-lead. However, right now, she needs some direction.

 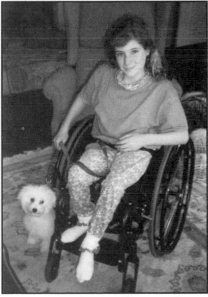

Leading with the Teaching Lead®.

Here's how to lead with the Teaching Lead®:

1. Make sure you are using the right training collar. (Remember, until your puppy is 16 weeks, use the regular buckle collar.) Please review Chapter 7, if necessary, to find the collar best suited for you and your puppy.

2. Slide the leash around your waist like a belt. Put the clip to your left side if you want your dog on the left or your right side if you want him on your right. Everyone who walks your dog must keep the him on the same side (do not have one person walk him on the left and another on the right). Connect the end clip to the appropriate waist hole and you're ready to begin!

3. To teach your dog proper leash manners and prevent pulling, take your dog to a hallway. Walk straight ahead, but watch your dog.

4. The second he walks ahead of you, call out his name as you pivot and dart in the opposite direction. Praise him, even though you may have pulled him. Continue to turn away from him until he pays attention to his name and stops trying to race ahead.

5. Now you're walking in style! Where you lead your dog must follow. This is your big chance. All household decisions are up to you. It may seem awkward at first, but soon you won't even know he's there. You might even call it fun! Remember, you're teaching your dog to follow *you*, so if there's a conflict of interest (he wants to go left when you're going right), go *your* way and encourage him to follow.

Sarah Says
Gauge your darting style for the dog's size. Do you have a monster? Dart big. A little guy? A strong step will do.

6. As you lead your dog around, start using commands conversationally. Encourage everyone around your dog to use them, too. Speak clearly, give your commands once, and enunciate your syllables; dogs understand sounds not words. Here are *five foundation* commands to get you started:

➤ **"*Name*, Let's Go!"** Give this command whenever you start walking or change direction. As you turn, hold your head high and don't look at your dog until he's turned with you.

➤ **"Sit."** Use this command whenever you offer your dog something positive like food, praise, a toy, or a pat. Say the command once, helping him into position if he doesn't respond. The most important rule of thumb is, say "Sit" once only! Dogs understand sounds; "Sit-Sit-Sit" sounds much different than "Sit."

➤ **"*Name*."** A few times each day, stand in front of your dog (proud and tall as a peacock!) and call out his name. If he doesn't look up immediately, direct his eyes toward you with a finger and a fun clucking sound.

➤ **"Wait and OK."** This duo is a real prize. Imagine getting your dog to stop before he races downstairs or across thresholds. Each time you're crossing a threshold or heavily trafficked area, command "Wait," and bring your dog behind you with his lead. He may get excited, but wait until he settles down before you command "OK." Make sure *your* feet cross the threshold first. Leaders must lead!

➤ **"Excuse Me."** Use this whenever your dog crosses in front of or behind you. Also use this if your dog presses against you or blocks your path. As you say "Excuse me," gently knock your dog out of your way. Remember, dogs respond to hierarchies, so you need to establish yourself as the leader.

If you feel like taking a break, you can do two things: have interactive play time in an outdoor enclosure or a using Flexi-Leash®, or station him as described later in this chapter (make sure his bladder is empty). There will be days when you station much more than lead—that's okay. Use both methods interchangeably, but keep that dog with you when you're home!

Everyone who can lead the dog around should! You don't want your hierarchy to become a dictatorship. The only unacceptable combination is small children and big puppies. Other than that, everyone should take part. If the lead is too long for a child, she can wear it like a banner across the chest.

Some dogs like to imitate *mules*. It's a passive form of resistance. Your dog is hoping that you will rush back and give him lots of attention, but please don't. There are two approaches to discourage this, depending on the dog and the situation.

➤ **Keep trucking.** Don't turn around! Praise the air in front of you and walk a little faster. When your dog catches up, praise him happily and continue. This method works well with large breeds who have a reputation of being stubborn.

➤ **Kneel forward.** If you have a more delicate breed or dog with a timid temperament, kneel down in front of your dog when he puts on the brakes. Tap the floor and encourage him to come to you. When he does, praise him warmly, then go to the end of the leash again and repeat yourself. He'll catch on soon. Remember, no attention for stubborn stopping and absolutely no pick ups!

Grrr

Some dogs love to walk their owners. It's enormously fun and reminds them of all those tug-of-war games you play together. The first step in correcting this problem is eliminating those tug-of-war games. When your dog takes the leash in his mouth, snap it back *into* the roof of his mouth (not out of his mouth) sharply and give a firm "No!"

Sarah Says

If your dog or puppy isn't leash trained, put some biscuits in a cup, place your dog on lead, and shake the cup as you walk around, encouraging him to follow by saying "Let's go!" Then, pick up the lead and walk around with the cup. Stop every ten feet or so and give the dog a treat.

Letting your dog run free in your house before he's trained can be a big mistake. He'll run wild, you'll chase him, and the whole thing will be remembered as one big game! He'll think dogs lead and people follow. Instead, leading will give you the upper hand. Your dog will learn to follow your lead and you'll be able to quickly discourage all inappropriate behavior and reinforce the good stuff!

Anchoring Your Dog

As you're leading, you may need to sit down to talk on the phone, do homework, talk to the plumber, or whatever. If you let your dog free at such a point, he might create havoc in his constant vigil to get your attention. Jumping on the counter or chewing the drapes can be real eye catchers, even when your attention is elsewhere. Instead of these habits, I advise you to create a more civilized routine. I call it *anchoring*.

Anchoring helps your dog learn to lie down.

With your dog secured to your side, slide the end clip around to your tail bone and sit on the remaining slack of the leash. Leave enough room for your dog to lie comfortably *behind* your feet and offer him a favorite bone to keep him occupied. Pet and praise your dog when he settles down or chews his bone.

Stationing

Stationing gives you the freedom to take your dog into each room of the house and show him how to behave there!

Stationing gives your dog an area to take it easy in.

To station your dog or puppy, you'll first need to select your areas. Go into each room you'd like your dog to behave in. Pick a good area for him to settle in—perhaps one near the couch in the TV room, but away from the table in the dining room. This will be his *station*. Eventually, he'll go there automatically. Right now, you must secure him on a lead.

Bet You Didn't Know

Dogs like to have a special place. Think of it on human terms; when you go into your living room, don't you have a favorite couch or chair?

Decorate each station with a comfy cushion or blanket and a favorite chew toy. This will help your dog identify his space. Ask your veterinarian for suggestions. Avoid rawhide bones with big knots—they can cause indigestion and other problems. Remove end fragments of hoofs or rawhide to discourage gulping.

Purchase and use a product like Bitter Apple® to discourage test-chewing of the surrounding furniture or rugs. You can find it at your local pet store.

Initially, tie your dog at his station until he learns his place. Wrap the Teaching Lead® around an immovable object and attach the top clip to the opposite end of the leash. Alternatively, you can screw an eye hook into the wall and clip the leash through it. When stationed, your dog should have no more than three feet of freedom; given too much room, he may piddle or pace.

If your dog chews on the leash, you can discourage him by rubbing Bitter Apple® Paste on the leash. It's vile tasting, but harmless. If Bitter Apple® is not effective, you can try a home-cooked mixture: some red pepper juice with a little garlic or Tabasco sauce. If all else fails, get a chain lead and temporarily station him on that.

If you must leave your dog, tell him to "Wait." Short departures are good because they get your dog used to being left alone and show him that you won't desert him. Go calmly. If he's excited when you return, ignore him. You don't want to reinforce that. When he's calm, give him attention.

When first practicing the stationing procedure, stay with your dog. Make him feel comfortable in the area and encourage him to chew his bone. Leave him only when he's busy with a chew toy or resting.

Bravely ignore whining or barking, unless your dog's communicating a need to go out. If he barks and you soothe him, you're teaching a lesson with headache written all over it. You may try distracting your dog by using a fancy long-distance squirt gun. (I found the Super Soaker to be very effective—long range and accurate, too!) But you must be very sneaky; he can't know where the water is coming from. Only release a dog from a station once he's calm and quiet.

As you lead your dog to his station, give the command to "Settle down" and point to his spot.

WARNING TO PUPPY OWNERS: Puppies can't handle being stationed too long. How long will depend on the age and mental state of your pup. A sleepyhead of any age can handle an hour or more. An older pup can handle more

Sarah Says
Your dog wants to be with you or another family member whenever you're around. The point of stationing is to teach him how to behave in social situations, so make sure you station him in a room with people.

Grrr
Some dogs panic when initially stationed. If you're concerned, determine whether your dog's reaction is really a panic attack or simply a persuasive protest. Ignore the protest. If he is truly panicked, initially station him only when you can sit with him. Encourage bone chewing and begin to leave his side only when he's sleeping. Pretty soon, he'll get the hang of it.

extended periods. The best gauge is your puppy; keep him stationed near you and be aware of his signals. If your pup has been napping at his station for an hour and suddenly gets up and starts acting restless, it's probably time to go to his bathroom spot. If your puppy chews on a bone for 15 minutes and then starts acting like a jumping bean, it's probably an energy spurt and time for a little play.

Other guidelines for stationing pups and older dogs:

➤ Your puppy must be at least 12 weeks old before stationing.

➤ Make sure the station is away from stairs, electrical cords/outlets, or entanglements like posts.

➤ Be sure the object you attach the dog to is immovable and sturdy.

➤ When securing your dog, attach the clip to the buckle or tag collar, never a training collar.

Problem Solving

The Teaching Lead® will also help you with many problem situations. Though we'll go into each issue in greater detail later, let me whet your appetite:

➤ **Housebreaking.** The leash follows the same logic as the crate; dogs don't like to mess in a confined area. By keeping your dog connected or stationed, you will be aware of his needs and know when he needs to go out. You'll quickly learn his "I've gotta go bad!" signal.

➤ **Jumping.** Some people advise that you knee or step on your dog's paws when he jumps on you. Aside from being potentially painful, those techniques are usually ineffective because both actions are interpreted as interactive. Again, the attention factor comes into play. Jumping is a big attention-getter—certainly worth repeating over and over if he gets a reaction.

With the Teaching Lead®, you can handle your dog's behavior without touching him. If he jumps up, grasp the leash and snap him down saying "Off!" in a very firm tone. Don't look at him or touch him until he calms down. When he does, command "Sit" and give him attention.

➤ **Company Acrobats.** Does your dog go nuts when the doorbell rings? When company arrives, station your dog where he can observe, but not influence, the situation. When he settles down, connect him to you and encourage your guests to pet him only after he is calm. If he jumps, correct him as outlined above. When you sit down, sit on the leash and give him a chew bone.

If your dog is secured around your waist (leading) when company arrives, ask them to please ignore him until he settles down. Offer a toy and correct him by snapping him back behind your feet until he's calm (it may take a while in the beginning).

➤ **Discouraging nipping.** Any time your dog is mouthing you or anyone else, remove his head from your hand and say "No." Do this by pulling his collar back sharply or by spritzing his nose with Binaca Mouth Spray® (found at your local pharmacy). If you pull your hand away or push your dog, you could inadvertently encourage rougher play.

➤ **Crunching habits.** Find a bone or similar chew toy that your dog likes. Buy the same one for every station, plus a few extras to keep handy when you're sitting on the leash. Too many different toys will confuse him.

Each time you give your dog his bone, say "Where's your bone?" Any time he shows interest in an inappropriate object, pull *him* back and say "Leave it." Pick up the offending object and correct *it* very sternly: "Bad sock! Shame on the sock!" Look at the sock, not your dog. Yes, you'll look silly, but this works wonders.

If your dog already has something in his mouth, tell him to "Bring it." Praise him when he does and ask "Where's your bone?" It's better to have a resident delivery service than a destruction crew.

➤ **Outside control.** Connect your dog to your side. Every time he gets distracted, call out his name and scurry in the opposite direction. Praise him immediately, whether he turned with you or was tugged by the leash. Continue this until he is attentive to you when you call out his name.

The Least You Need To Know

➤ The Teaching Lead® doesn't take the place of the crate. Crates are still good to use when leaving your puppy or untrained dog for up to six hours and for housebreaking purposes at night.

➤ You can purchase the original patented Teaching Lead® (using the order form in the back of this book) or create your own as described earlier in this chapter. Whatever your decision, start using the training techniques today!

➤ When training your dog how to behave in the house, don't give him full freedom. Use the three applications of the Teaching Lead®—leading, anchoring, and stationing—to structure his behavior.

Housebreaking

Teaching your dog how to behave in your house is no small trick. Think about it; they're dogs. They're genetically predisposed to cave-life, a free-ranging toilet, nature's toys, and an interactive community. They're not too home proud. Sure, we've pulled a domestication trick or two, but we cannot transform a whole species. Be patient with your dog. Don't take anything for granted. Sure, dogs shouldn't soil the house, but some do, especially pups. This chapter introduces you to techniques you can use to housebreak your dog.

Not on the Rug!

Dog-do on the carpet is perhaps one of life's more wrenching sights. I hear the following quote daily from my clients: "She knows it's wrong! Just look at her eyes; guilt's written all over her face."

Sarah Says
Use a word like "Outside" as you lead your dog to her potty area.

No it's not—dogs don't feel guilt. They really don't. You might be noticing fear and confusion, but after-the-fact corrections won't help your long-term goal. If you have a housebreaking problem, you need to accept that your dog doesn't know much about your home. Approach this project with a level head. Your dog isn't human—never will be—but, fortunately, she can be potty trained to go outside or on papers. Here's how.

The Outside Routine

The most important aspect of housetraining is establishing a routine, as follows:

1. **Select a spot.** Pick an area to potty train your dog. If it's outdoors, you must take your dog there before you walk him.

2. **Blaze a trail.** Be consistent. Follow the same path to your dog's area each time you potty her. Use the same door.

A structured routine is a must!

START HERE

SAME SPOT

3. **The attention factor.** Don't greet or praise until after your dog has pottied.

4. **The command.** As your dog is eliminating, say "Get busy." Eventually, he'll go on command. It's no small miracle.

5. **The reward.** Once he's pottied, greet, praise, and walk him as usual!

Grrr
Do you have a small dog or young puppy? Don't carry him to his area. Let him walk so he can learn how to navigate on his own.

Your pup will need to go after feeding, exercising, napping, and isolation. Use table 9.1 as a guide.

Table 9.1   How Many Times a Day Your Dog Will Need To "Go"

Age	Trips to the Spot
6 to 14 weeks	8 to 10
14 to 20 weeks	6 to 8
20 to 30 weeks	4 to 6
30 weeks to adulthood	3 to 4

Lay Off Corrections

Getting mad makes you look foolish. You're getting mad at a dog. As much as you think she's human, she isn't. Even though I've heard it a thousand times, I'm still not convinced that "dogs understand." You can interrupt the process if you catch it, but lay off all other corrections.

Interrupting the Process

If you catch your dog in the process of eliminating in the house, startle her. Clap your hands as you say "Ep, Ep, Ep!"; jump up and down like an excited chimp—whatever it takes to get her to stop. Then direct her to the elimination area like nothing happened. Praise her for finishing.

Keep Your Dog Confined

Use your Teaching Lead®. Crate your dog when you're out and at night, if she's not stationed. You'll be able to grant her more freedom after she learns the rules, but not now.

Keep the Diet Consistent

Avoid changing dog food brands unless directed to do so by your veterinarian. Dogs don't digest the way humans do. Their stomachs can get upset if you change their diet. Lay off treats for a while until they're housebroken. (See Chapter 17 for nutritional hints.)

Watch Water Intake

Dogs, especially young ones, drink water excessively if they're bored or nervous. If your dog is having peeing problems, monitor his water intake by giving your dog access during meal times and as you take him to his area. Be careful not to dehydrate your dog. If he looks thirsty, let him lap! Remove water after 7:30 p.m. Give him ice cubes, which absorb faster into the bloodstream, if he needs a drink.

Sarah Says
Is your dog just too polite to rock the boat? If you can't get your dog to articulate a signal, try hanging bells from the door. Each time you pass through the door, slap the bells with your "paw" and say "Outside." Soon your dog will join in the fun.

Learning Your Dog's Signal

Once you have the routine down pat (give it about a week), interrupt it. Instead of chanting "Outside," lead your dog to the door. Wait until she gives you a signal to continue. If her signal is subtly staring at the door, call her back to you and pump her up, "What is it? *Outside*? Good dog!" and out you go. Repeat the process in rooms farther and farther from the door or her papers.

Puppy Considerations

Puppies need to go out more frequently than older dogs. Really young puppies, younger than 12 weeks, may need to go out every hour or two. Believe it or not, there is a pattern to their elimination habits. Puppies go after they sleep, play, eat, and after long bouts of confinement. Be patient. Some train in days; others take months.

Still Having Difficulty?

If you're still having problems, go through this checklist to ensure you're doing everything by the book.

✓ Limit your dog's freedom unless he just pottied in the right place and you can watch him 110 percent.

✓ Crate or isolate your dog when you're out.

✓ Use the Teaching Lead® to keep your dog with you when you're home.

✓ If your dog eliminates when stationed, you may be giving him too much freedom. Two to three feet is appropriate, depending on the size of your dog.

✓ Are you giving the dog attention before she eliminates? Wait instead and let the dog earn your love by eliminating in the right place!

✓ Give your dog five minutes to do her business. If your dog lingers, crate her for 15 minutes and start from the top.

✓ Are you following a consistent routine and encouraging everyone to do the same? Consistency is key!

If you're still having problems, seek a professional animal trainer or behaviorist. Good guidance will leave you wondering why you didn't opt for it months ago!

The Least You Need To Know

➤ Dogs aren't born knowing inside from outside. You must show them the ropes!

➤ Housetraining is a matter of order and cleanliness. Dogs like both. Keep them confined and give them a routine to follow.

Chapter 10

Other Horrors

In This Chapter

➤ How to curb nipping, chewing, and barking

➤ When your dog's idea of fun isn't fun for you

➤ Four paws on the floor: redirecting your jumper!

Order in the house! Order in the house! Sometimes you'd like to yell it and have it be so. Teaching household etiquette may be the most trying time for you and your dog. While your dog is trying to figure out what you want, you've been reduced to pleading for cooperation: "I'll give you a biscuit. Biscie Boomer. Please, Boomer, please? I'm late for work."

It's embarrassing. You need some guidelines to get on the right track. In this chapter, I'll cover chewing, the infamous grab-n-go, jumping, barking, and nipping. (The more serious infractions will be covered toward the end of the book.)

Stop Chewing!

Chewing is a dog thing. It's nothing personal. They don't know a stick from furniture or a doll's head from a chestnut. Fortunately, they can be rehabilitated. If you have a habitual chewer on your hands, however, you'll need to be patient and use some of the tried-and-true techniques described next.

Bet You Didn't Know

Just like kids, pups are curious about the world around them and they love to explore. Kids use their hands; puppies use their mouths. Additionally, pups between 3 1/2–8 months are teething. Your puppy might chew on the furniture or your favorite shoes to alleviate discomfort. To ward off possible destruction, supply and encourage the use of appropriate chew toys.

Buy Stock in Bitter Apple®

Bitter Apple® is nasty tasting stuff you can buy at most pet stores that you can spray on items to prevent your dog from chewing them. If you notice your dog chewing on the furniture surrounding her station, spray everything but her bed and bone. Believe it or not, some dogs like Bitter Apple®. If this is your dog, try a Tabasco sauce mixture.

Provide One Main Toy

Having too many objects to choose from can confuse your dog. Pick a bone or toy that will satisfy your dog's penchant for chewing, buy multiples of that item, and spread them around the house for quick access. Do the same for play toys.

Choose one good chew toy and one good play toy and stick with those!

Chew toys

Play toys

Avoid Prize Envy Confrontations

Don't yell at your dog after she's begun or after she's finished chewing. It's too late. If you chase a dog who has something in her mouth, she'll be thinking, "Wow, what a great prize...everybody wants to take it from me!" (This is called prize envy.) Instead, learn about the treat cup and use it effectively.

Create Treat Cups

Making a *treat cup* is easy. Break up your dog's favorite treats in a cup. Shake the cup and offer your dog a treat. Continue this until your dog associates the sound of the cup with getting a treat. Now spread treat cups all over your home and be consistent. Use the same kind of cups. Party cups or deli containers work best.

Anytime your dog is chewing on an *acceptable* object, go over with the treat cup, say "Out," offer her a treat, and leave. When your dog's eating a meal, shake the cup, say "Out," offer her a treat, and leave. Now that you've communicated that your approach is not threatening, the next time your dog grabs something, find a treat cup and say "Out." Treat all objects she grabs, good or bad, as treasures and she'll be much more cooperative. Praise her when she releases the object and help her find a chew toy: "Where's your bone?"

If It's Gone, It's Gone

If your dog has destroyed something, let it go. Yelling or hitting your dog will only make him nervous and frightened, which leads to more chewing. Any dog owner can commiserate and I know first hand how angry you feel, but don't take it out on your dog. He doesn't know any better. Remember, your dog's mouth is equivalent to your hands; if your dog is nervous or fidgety, he'll chew. I'm sure if your dog could surf the Net, scan the soaps, or pull his hair out, he would, but since he can't, chewing will have to do.

Catch Your Dog in the Thought Process!

Set up a situation with something your dog's obsessed with—tissues, shoes, a Barbie doll, whatever her fancy. While your dog's resting in another room, set the object in the middle of the floor. Now bring your dog to it on her Teaching Lead®. The second your dog notices the object, say "No," and snap back on the leash. Next, pick up the object and shout at it. You read right. Get angry at the object, not your dog. You're doing the dog version of telling a child the stove is hot. Now walk by the object again. Your dog should avoid it like the plague. Use this technique to catch your dog in the thought process; if your dog already has an object in her mouth, you're too late.

Still Having Difficulty with Your Chewer?

If you're still having problems with your dog chewing, go through this checklist to ensure you're doing everything by the book. If you're following the list but are still having problems, call a professional.

Sarah Says

Remember, you're correcting the object, not your dog! Don't even look at your dog as you mouth-off to the naughty thing. Your neighbors may commit you, but your dog will love you for it. Do not practice this exercise off lead. Your dog will think the object's a mouse and join in the kill.

✓ Limit your dog's freedom around the house until she's a respectable chewer.

✓ Avoid the infamous "grab-n-go." This is when your dog grabs an object just to get you to chase him. It has dog-fun written all over it. Decide on an alternative game plan and teach everyone to follow the same routine.

✓ Don't yell at your dog after the fact. She'll consider your aggressive interest a sign that whatever she's found must be valuable because you're willing to challenge her for it.

✓ Treat cups and discipline don't mix. Treat cups encourage your dog to show you her treasure. Don't correct her (or the object) after she's given it up or she won't bring it to you again.

Jaws Junior: Nipping and Mouthing

Mouthing and nipping are two different issues. *Nipping* is a puppy thing; it's interactive and playful. *Mouthing* is a lesser infraction; it's more of a communication skill to get you to do a particular thing. Less pressure, less annoying, but still not a charming habit. If you have an older dog who still nips, read the section on aggression. Nipping dogs are bossy and manipulative and need a firmer regime.

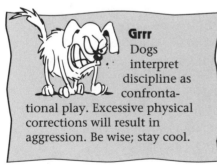

Grrr

Dogs interpret discipline as confrontational play. Excessive physical corrections will result in aggression. Be wise; stay cool.

Mouthing is an attention getting behavior. If your dog uses it to communicate a need to go out, respond. If your dog is mouthing you for a pat, please ignore it. Pretend she isn't there. If she becomes too annoying, get Binaca Mouth Spray® and spritz her discreetly, hiding the Binaca in your hand, avoiding all eye contact, comments, or pushing.

Nipping with sharp little needle teeth can hurt! It's another one of those dog-things that you'll need to refocus. Consider this: When your puppy still hung out with her littermates, she nipped during play and to determine her rank. She also soft-mouthed her mother affectionately. When you bring your puppy home, what happens? This behavior continues. What your puppy wants to know is who's a puppy and who's not. This determines the type of mouthing or nipping: soft or playful. Usually, everyone gets categorized as a puppy. *Why?* Well for starters, most people pull their hand away when nipped. To a human, it's self-defense. To a pup, it's an invitation to play. Even if you were to correct your young puppy, she wouldn't get it; it's like correcting a one-year-old baby for pulling your hair. So what should you do? Good question. Your approach will depend on your puppy's age.

Younger Than 14 Weeks

Young puppies mouth a lot. They mouth when playing; they also mouth to communicate their needs, just like a baby cries. If your puppy starts mouthing, ask yourself: Is she hungry or thirsty? Does she need to eliminate? Is she sleepy? Does she need to play? Next, follow the checklist to control mouthing and nipping!

✓ Whenever your puppy licks you, say "Kisses" and praise her warmly.

✓ Hold your attention when your puppy nips softly. Keep your hand still. Don't forget, hand withdrawal is an invitation to play and nip harder.

✓ If your puppy starts biting down hard, turn on her quickly, say "Ep, Ep!" and glare into her eyes for two seconds. Go back to your normal routine.

✓ Remember, puppies nip when they feel needy (just like a baby cries). If your puppy won't let up, ask yourself if she wants something, like an outing, exercise, or a drink. If all checks out and your puppy won't quit, crate or isolate her with a favorite bone. Do not scold your puppy as you isolate her. Calmly place your puppy in her area.

Training Your Puppy around Kids

Kids act a lot like puppies. They're always on the floor and into everything. If you have children, teach your puppy not to mouth them from the start. Here's how.

Leave your puppy on a one-foot long nylon leash whenever she's with your children. If she starts playing too rough, pick up the leash, snap back, and say "Ep, Ep." If you're still having trouble, buy a super soaker or plant mister and fill it with water and vinegar. Spray your dog discreetly when she starts getting riled up.

If all else fails, give the puppy a time-out attached to you, stationed, or crated. Help the kids see that their restlessness leads to puppy-withdrawal.

Older Puppies

Do you have a Peter-Pan pup, one who still nips past her time? Well, the buck stops here. After 14 weeks, there's no excuse. If your puppy's still nipping, it's likely that you've taught her, so it's you who'll have to mend your ways:

➤ Stop all challenge games. These games include wrestling, tug-of-war, chasing your dog around, and teasing. You're sending the wrong message.

Tug-of-war sends the wrong message.

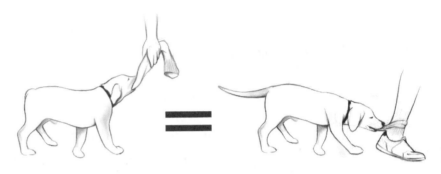

Grrr
No tug-of-war or rough wrestling matches please! These games teach dogs to clamp down hard on any object and challenge. This could be a leash, the laundry, your shirt, or even your skin. For game alternatives, see Chapter 24.

Sarah Says
If things get out of hand, avoid yelling at the kids. It sounds like barking to your dog and ups the fun ante. Calmly station, crate, or isolate your puppy until she mellows.

➤ Correct all nipping, whether it's a bite on your arm or a nibble on your finger. Teeth do not belong on human skin, period.

➤ Put the Teaching Lead® applications in Chapter 8 into action. It's time for you to step up as the leader!

➤ Purchase a few weapons to use in defense, such as Binaca Mouth Spray®, Bitter Apple® spray, or a long-distance squirt gun.

➤ Give yourself something to grab. If your dog's not wearing the Teaching Lead®, place a short lead onto her buckle collar.

➤ If your dog begins to mouth, turn to her, use a lead or collar to snap her head from your body, and say "Ep, Ep!" Glare at her for a second and then go back to business as usual.

➤ If she continues to nip, ask yourself: Do I look convincing? Am I snapping or pulling? (Pulling encourages play.) Is my dog taking me seriously? You may need more training before you earn her respect.

➤ Carry Binaca Mouth Spray®. Spritz your dog whenever she's mouthing and say "Ep, Ep!" Spray her nose once or twice. After that, you can spray the air above her head; the blasting sound will warn her off.

Curing the Chase and Nip

There are two categories to cover here:

➤ **The bathrobe assault.** If your dog's a clothing grabber, dilute some Bitter Apple® spray in a plant mister and carry it with you when you suspect your dog will pull this assault. Do not turn and face your dog when she jumps; this is interpreted as a challenge. Without looking or responding, spray your dog and continue walking. If this problem persists, get help now. It can develop into post-puberty aggression. No joke.

➤ **The child chaser.** Kids running around the yard, apartment, or house are a big temptation. If you were a dog, you'd be jumping and nipping too. Because you can't teach kids to stop being kids, you need to help your dog control her impulses. Put your dog on the Teaching Lead® and ask the kids to race around in front of you. Anytime your dog looks tempted to lunge, snap back and say "Shhh." Repeat as often as necessary to gain control.

Still Having Difficulty with Your Nipper?

If you're still having problems keeping your dog from mouthing and nipping, go through this checklist to ensure you're doing everything by the book. If nothing else works, get professional training help.

✓ Do not yank your hand away from your dog's mouth.

✓ Avoid physical corrections. They often encourage dominant play and lead to more aggressive reactions.

✓ Permit young puppies to mouth softly. Correct hard bites by emitting a startling vocal sound and either snapping their head from your hand or spritzing their mouth with Binaca Mouth Spray® or diluted Bitter Apple®.

✓ Do not allow mouthing after 14 weeks.

✓ Kids aren't for mouthing. Period. Let your dog drag a leash when they play together and correct all rough play.

Two Feet, the Joyous Jumper

Everybody knows a jumper—a knock-you-over-when-you-come-in jumper, a muddy-paws-on-the-couch jumper, a counter cruiser (a dog who likes to sniff along counter tops). Jumping is a sure-fire attention getter. So what gives? The first step in solving your problem will be to understand how it became a problem in the first place. Once again, your dog's not to blame. Let's hop into his paws and see what's going on.

Dogs see us as other dogs. Eye contact is a big method for canine communication. Our eyes are up, so to be gracious and greet us properly, dogs must jump. The first time this happens, often in puppyhood, a hug follows. "Isn't that cute?" After about the tenth jump, it's not so cute. So the dog usually gets a shove. But what's a shove to a dog? Confrontational play. The dog jumps higher and harder the next time. So the human tries a little toe stepping, paw grabbing, yelling, all with the same effect; dogs think jumping is very interactive and very fun.

Counter jumping is another favorite pastime. After all, we're looking at the counter constantly, so why shouldn't the dog do so as well? When a dog jumps up, the human reacts by shouting and shoving. The dog interpretation? Prize envy. The dog thinks, "Whatever I was reaching for must be excellent because everybody raced over for it." So the dog reconsiders. He jumps when your back is turned or you're out of the room. Is this behavior spiteful? No, just plain smart. Now let's dissect and correct this problem one jumping situation at a time.

Your Homecoming

The best way to remedy jumping when you come home is to ignore your dog. Try it for a week. Come home and ignore your dog until she's given up the jumping vigil. Keep a basket of balls or squeaky toys by the door. When you come in, toss one on the ground to refocus your dog's energy. If your dog's crated, don't let her out immediately; wait until she's calm.

If you have a big dog or a super persistent jumper, put on an overcoat to protect yourself. Whether it takes two minutes or 20, go about your business until your dog calms down.

Do you have kids? Tell them to look for rain and do the same. Cross your arms in front of your chest and look to the sky. Don't look down until the coast is clear. Consistency is key. If one family member follows the program but the others encourage jumping, your dog will jump-test all visitors.

Bet You Didn't Know

Dogs mimic their leaders' energy levels. If you come home to an excited dog and you get excited, what message are you sending? Instead, come in calm and wait to greet your dog until she's settled down too!

Ignore a jumping dog.

When Company Arrives

CHARLIE (the dog): Oh boy! The doorbell. What fun! All eyes are on me. Paws flying everywhere! Oh no! Why are you putting me in the basement? What did I do? Bummer.

COMPANY: Oh my gosh. This crazy dog. Why don't they train her? How unsettling.

It's a common routine. Nobody's in control. Nobody's comfortable, except maybe the dog. But even that passes if you have to isolate the dog. Fortunately, there's a better way. Remember the idiom "Good manners start at home?" Well, the same rule applies for dogs.

First, be stern with your regimen and train your company how to act around your dog—and you thought training your dog was tough.

➤ **Practice doorbell set-ups.** Put your dog on her Teaching Lead®. Position someone at the door and ask him to ring the bell 10 times at 20-second intervals. Tell the visitor to come through another door when he's done. Each time the bell rings, call your dog's name and walk away from the door. If your dog is a real maniac, try the chin lead (described in Chapter 7) and discreetly spray her nose with Binaca Mouth Spray® as you say "Shhh." Practice these set-ups twice a day until your dog tones down her reaction.

> **Sarah Says**
> If you're sitting down, anchor your dog until she's calm enough to greet your guests.

> **Doglish**
> OOOH...
> The *fly flick* says "how dare you" in the most passive manner. It's not tough or abusive. You just grasp the collar or leash with your thumb and forefinger and flick your dog off to one side. You might need to do it several times before your dog gets the message. When he finally sits down perplexed, give him a great big hug!

➤ **Create a greeting station.** Designate an area by the door to send your dog when company arrives. Secure a leash to the area and place a favorite ball or toy there. When the bell rings, station/secure your dog as you instruct "Go to your place" and answer the door. Instruct your visitors to ignore the dog while greeting you. Wait until your dog has calmed down to introduce her, even if it takes an hour.

➤ **Designate a greeting toy.** If your dog's a real tennis ball fanatic (or any other toy), withhold it until you have company arriving. Each time you enter your home or company arrives, say "Get your toy" as you toss it on the floor. Spritz your dog if she jumps and continue to ignore her until she's settled down.

Calming Attention Jumpers

If you can ignore your dog, the silent treatment is your most effective response. If I kept bugging you for a game of Parcheesi and you didn't look up once, I'd go elsewhere for fun. Once your dog lets up, encourage her by saying "Get your toy!" and let her pay attention to that. If your dog's a real nudge, keep a lead (short or long) attached to her collar. When she jumps, grasp the lead and snap your dog sideways quickly (this is called a *fly flick*) as you continue to ignore her. Give no eye contact, body language, or verbal corrections.

Discouraging Counter Cruisers

Do you have one of these? Counter cruising is a bad habit that's hard to break. Corrections actually encourage sneaky behavior. Though I've heard it a thousand times, your dog's not grabbing out of spite. The reason your dog grabs when your back is turned or you leave the room is so that she can avoid a challenge. Let me expand: Your dog sees your eyes and mouth (hands = mouth) interacting with objects on the counters all day. When she copies you, you bark (shout = bark) and challenge her for whatever the prize is. Canine message? Whatever is on the counter must be great, but I better grab it when all backs are turned or they're out of the room or I'll have to give it up. Let's try to solve this problem with dignity:

Sarah Says
If mealtimes are too distracting to your dog, station your dog while you cook.

1. With your dog on the Teaching Lead®, place something tempting on the counter.

2. The instant your dog looks up to sniff the counter, snap the lead back, say "Ep, Ep," and shout at the counter "Bad turkey!"

3. Continue to work in the kitchen, correcting your dog whenever she even thinks about approaching what's on the counter.

If your dog's already on the counter, you're too late to correct her; instead flick her off by curling a finger under her collar or grabbing her lead. Do not yell at your dog once she's on the counter. Do not lurch, shove, snatch, or hit. Touching reinforces behavior. After all, a touch is attention. If you push your dog, you'll reinforce her behavior. Remember that!

Furniture Fanatics

Most people invite puppies on the furniture only to regret it later. If you have a puppy and you don't want him on your furniture permanently, do yourself a favor and discourage it from the start. If you have a delinquent furniture lover, the problem's not too hard to break. You'll just need to be consistent.

Place your dog on the Teaching Lead® and walk up to your couch or bed. The second your dog prepares for the jump, snap back and say "No!" Encourage him to "Sit" and pet him. Walk back and forth until he sits automatically. Try the same set-up with a family member on the couch. Next, lead your dog up and sit down yourself. If he goes to jump, snap sideways and ignore him until he sits quietly. Reward his cooperation with a chew toy.

Still Having Difficulty with Your Jumper?

If you're still having problems with a jumper, go through this checklist to ensure you're doing everything by the book.

✓ Correct jumping before the jump! Nip it in the excitement phase.

✓ Control yourself! If you want your dog to stay calm, you must set the example.

✓ Train visitors to ignore your dog until she's calm.

✓ Use your Teaching Lead® to lead and station your dog around temptations.

The Bothersome Barker

A barking dog's a real headache—a complete nightmare. How you handle the situation will depend on what's prompting it in the first place. In the meantime, you need to watch your reaction. The cardinal sin when rehabilitating your barker is for you to yell. When you yell, your dog thinks you're barking, which leads to—you guessed it—more barking. A bark-along. To solve your problem, stay cool.

At the Door

Almost everyone appreciates a dog-alarm at the door—a few woofs to announce new arrivals. It gets annoying, however, when the alarm can't be shut off. The optimal situation would be to have an alarm bark with an off switch. Here's how:

Doglish

To make a *penny can*, fill an empty soda can with ten pennies and tape the top. The shaking sound startles many dogs.

1. Place a penny can or spray bottle (filled with a 50/50 mix of vinegar and water) at the door.

2. Position someone outside the door and ask him to ring the bell 10 times in 20- second intervals.

3. When your dog starts barking, approach the door calmly. Spray her nose or shake the penny can discreetly as you say "Shhh!!!" and instruct "Back" to clear the greeting area. Approach the door calmly.

4. Keep your dog behind you as you open the door. Never hold your dog while you open the door. It will make her more wild.

Keep your dog behind you as you open the door.

5. Repeat as often as necessary to condition respect.

6. Now try it with the real McCoy!

If your dog is aggressive, please consult Chapter 25 on this subject and call a professional. Aggression is a serious problem.

The Territorial Terror

Do you have one of these? Does your dog bark at everything he sees and hears? Nothing goes unnoticed—a biker, the neighborhood kids, or little tidbits passing through your yard. For some people, after a while, it can seem as much a part of their daily routine as the wind passing through the trees. For those of us who don't fall into that category, however, perpetual barking is a big pain.

> ### Bet You Didn't Know
>
> Barking has an added lure. Whenever your dog barks at something, whether from the window or the yard, it goes away. Sure, you and I know that the postman's going to keep moving, but don't tell your dog. She thinks her strength and prowess drove the postman away. It's quite an ego boost. Dogs who bark at everything perceive themselves as your leader. One of the leader's duties is to guard her territory and her group from intruders.

Start training immediately. Your dog needs to understand that you're the boss. Avoid leaving your dog alone outdoors for long stretches of time. Unsupervised confinement often breeds boredom and territorial behavior. Put those two together and you're likely to end up with a barkaholic. Block off areas that your dog uses as lookout posts such as a living room couch or windowsill. If she's a night watchman, secure her on-lead in your room at night. Give her 3 feet of freedom—just enough to lie comfortably on her bed.

Screaming at your dog will be translated into barking. Your dog will feel supported and her role as leader (she barked first) will be reinforced. Anytime you see (or hear) your dog start to perk up, say "Shhh" and call her to your side. If she ignores you, place her on the Teaching Lead® or let her drag a leash so you can quickly gain control. Use spray misters or penny cans to reinforce your verbal "Shhh!!!"

Car Problems

Being locked in a car with a barking dog is my version of purgatory. The car creates a "fish bowl effect," similar to the territorial situation just described. Your dog barks and the passing object disappears, only faster in the case of a moving car! Yelling at your dog isn't the thing to do. Pleading won't win you any brownie points. This problem tends to disappear slowly as you progress through training, although there are a few things you can do in the interim to discourage this behavior:

➤ Have your dog pause before you let her enter or exit the car. Instruct "Wait" and give her permission to enter with "OK." It's your car, not hers!

➤ Enforce stillness while you drive. Station your dog in the car with a Seat Belt Safety Lead (SBSL)™ (described in Chapter 7).

➤ Is your situation unbearable? Secure your dog on a chin lead (see Chapter 7).

➤ Ignore the barking if your car's moving. Driving is a job in itself.

➤ If you're stationary, spritz your dog with a plant mister or shake a penny can and say "Shhh."

➤ If your dog barks at gas-station or toll-booth attendants, ask them to toss a piece of cheese into the car window from afar. Hopefully, your dog will make a more positive association.

Attention or Protest Barking

Some dogs don't like to be left alone. This is especially true with adolescent dogs, but is also the case when older dogs have been pampered every time they barked. If you soothe a protest barker or dog that's barking for attention, you'll end up with a real spoiled brat on your hands. If you ignore the situation, your partner may threaten to leave you. Is there a happy medium? Well, not really, but I'll give it my best shot:

➤ Ignore it if you can. Never yell.

➤ Avoid grandiose departures and arrivals. They're too exciting.

➤ Dogs like to be with you. Avoid problems in your home by using the Teaching Lead®.

➤ Place peanut butter in a hollow bone and give it to her as you leave.

➤ Use a water pistol or toss a penny can toward (not at) your dog when she starts up. Be careful though, she can't know where it's coming from.

➤ Return to your dog only after she's calmed down. If you must interfere with her barking tantrum, go to her quietly without eye contact or comments, place her on the Teaching Lead®, and ignore her for half an hour while you lead her around.

Still Having Difficulty?

If you're still having problems, go through this checklist to ensure you're doing everything by the book.

➤ Never yell at a barking dog.

➤ Make sure you place your feet in front of your dog's paws before a correction.

➤ Don't focus on your dog or make prolonged eye contact when giving a correction. Eye contact reinforces behavior.

➤ Once your dog quiets down, respond by refocusing his attention or praising.

The Least You Need To Know

➤ Excessive corrections or physical discipline makes dogs nervous, encouraging more problem behavior and solving nothing. Stay calm.

➤ Avoid prize envy confrontations with your dog. Use treat cups to teach your dog to show you her treasures.

➤ If you catch your dog thinking of approaching an object, correct the object, not the dog! After-the-fact corrections don't work.

➤ Nipping is encouraged by physical discipline. You must teach your puppy to withdraw her mouth from your hand. Leash jerks and spritzers are good tools.

➤ Never push or look at a jumping dog! You're interacting and encouraging rougher play. Leave your dog on a leash and correct jumping the second you see it in her eye!

➤ To resolve a barking problem, stay cool, start training, get in front of your dog, and refocus her energy.

Chapter 11

Help

In This Chapter

➤ Talking to non-professionals

➤ Seeking advice from your veterinarian, groomer, or pet store

➤ Finding a class to fit your needs

➤ How to recognize a good trainer

➤ Behavior and drug therapy

Finding the right help for training, if you need it, is essential. Training is a joint effort for you and your dog. My clients would be the first to tell you that it's a blend of the right actions—from how you hold the leash to your tone of voice to the way you stand—that helps your dog learn what you are trying to teach. When I'm training people to work with their dogs, I harp on the little things until they are doing them instinctively. If my harping doesn't come through in the pages of this book clearly enough, get help—the right help, as described in this chapter.

Amateur Trainers

It's funny, actually. As soon as people know you have a dog, they become experts. Promise me one thing: no matter what they say, no matter how convincing, regardless of how many parlor tricks their dogs know, don't listen.

Grrr
Free advice never pays. If you try a little of this and a little of that, guess who's going to suffer? You'll make your poor dog crazy.

Veterinarians, Groomers, and Pet Stores

Ask for training advice from a vet, groomer, or pet store owner, and you may get an off-the-cuff, routine answer, but nothing that is tailored for your individual situation or dog. Instead of asking these other professionals for training tips and solutions, ask where you might find a reputable trainer or classes in your area.

Sniffing Out a Good Dog Trainer

Finding a good trainer—one who is well-rounded in his/her knowledge of dog behavior—can be a real lifesaver. Many clients call me at their wit's end and I discover a wonderful dog who's just dying to come out. It's usually the owner who is confusing the dog. So, I train the owner and the dog behaves. It's often just as simple as that. If you need help training your dog, scout out professionals in your area to get some good leads and call today. You and your dog will be glad you did! The following sections look at a few of the training options that are available to you.

Personal Trainers

I'm a personal dog trainer. I train more than dogs though; I train people. When looking for a personal trainer, you're looking for someone to train you (as well as your dog). These are some of my training ethics, which I recommend looking for in any personal trainer:

➤ Put yourself in your client's shoes.

➤ Know that the client is trying to do the right thing.

➤ Understand the dog's personality and listen to what the dog is trying to say with his behavior.

➤ Know when you can't help. Be honest with your client.

➤ Help your client understand why the dog is behaving inappropriately. Help the client think for his dog.

➤ Teach the client Doglish so he can communicate with his dog.

➤ Help the client structure his home.

➤ Teach the client patience, tolerance, understanding, and sympathy. After all, he loves his dog.

Not all trainers are in this profession because they love dogs first and foremost. Some are in it primarily for the money. Beware. I'll tell you a personal story to make my case. A veterinary hospital asked me to evaluate an aggressive Old English Sheepdog, whom I'll call Arnie. Arnie was five years old. He belonged to a couple who was about to have a child. He had been threatening the wife and household company for two years. He had bitten twice. As usual, in my consultation, I tested the dog to see at what level the aggression response existed by removing a bone, snapping the leash, and refusing entrance without permission.

Arnie flunked in a big way. He was so assertive, he knocked me on the floor, threw out my back, and (I'm convinced) would have crunched a body part had the owner not removed him. My diagnosis was clear. This was a dangerous dog—not one to be messed with, not one to have with children, and not one to be given away. Someday, this dog was going to bite and it would be severe. I shared my opinion with the clients and the veterinarian. That's the last I heard of them for two years. The veterinarian stopped referring me. The clients did not call or return my phone calls. I later found out the people had found another trainer who worked with them weekly for nearly a year. Supposedly, she had "turned the dog around." Nearly two years from the day they met with me, the dog mauled the wife and attacked the baby.

I was sorry, but I was also angry—angry at the clients for putting their helpless child in jeopardy, angry at the trainer who had no idea what she was dealing with and should never have taken a cent of the people's money, and angry at the animal hospital who so easily disregarded my expert opinion after years of mutual respect. And what happened to Arnie? Not the responsible action of euthanizing a dangerous dog. They gave him away. I don't even want to think about it.

Group Training

Group training class can be a real blast. It can also be a dog owner's worst nightmare. So what's the deciding factor? The instructor. No, it's not your dog—no matter how badly behaved he is around other dogs. A good instructor expects that and will know what to do. When exploring different classes, talk to the instructor and get a feel for his/her style of training. Here are some questions you can ask:

➤ How many dogs are in the class?

➤ Are the classes divided by age?

➤ Do you have a favorite breed of dog or do you have experience with a wide variety of breeds? This can indicate a strong bias on the part of the instructor.

➤ What do you teach in class?

➤ Are the classes indoors or outside?

Group class is great for socialization and training.

➤ Do you have different class levels?

➤ Are behavior problems discussed?

➤ Do you have a make-up policy?

➤ Is family participation encouraged? Can the kids come?

Sarah Says

People often ask me what the best way to train is, group or private? Honestly, it's a combination of the two. A private consultation lets me see how things go on a day-to-day basis. Class gives me the opportunity to follow up on that session while the dog learns around distractions.

The class size should be limited and must be divided by age and experience. I offer Puppy Kindergarten classes for dogs under six months, Grade School for inexperienced pupils, and High School and College for advanced students. I limit my class size to eight. Make sure your instructor is not breed-biased. Your dog should be seen as a unique and special personality, not a stereotype. Your instructor should be versed in breed-specific tendencies, however, and help you understand your dog's individual character. He/she should also help you understand how your dog relates to your entire family and encourage them to participate in the training.

The Do-It-Yourself Route: Books and Videos

Are you a do-it-yourself person? I'm all for it as long as you follow the right advice. Obviously, since you're reading this book, you have some faith in my methods, but not everyone suggests a positive approach to training. Be selective when choosing your reading material and call for some help if matters don't improve. You'll only train your dog once, so do it right!

> **Sarah Says**
> Videos are the wave of the future! They're easy to follow and can be watched by the whole family. There's even a companion video that goes with this book. Refer to the order form in the back of this book.

Boarding School

Sending your dog off for training is an option. It's not one I'd recommend, but it has pros and cons.

Some pros include

➤ Your dog's not around.

➤ You won't be part of your dog's education.

➤ Your problems are solved—temporarily perhaps, but you'll have some immediate gratification.

➤ If you follow through, your dog will respond to the training.

➤ Certain problems may disappear.

Cons include

➤ Your dog's not around.

➤ You won't be part of your dog's education.

➤ It's expensive.

➤ Problems can resurface or may get worse because of the structure provided in the training environment.

➤ Training is quickly forgotten if you don't follow through.

If you're considering this route, visit the facility first and remember that your dog isn't a machine. Sending him off to school isn't like dropping off the car for a tune-up. You must follow through!

Behavior and Drug Therapy

A *behaviorist* is someone who teaches dogs and has a degree in veterinary medicine. Behaviorists focus less on "dog training" and more on problem-solving. If you seek out a behaviorist, be selective. They're very costly and may not be any more effective in modifying your dog's behavior than a good trainer who's done his/her homework.

Many behaviorists use drug therapy to modify dog behavior. Though I'm not an advocate of this, in some cases, drug therapy can be effective.

The Least You Need To Know

➤ Ask your veterinarian to recommend a trainer or behavior specialist.

➤ If you decide to call a few trainers, have a list of questions prepared to ask them. Use the trainer who makes you feel most at ease, not the one who's the cheapest.

➤ Group classes can be a lot of fun. Get to know the trainer's methods and class structure before you sign up.

➤ If you opt for doggy boarding school, visit the facility before sending your dog there.

➤ Training isn't like having the car fixed. You need to follow through and use commands to interact with your dog.

Part 4
Just the Basic Training Course, Please!

Let the training begin! As you work with your dog, don't be too heavy-handed. Your dog won't learn everything in one day. If you put too much pressure on him, he won't like working with you at all. You should have fun training—yes, fun. I'm still fascinated with the whole process.

You must take it slowly; you should approach training with patience. Let your dog be successful in the beginning with small, simple steps. He'll work to understand you as training progresses. In this section, I'll walk you through each of the training stages, from teaching your dog the basics to handling him in public and encouraging off-lead focus. Just remember, it's a process, so take it slow!

Chapter 12

What Good Dogs Know

In This Chapter

➤ Here at my Heel

➤ What "No" really means

➤ Don't move an inch: Sit and Stay

➤ Come (please)

➤ Hit the dirt: Down

Here are the basics. These are the bare-bone facts your dog must understand and you must learn how to teach him. I'll walk you through each command one step at a time. I suggest you practice each command five minutes a day. Your dog may pick up certain things quickly and take weeks to learn others. That's how it usually goes, so don't get frustrated. Think of what you're accomplishing. You're teaching another species your language. Be patient. Dogs learn best from an understanding teacher.

Heel

It's a beautiful thing to watch: a dog standing calmly at his owner's side, walking when he moves and sitting when he stops. Yes it can happen to you too if you're patient. Though it takes a while to synchronize, eventually you'll be maneuvering through crowded streets and calling your dog to heel at your side from a distance. Sound miraculous? It all starts with one small step. Use the exercises described next to train your dog to stay at Heel.

Walk here at my Heel.

Bet You Didn't Know

How many ways were you taught to sit at the dinner table? One. Guess how many ways there are to sit at Heel? You're right—one! Picture this: your dog at your heel, toes aligned, heads facing in the same direction. Such a pretty picture!

The Merry-Go-Round

Practice this heeling exercise in a non-distracting environment (it can be indoors or outside). Clear an area to walk in a circle. Position your dog in the starting position: sitting straight at your left side, toes aligned, your heels ahead of the dog's front paws. You're ready to begin!

1. Relax your arms, let them hang straight at your side, and keep your thumb behind your thigh. Use a snap correction the instant your dog wanders from the heel spot.

2. Command "*Name*, Heel" as you begin to walk in a counterclockwise (dog on the inside) circle.

3. Walk in a forthright manner—head held high and shoulders back—to communicate leadership.

4. Praise your dog for watching you or snap the leash to encourage focus.

5. Stop after each circle by slowing your pace and reminding "Heel." Place your dog into a sitting position. (To position your dog when you stop, grasp the *base* of the leash [where it's attached to your dog's collar] with your right hand and use your left hand to position his hind quarters.)

6. Practice five circles twice a day.

Grrr

If your dog turns to face you when you stop, guess what? He's facing off. Another attempt for control. To discourage this habit, grab the base of the leash with your left hand. Step back on your left foot and swiftly swing your dog into the proper position. Now you can praise!

Float the Finish!

When you're preparing to stop, lift your left foot high in the air (like you're marching) and stamp it lightly on the floor. This will give your dog an added clue that he's suppose to stop and sit.

Change Your Pace

Move faster by trotting. Slow your pace by lengthening your stride. Make sure you change gears smoothly and indicate the change by saying "Easy." Remember your dog's a dog, not a Porsche!

About Face

At normal speed, command "Heel" and pivot to the right. To help your dog follow you, slow down as you turn and cluck, bend your knees, or slap your leg. Make it interesting!

Avoid choking him through the turn—that's no fun! Walk on six paces and stop and hug your dog—good job!

Big Time Heeling

You'll know you're ready to practice the Heel command in everyday situations when your dog responds without pressure on his collar. Then, try it in new situations.

For example, keep a short lead on your dog around the house. Pick it up and command "Heel" as you're walking around. Have your dog finish in the proper sitting position. Then release him by saying "OK" and give him a big hug! Or, practice heeling for 1/4 of your morning walk. Keep your hand behind you. No sniffing or lunging at neighborhood pals. Finally, you can practice in a parking lot. Make sure it's not too crowded.

Do things get out of hand when you're in public? If so, calm down! If you yell "Heel, Heel, Heel" and jerk your poor dog back and forth, of course he'll get excited. Wouldn't you? Ask yourself, "Am I asking too much too soon? Does my dog need to exercise more before we practice in public? Is my left arm straight and behind my back?" If your left hand is in front of your thigh, your dog will be too. Then he's the leader, not you!

No

Many dogs think "No" is the second half of their name: "Buddy No! Tristan No! Molly No!" There are a few inconsistencies with the way people use this little word that leaves dogs baffled as to its meaning.

For starters, "No" is usually shouted. Shouting to a dog sounds like barking. Would barking excite a situation or calm it down? "No" is used with the dog's name. In my book, you should only use your dog's name when you're happy, not mad. "No" is said after the action has occurred. If I yelled at you after you ate a bowl of soup (or even while you were eating it), would you understand that I was upset at you for opening the can? "No" said at the wrong time communicates nothing. Finally, "No" is said repetitively; "No, No, No, No," sounds different than "No," again confusing dear doggy.

Sarah Says
If you don't like to say "No," use another word or sound. Just be consistent. Personally, I like "Ep, Ep." It sounds softer, but the dog gets the message "Don't even think about it!" loud and clear.

What's an owner to do to teach a dog not to get into trouble? Fortunately, I have the answer. To teach your dog this concept, you must set up situations to catch your dog in the thought process. First we'll work indoors; then we'll go out.

Indoors, put your dog on his Teaching Lead®. Have someone secretly place a piece of cheese on the floor in a neighboring room. This is your prop. Follow these steps and pay attention to timing!

1. Bring your dog into the heel position and casually walk toward the cheese.

2. The second your dog notices the cheese, snap back on the lead and say "No!"

3. Continue to walk like nothing has happened. Remember you're the boss. No means No.

4. Walk by the cheese several times to ensure that your dog got the message.

Bet You Didn't Know

Your dog has a built-in antenna system. Can you guess what it is? It's his ears. If his ears perk up, your dog is alert. When teaching "No," watch your dog's ears. Correct your dog the second he is alerted to something inappropriate.

After your indoor training, practice "No" when you're out for a walk. When your dog notices a passing jogger, car, kid, another dog, or two tidbits climbing a tree, say "No" just like you did with the cheese. Sidestep away from the temptation to emphasize your snap. Continue to snap each time the antennas flicker. Praise your dog for focusing on you and relaxing his radar system.

Stay

Is this your dream command? You're not alone. I'm not sure why people have so much trouble teaching this one, but it's probably because it's rushed. They teach it one day and expect their dog to stay while they welcome company or walk into the kitchen for a sandwich. Promise this: you won't rush. Taught progressively, this one's a real winner. To prepare for your first lesson:

➤ Take your dog into a quiet room. No TV. No kids. No cats. Just you two.

➤ Slide your dog's neck collar high near your dog's head and center it between his ears.

➤ Fold the leash in your left hand to hip level.

➤ Position your dog behind your heels.

Now you're ready to teach your dog his first lesson! You'll do six commands. No more, no less. Here are a couple of rules for your dog's sake.

Look over your dog's head when you practice; never look directly into his eyes. It's too daunting. Stand tall. When you bend, it looks like you want to play. Stay close to your dog when you start out, about six inches from toe to paw. Creating too much distance too soon can be really scary. While doing each exercise, hold the lead directly above your dog's head. If he confuses "Stay" with "Go," you'll be ready for a quick correction. Vary the length of each pause. If you don't, your dog will think smart and break ahead of time. He's just trying to please! Resist petting your dog until you finish the following steps. Too much petting will ruin his concentration.

1. Command "Sit." Align your dog with your ankles.

2. Command "Stay" as you flash your hand in front of your dog's nose. Remove the signal and pause for five seconds. Command "OK" as you swing your arm forward and step out of position.

Sit down and Stay put.

3. Again! Command "Sit, Stay." This time, pivot to face away from your dog and pause ten seconds. Return to the starting point, and release. "OK!"

4. Back again. Command "Stay." Pivot in front of your dog. Pause. Now march. Yes, march, slowly at first, like you're sleepwalking. Once your dog holds still for that, start marching like a proud soldier.

5. Command "Stay" and pivot and pause. Now try jumping and waving your arms. Go slowly at first; ease into it.

6. Now for some noise. Pivot, pause, and then bark at your dog. Remember, no staring; keep looking over his head. Add a meow or two when he can handle it. Return, pause, and release!

7. From your starting position, command "Stay," pivot in front, and pause for 30 seconds. Stand up tall, relax your shoulders, and keep the leash above your dog's head just in case he's tempted to break. When the time is up, return to his side, pause, and release with "OK!" Now it's time to hug that dog.

Practice this simplified sequence twice a day until your dog's feeling mighty fine about his accomplishments. Now you're ready to increase the three Ds: duration, distractions, and distance! First start with distractions. Step up your march, add a new aerobics twist, walk around your dog full circle, and chant like a chimp. Can you do all this without tempting your dog to move? If so, increase the duration, extending your 30 second stand-still to two minutes. Increase your distance from your sitting dog—just a foot initially. When you increase your distance, go back to simple distractions. Then increase them. Now the two of you should feel like pros!

Are you wondering why you're jumping around and making noise while your dog's expected to stay? Eventually, your dog will have to concentrate around motion and sound distractions; you're helping him get started on the right paw!

Bet You Didn't Know

Your dog can start learning hand signals, which will help him focus on you. Use hand signals in front of your dog's nose to direct his attention to you. Here are three to start with:

Sit. Swing your right hand from your dog's nose to your face, like your scooping his attention toward you, and say "Sit."

Stay. Flatten your palm like a paddle. Flash it quickly in front of your dog's nose and say "Stay."

OK. Swing your right hand out from your dog's nose as you step forward. "OK" should be used to say "Job well done!"

Come

Now for everybody's most desired command. First you need to ask yourself a couple of things. Have you said "Come" more than once and yelled it repeatedly? Have you chased your dog and bribed him with his favorite delicacy? If so, trouble is brewing. Your dog thinks "Come" means disobedience; Come = Game Time! Fortunately, you can straighten him out, but it will take some time, concentration, structure, patience, and a lot of praise. If you think you have what it takes, read on!

Come Front

Like "Heel," "Come Front" is taught as a position near you. This time, your dog should be facing you and looking up. Whether you're calling your dog from two feet away or across the yard, he should come and sit down, paws facing toes, eye to eye. To teach your dog what "Come" is all about, start with a simple exercise that you'll use throughout the day. Practice it in the house to start.

Grrr
If you must position your dog, lift his collar gently and squeeze his waist muscles below his ribs as you press down. Avoid jerky motions and pressing his backbone. Do not command as you position.

1. Walk in front of your dog while he's standing calmly.

2. Standing tall, say *"Name,* Come" as you tap your foot and zip your finger up your belly from his nose level to your eyes. Make a funny sound to encourage focus.

3. If he comes but doesn't sit, guide him into the proper position by lifting up on his buckle collar and tucking his hind quarters into position.

4. Once your dog sits and makes eye contact, give him a big hug!

Repeat this exercise throughout the day, whenever you have something positive to share—a pat, treat, dinner, or toy. Make sure your dog's first associations to this word are warm and welcoming.

Distance Control

No, you're not off-lead yet. Be patient. Prerequisite? Your dog must understand that "Come" means a specific spot in front of you, looking up. Mission accomplished? Practice this exercise in a quiet room. No TV. No kids. No cats. Keep your lesson short and upbeat:

1. Practice three regular "Sit-Stays." Return to your dog's side and release him with an "OK!"

2. Leave your dog in a "Stay" and walk out to the end of the leash.

3. Pause. Vary the duration each time.

4. Call *"Name*, Come!" in a directional tone. Signal it by sweeping your right arm across your body.

Use a sweeping gesture to tell your dog to come.

5. As soon as you've issued the command, scurry backward and reel in the leash.

6. When he gets near your feet, signal up your belly and tap your heel to the floor (as described earlier) to encourage a "Sit" finish.

7. Encourage eye contact by standing tall and making kissing sounds.

8. Release him with "OK." Good dog!

Practice "Come" three times per session. That's all. More is stressful. Remember to blend each "Come" call with a few regular "Sit-Stays." If you don't, your dog will break his "Stay" early to please you. Sweet thing.

Troubleshooting the Come Command

Here are a few things to remember when teaching this command:

Use it sparingly. When it's over-used, dogs stop paying attention.

Don't chase your dog if she doesn't respond! Practice *on-lead* for now.

Never call for negatives. Do you have to brush, bathe, or isolate your dog? Don't use "Come." Avoid using it if you're angry. You'll only freak her out.

If your dog runs away, don't repeatedly call or correct her! I know the frustration of marching around in the middle of a cold, wet, rainy night looking for your dog, but if you call or discipline your dog, you'll only be teaching her to run from you.

Use a different command to bring your dog inside. Coming in from outdoors is a big drag, paralleled with being left alone or ignored. Using the command "Come" would make it a negative. Instead, pick a command like "Inside." Start using it on-lead when bringing your dog into the house. Quickly offer a treat or ball toss.

Are you having some problems with these first few exercises? Here are some situations my clients complain of:

My dog comes, but he's so excited that he jumps all over me! That reminds me of Jerome, a big chocolate Labrador Retriever, whose enthusiasm could knock anyone flat. When his owner called him in group, the entire class—dogs, people, and all—ducked for cover. It's a positive problem, though, so don't get me wrong. To tone it down, command in a calmer voice. As your dog comes, lean forward with your arms outstretched like an airline flagger. This blocking posture slows the dog down. Stand as she approaches. Say "Shhh" as she gets closer. Stand tall and click your heels to finish.

My dog stops three feet in front and either veers to one side, licks my face, or tinkles. You're probably bending over. Try leaning back when you call. Bent postures communicate play, confrontation, or submission. Straight posture communicates leadership.

My dog comes too fast for me to reel in the lead. Another problem with an easy solution. As soon as you've said your command, scurry backward. This will give you added time to reel in the lead.

My dog looks so depressed when I call her. Either you're commanding too harshly or not enthusiastically enough. Use low tones, not cross ones. Also increase your animation. Make it seem like more fun. Say "Come" and run backward or kneel down for the big effect.

Distraction Come

Does your dog get excited when she hears "Come"? Good job. Now you can start encouraging focus around low-level distractions and increasing the distance from which you call her. Here are some ideas (see if you can add to the list): try it in front of the TV, in the backyard, in front of the kids, and during mealtime. In a quiet hallway/garage, attach the Flexi-Leash® and increase your distance slowly.

Using the "Come" command around distractions is a taller order than your living room version. Most dogs try to pay attention to the distraction and you at the same time, which is impossible. If your dog's torn, say "No" and snap the lead when your dog turns toward the distraction. Praise him when he focuses on you: "Good Dog!"

Though "Come" is the command of the hour, don't forget to sandwich each exercise between a couple of normal "Sit-Stays." If you call your dog from each "Sit-Stay," he'll anticipate your request and since you can't correct a dog that's coming at you, you're stuck. Prevent the problem by working a few "Sit-Stays" between each "Come" command.

Are you having trouble getting your dog's attention around distractions? You're not alone. It's a hard nut to crack. My advice: stick with it. Don't give up. You must communicate that there's only one way to "Come" and that is to sit directly in front of you. Practice in a quiet room for a day, enthusiastically praising your dog's focus. Next try it with your TV on:

➤ Leave him: "Stay."

➤ Pause at least a minute (building up anticipation).

➤ With a straight back, deep voice, and gigantic hand signal, call "*Name*, Come!"

➤ Flag him in. If he sits straight, praise him happily!

➤ If not, side-step from the distraction, snap the chain firmly, and say "No."

➤ Encourage and praise any focus immediately.

Work up the distraction chain slowly. If your dog's too stimulated, practice around simpler distractions for a while. There's no rush. It's not a race. And whatever you do, don't get frustrated! Frustration kills enthusiasm.

"Come" is a funny thing. If used too much, dogs resist it. When your dog understands the command, avoid using it all the time. Say it infrequently and make it extremely rewarding! (Don't forget your other commands too: "Inside" for coming indoors, "Let's Go" for follow me, and "Heel" for staying at your side.)

Use "Come" in two of the following situations daily. You can add to the list (only two "Comes" a day though): when your dog's distracted on a walk; during regular teaching or with the Flexi-Leash®; indoors, as your dog's waking up from a nap; as your dog's getting out of the car; or when the neighbor's jogging by.

Here are a few more common questions:

My dog comes on the Flexi, but then veers by me. Are you fudging on the final step? Your dog must return to you, sit in front of you, and look up. Remind him with a few beginner "Come" exercises on his Teaching Lead®. When he's cooperating, go back to your Flexi-Leash® and correct him if he races by with "No" and a leash snap. Bring him into the proper position and praise as usual.

My dog looks at me like she's too busy to be bothered. Kind of amazing to see her thought process. Just tug the leash, say "No," and encourage her to you with praise.

If there's a distraction, my dog will walk sideways and sit on my feet to keep focused on it. Clever dog. Trying to please everyone. Not exactly what the dog trainer ordered! When your dog takes his eyes off you, side-step away from the distraction as you snap the lead and say "No!" Keep stepping and snapping until you get through. Don't settle for less than perfection if you're striving for that off-lead "Come!"

Down

Whoa Nellie! That's what the "Down" command says. Once you can get your dog to do this, you're really on your way. "Down" is also a sign of respect. Sound dreamy? It's easier said than taught, however, because the issue of trust also comes into play. For a dog to lower himself into a submissive, vulnerable position, he must be really sure you're the competent leader you say you are. Will you stand up to the scrutiny? We'll see...

Your dog's first "Down" lesson will be simple. You expect nothing; you're just showing your dog what the word means. You say it and help him into position over and over until he gets the picture. There are different strokes for different folks; pick the procedure that suits you best. Once you decide, practice 2–3 times daily, four "Downs" per session.

Sarah Says

Training a young dog makes it easier. Young, passive dogs are the easiest to persuade. Brutes, young and old, are more difficult. Am I giving you nightmares already? Good. Now that you're prepared for the worst, you may be in for a pleasant surprise.

The Easy Slide. This one is great for easy-going dogs or pups.

1. Instruct "Sit" and kneel down at your dog's right side.

2. Draw a quick line from your dog's nose to the floor and say "Down."

3. Place your left thumb between his shoulder blades and...

   Gently lift a paw forward with your right hand as you firmly press between the shoulder blades. Your dog should slide himself to the floor.

4. Don't pet your dog yet! Pause five seconds, verbally praising him quietly.

5. Release with "OK," stand up, and hug. Good dog!

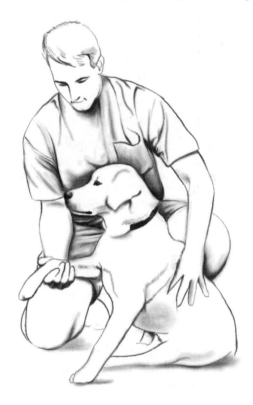

Teaching an easy-going dog to lay down.

The Side Swipe. If your dog locks up on the Slide, try this method:

1. "Sit" your dog and kneel at his right side.

2. Draw a quick line from your dog's nose to the floor and command "Down."

3. Reach your left arm over your dog's back and place each hand on a corresponding paw.

4. Lay your left forearm across his shoulder blades.

5. Gently lift your dog's paws as you apply pressure with your forearm.

6. Re-command "Down" as you're positioning.

7. Pause five seconds, while praising verbally.

8. Release with "OK," stand, and praise.

Look, No Hands! Does your dog think he's Jaws? If so, try this option:

1. Sit your dog and stand perpendicular to his right side.

Sarah Says
Once your dog begins cooperating, use "Down" for everything: before treating (hold the treat to the ground and command "Down"), dinner (cover the bowl with your hand and, as you put it down, say "Down"), or a Toy Toss (hide it in your hand, hold it to the ground, and command "Down").

2. Drop the leash-slack on the floor and calmly slide it under your left foot. Fold the remaining slack in your left hand.

3. Command "Down" as you point to the floor.

4. Pull up on the lead continually, forcing your dog's head down.

5. Most give in at this point. If yours does, praise verbally, pause, and release with "OK!"

6. If your dog doesn't respond, press his shoulder blades until he collapses into position. Hold the slack under your foot for five seconds. Release and praise.

Troubleshooting the Basic Down Command

Here are a few questions you might have:

What if my dog growls when I'm positioning him? Go to the phone immediately and get help from a professional dog trainer or behaviorist. You have a dominate dog who may bite when he doesn't agree with you.

What do I do when my dog mouths me? First of all, don't try to correct him! It turns the command into a challenge game. Your dog's anxious. Let him know there's nothing to fear by ignoring it. Yes, I'm serious. Allow your hand to go limp, stare at the wall in front of you, and ignore the situation until he settles. You're reassuring your dog that everything's cool. If it really hurts, take your hand away slowly and try the "Look, No Hands" method.

What if my dog rolls over when I give the "Down" command? Whatever you do, don't pet his belly! You're falling into the "game" trap. Stare at the wall and ignore the situation until he's upright. Then praise him quietly. Release him only when he's in the proper position.

My dog's a pop-tart! She goes down, and then pops right up again. As soon as she's down, hold your hand to her shoulder blades and slide the lead under your foot so she can't move. Release and praise her warmly after she stops struggling.

Can you command "Down" more than once? No. "Down" is like "Sit." If you keep repeating it, it becomes a different issue altogether.

The Upright Down

At this point, your dog should go down whenever you give the command—if company is visiting or when you're eating dinner, out in the yard, or at the veterinarian. Remember, "Down" communicates two things: "Calm Down" and "I'm the Leader." Now that he's had time to learn the word, you can give this command from a normal upright position:

1. Sit your dog, pivot perpendicular to him, and casually slide the lead under your left foot (gathering the slack in your left hand).

2. Stand straight and point to the ground as you command "Down" sternly. DON'T BEND! Pull the lead under your foot continually.

3. Praise for cooperation, pause, and release with "OK." (If your dog refuses, press down on his shoulder blades.)

4. Now it's time to change your position! Pivot six inches in front of your dog.

5. Slide the lead under your foot.

6. Lift your arm above your head. Point swiftly to the ground as you command "Down." Pull the lead gently if necessary. Press his shoulders if he refuses.

7. Pause, praise, and release.

Once your dog's responding well at six inches, pivot out one foot and repeat the above. Then pivot two feet, four feet, six feet, and so on. You're on your way!

Once you can instruct your dog "Down" at three feet, you're ready to start using the command in some everyday situations. Here are some ideas (add to this list): before you sit down to pet your dog, at night while you're watching TV or reading, or when your dog comes over for his good night kiss.

Now we're talking! Start using the "Down" command to settle your dog whenever he gets restless or a situation feels too out of control. Here are some things that flash to my mind (add to the list!): when company's visiting, at the veterinarian, when there's a sudden change in the environment, outdoors, when he gets over-stimulated, and so on. Start with

Sarah Says
Remember the ratio: one command = one action. If your dog responds, praise him lovingly. If he doesn't, position him calmly. Avoid getting frustrated; it only adds fear to an already stressful situation.

small distractions, such as squirrels, and work your way to big ones, such as other dogs, the mail carrier, and joggers!

More Challenging Questions about Down

Here are a few more common questions:

Should I practice "Down-Stay"? Once your dog goes "Down" willingly, you can practice "Down-Stay." Copy the "Sit-Stay" procedure.

My dog scoots forward when I command "Down" at a distance. What should I do? You may be moving out too quickly. Scooting is often a sign of separation anxiety. Corrections only intensify it. Return to a distance that your dog's comfortable with and work back slowly. If the scooting continues, however, you may try the following: Just before you give the command, lean forward, and re-command "Stay." Quickly command "Down" with a big hand signal. If your dog responds, stand straight, pause, and return to release. Position your dog in the original spot if necessary.

> **Sarah Says**
> You can correct your dog now that he knows better. If your dog blows you off defiantly, say "No" as you snap the leash and position firmly. If your dog is a real sweetie, don't correct very hard; just look disappointed.

Why do you start using discipline at this stage? If you keep positioning your dog, he won't learn your expectations. It's like teaching a child to tie her shoe. Eventually, she's going to have to tie it on her own. "No" lets your dog know your expectations.

We learned "Settle Down" with anchoring in Chapter 10. When do we use it versus "Down"? "Down" is given when you're requesting an immediate response. "Settle Down" instructs the dog to move to a specific spot and stay until released, whether that spot is the dog's bed across the room or by your side when the situation calls for it.

My dog scoots around on his belly when there's something stimulating. How do I correct him? You try not to. Ignoring often helps, unless he scoots completely out of place. Then stepping on the lead can do the trick. If all else fails, wait until he's out of place, act astonished, and reposition him sternly with "Shhh!"

My dog doesn't listen when other dogs are around. Join the club. A class taught by a competent teacher is your best bet. It's a lot of fun, great socialization, and very helpful if you have the right teacher. Ask around your neighborhood or call your veterinarian. If you have some choices, view ongoing classes before you select one.

My dog is very fearful at the veterinarian. Should I force him "Down"? You can use a "Town Down" once you've practiced it at home. I love this application. Here's how it goes: Place a chair in the middle of a room. Fold the lead up neatly in your left hand. As you sit, point under the chair and command "Down." Grasp the lead under your knees and thread him into position. Slide the leash under your foot and command "Stay." You've done your first "Town Down," so called because it works great when you're out on the town. Once you've mastered it at home, try it on the park bench, at a barbecue, when visiting a neighbor, or in your veterinarian's waiting room!

The Least You Need To Know

➤ You are the biggest factor in training—not your dog's age, breed, or sex. Though these factors are important, how you approach the training process is critical.

➤ Learning takes time. Don't rush the process. Go one step at a time. Be cool.

➤ Straighten your back when giving commands. Look confident and strong. You're the leader!

➤ Watch that tone! Watch that tone! Watch that tone—it can't be overemphasized, although I've tried. Keep your voice strong and serious when giving your commands. Use a happy high-pitched voice to praise him for a job well done.

Tricky Bits

Dogs love to laugh—yes, laugh. Oh sure, some would argue they can't, but I've laughed with my dog and I'll bet you have, too. Take tricks, for example. They're a challenge to learn, but once that phase is over, they're a real delight. Training doesn't have to be all work, work, work and structure, structure, structure. Once your dog knows the basics, you can have some fun and teach him tricks that will bring a smile to every face!

Stand Still

This trick is great for wiping muddy paws and grooming. Fortunately, it's not too tough to teach.

1. Kneel down on the floor next to your dog.

2. Place your right hand, palm out, on your dog's buckle collar.

3. Slide your left hand under your dog's belly.

Stand still, sport!

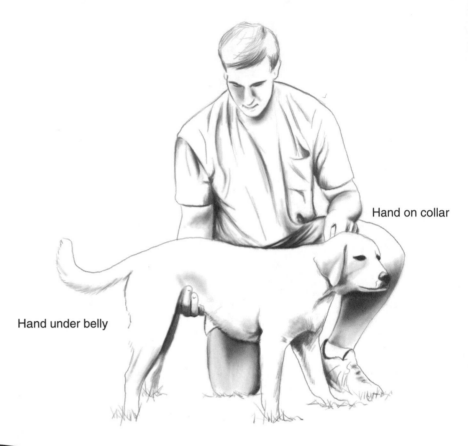

Hand on collar

Hand under belly

Sarah Says

Does grooming your dog give you nightmares? Try peanut butter. Rub some on the edge of your bath tub or the side of the refrigerator as you brush. Say "Stand still," as your dog licks away. Most dogs get so carried away with licking, they don't even notice what you're doing. (If peanut butter doesn't work, try margarine or butter.) Soon, you can ease off the peanut butter; just say "Stand still" as you brush.

4. Command "Stand still" as you prop your dog into a standing position.

5. Relax your right hand and slide your left to rest on your dog's thigh.

6. Pause 2, 3, 4, 5...and release with an "OK!"

7. Increase the time to one minute.

8. Repeat the above steps from a standing position.

9. Now you're ready to let go, so prop your dog into position.

10. Remind "Still" and slide your left hand away from your dog.

11. Once you're successful, slide you right hand from the collar. Remind "Still" as often as necessary.

Once your dog catches on, begin using this command whenever the situation calls for it. Does your dog have muddy paws? Have him "Stand still." Sure, your dog may be fidgety; just say, "Shhh…Stand still." For brushing, try the same thing.

Other Tricky Bits

Here are a few tricks that are nonessential, but fun. You don't need to teach your dog all of them—just those your dog picks up easily. For example, if your dog's paw expressive, he'll definitely get into the "Paw" or "Wave." Teaching a trick or two spices up the normal routine.

Paw, High-five, or Wave

Is your dog paw expressive? Does he always slap you for a pat while you're trying to read the paper or talk on the phone? You need to redirect his habits. What better way than a good old-fashioned parlor trick?

Bet You Didn't Know

A dog can learn many tricks from one action. With pawing, for example, you can teach your dog to shake your hand, wave a big hello, or slap your hand for a high-five!

Teaching your dog to Paw is easy and fun! Start from a sitting position and follow these steps:

1. Say "Paw" or "Shake" as you extend your hand in front of your dog.

2. If your dog looks puzzled, press his shoulder muscle with your other hand.

3. Take his paw the instant he lifts it off the ground and praise him. Soon he'll be reaching out for you.

All of my dogs have mastered the Wave. It's a real charmer, especially for kids. Teach it using these steps:

1. Sit your dog. Hold a treat inches from his nose and say "Wave" as you wave your hand in front of him.

2. Praise and treat him the instant he lifts his paw.

3. Encourage more enthusiastic waving as he catches on.

Your dog's going to have to reach to learn the high-five. What's the prerequisite? He must be a champion paw-er. Follow these steps:

1. Do two Paws. Be an enthusiastic praiser.

2. Hold your hand up and out for the high-five. Say "Paw, high-five!"

3. Lower your hand if your dog makes an attempt. Soon he'll be bringing that paw up enthusiastically!

Ask Nicely

Good balance is a requirement for the Ask Nicely trick. You're asking your dog to tilt back from a sitting position and balance on his hind paws, like the old begging routine. Here's how:

1. Break up five favorite treats.

2. With your dog in a sitting position, place a treat centimeters above his nose.

3. Command "Ask nicely" as you bring the treat back toward his ears.

4. If he tilts back for a split second, treat and praise him. *Encourage the slightest effort; increase your expectations slowly!*

5. If your dog's trying, but can't seem to balance himself, stand behind him with your heels together near his tail. Draw the treat back and catch his chest, leaning his body against your legs. Repeat the command as you hold and treat him. Then praise him.

Bowing Out

Does your dog love a good stretch? Betcha didn't know you could turn this one into a trick:

➤ As your dog's stretching, bow toward him and say "Bow!"

➤ Praise your dog like he just invented the dog biscuit!

➤ Repeat this each time your dog stretches.

Soon he'll be bowing on cue!

Roll Over

Everybody wants his/her dog to roll over. Few dogs are so impressed. Does your dog roll over on his own? Does he shift from side to side with ease? If so, he'll like doing this trick. If not, find another trick to impress your friends.

1. Get a handful of treats and encourage your dog into a down position.

2. Scratch your dog until he rolls to one side.

3. Take the treat and circle it from your dog's nose to the floor.

4. Say "Roll over" as you circle the treat around his nose toward his chest. It's hard to visualize, I know, but imagine a string tied from the treat to your dog's nose; you're trying to pull his body over.

5. If he seems to lean into it, praise him and flip his paws over. Praise him wildly and encourage him to jump up!

Nap Time!

I've always thought the trick Play Dead was a little depressing. It is clever though, so I simply switched the command. This one's easy if you have a calm dog and it's good practice for the high-energy ones:

1. Command "Down." Encourage your dog to rest on one side.

2. Kneel next to your dog, but don't look at him.

3. Tap the floor near his head and say "Nap time."

4. Gently apply pressure to his shoulder and help him rest his head on the floor.

5. Keep his head in place by stroking it gently while commanding "Stay."

6. Release your dog once he's still, increasing the still time gradually.

Once your dog cooperates, take your hand off his head slowly. Eventually, stand up. Do everything gradually. Remind him "Nap, Stay" as needed.

> **Sarah Says**
> Never practice tricks during lesson time. You'll be turning serious work into a game.

Break Dance

This is a clever trick. Do you have a dog who has a perpetual back itch? Scratching is a common ploy dogs use to escape lessons; however, it can be an awfully cute trick, too.

1. When your dog starts to roll on his back, say "Break dance!"

2. Bend over and scratch his belly as you praise him.

Repeat this process again and again until you're able to command him on cue! This trick is a real crowd pleaser.

Head Down

Is your dog a head knocker? Does he always nudge your arm for attention, especially when you're trying to enjoy your morning coffee? Believe it or not, you can redirect this misguided behavior.

Each time your dog butts his head against you for attention, say "Head down," and encourage your dog to lay his head in your lap (holding his head still if you must). Though he may resist in the beginning, be diligent. Pet your dog when his head rests in your lap.

Soon, he'll have a new and more polite way of demanding your attention and you'll be able to enjoy your morning coffee again!

The Least You Need To Know

➤ Training doesn't always have to be work, work, work. Once your dog knows the basics, you can have some fun.

➤ When teaching tricks, stay positive—no discipline allowed.

➤ Use treats to encourage cooperation. Sometimes tricks can be confusing.

➤ Laugh a little.

Chapter 14

Advanced Moves

In This Chapter

➤ Steady an off-lead "Stay"

➤ Get your dog's attention at a distance

➤ Work all commands off-lead

➤ Teach and use an Emergency Down

No one can underestimate the pleasures of a well-trained dog. In Chapter 12, we went over leash training techniques. Master these before you begin the exercises described in this chapter. As you work toward off-lead control, don't get too bold. You'll have less control. Your dog has a choice. If he doesn't want to come and he's free to run, you may be standing there helpless. Off-lead work means constantly reading your dog and being aware that your dog is reading you. To have control, you must look like a leader; be confident and self-assured, so your dog will want to trust your judgment.

To further your mental preparation, keep these three steps in mind:

➤ **Stay Cool.** Frustration makes you look weak. As you wean your dog to off-lead commands, your dog may act confused and unresponsive. There is a reason. The guidance step of the command sequence is gone. You used to give the command

and guide her with the lead. Now, something's missing. It will feel awkward. Whatever her reaction, stay cool. Any corrections will add to her confusion. Jazz up your body language and use some pep talks to encourage her toward you.

➤ **Stay Focused.** Eye contact communicates control. Your dog should be watching you. If the reverse is true, you're the follower. To avoid this, make sure you're working in a confined area so that you can ignore your dog when she disobeys. If you're near your house, walk inside. A graceful retreat is not a failure.

➤ **Step Back.** Your dog is responding off-lead beautifully until...someone rings the bell, a chipmunk runs across the drive, or another dog's around; then everything's out the window. You're back to being ignored. Let me tell you a secret. Off-lead control takes time. If your dog is good, but still having trouble in a stimulated situation, use your Teaching Lead®. Using it helps control the situation while simultaneously conditioning more appropriate behavior.

Using Some New Equipment

As you work toward off-leash obedience, you'll be practicing exercises that extend your control to farther and farther distances. Before you start, round up these items:

➤ **Flexi-Leash®.** This retractable leash is invaluable for advanced work. The longer, the better.

➤ **Tree Line.** You attach this line to a tree and practice distance command control. Purchase a canvas leash or make your own out of a clothes line attached to a dog clip, which you can purchase at a hardware store.

➤ **Long Line.** You'll be using this for distance control with "Wait," "Heel," "Down," and "Come" commands. Purchase a canvas lead or use a clothes line.

➤ **10-foot Line.** Make this in the same fashion as the 30-foot line. You'll use this line to reinforce house control.

Grrr
Attach all lines to your dog's buckle collar, not her training (choke) collar.

➤ **The Short Lead.** This is an additional training tool. It should be long enough to grab, though short enough not to distract your dog.

Off-lead dogs aren't created overnight. Training is a step-by-step process. You'll be using your new equipment to increase your dog's focus, but don't get itchy fingers. Just because she behaves well on her Flexi-Leash® one day doesn't mean she's ready for an off-lead romp the next. Take your time. Though I'll explain how to train with each piece of equipment separately, you should use them interchangeably in your training exercises.

Training with the Flexi-Leash®

This leash is a great exercising tool. It allows freedom to explore, while still leaving you in complete control. As a training tool, you can use it informally during walks to reinforce the following commands:

*"**Name**."* Call out your dog's name enthusiastically: "Daisy!" If she looks at you, praise her. That's all that's required. Just a glance. If she ignores you, snap the leash, say "No," and then praise her once you have her attention.

"**Wait**." Begin to command your dog to stop three feet in front of you with this command. If your dog continues forward, snap the leash and say, "No, wait." Increase your distance to 6 feet, 8 feet, 12 feet, 16 feet, and 26 feet in front of you.

"**Sit-Stay**." Use the Flexi-Leash® to increase your distance control. Increase your distance incrementally.

"**Heel**." Use this command to call your dog back to your side. Call out her name and then command "Heel" as you slap your leg. Praise your dog as she responds, then walk a short distance before you stop to release her.

"**No**." Whenever your dog's focusing on something she shouldn't be, snap the leash and say "No!" Immediately refocus her attention with a toy, stick, or command.

Training with the 10-foot Line

Use this line while you're keeping an eye on your dog. Every couple of minutes, stand by the line and give a command ("Sit," "Down," "Wait," "Come"). If she looks confused, step on the line, and praise her anyway as you help her into position. For example, if you command "Down" and she gives you a blank stare, praise her as you guide her into position. Your understanding will help her overcome her off-lead confusion.

If your dog gives you some defiant canine back talk (a bark or dodge), step on the lead, snap it firmly as you say "No," and station and ignore her for 15 minutes. She's been grounded with no TV!

*Control with the
10-foot line.*

Practice Indoors with the Short Lead

Use the short lead indoors after your dog's reliable on the ten-foot line. When it's attached to your dog's buckle collar, you can use it to reinforce your stationary commands: Sit, Stay, Down, Wait, Heel, and Come.

In addition to using the short lead around the house, do a lesson once a day. Bring your dog into a quiet room and practice a command routine. Initially, hold the short lead, but then drop it once you've warmed up. Slap your leg and use hand signals and peppy body language to encourage your dog's focus.

Branching Out with a 20-foot Tree Line

Tie this line to a tree or post. Secure all knots. Leave the line on the ground and follow the sequence described next.

Working your dog with the tree line.

Warm up with five minutes of regular on-lead practice. Stop your dog next to the 20-foot line and attach it to your dog's buckle collar discreetly. Remove her regular lead and place it on the ground in front of her. Keep your hands free.

Command "Stay" and walk 10 feet away. Extend your distance as she gains control. Run your fingers through your hair and swing your arms gently back and forth to emphasize that your dog is off-lead. As your dog improves, practice an out of sight "Sit-Stay." Practice "Down" from a "Sit-Stay" and a "Down-Stay." The command "Come" can also be practiced, but never call at a distance greater than the line will reach.

If she falls for this and darts for a quick get-a-way, wait until she's about to hit the end of the line to shout "No!" Return her back into position and repeat the exercise at a closer range.

If your dog disobeys, determine whether her response is motivated by anxiety, confusion, or defiance. If she's confused or anxious, do not issue a correction. Calmly return to her side and reposition gently. Repeat the same exercise at close range. If your dog breaks defiantly, however, either shout "No" as she hits the end of the line or, if she's baiting you, return quietly and snap the lead as you say "No." Reposition and repeat the exercise at close range for quicker control. Good luck!

The Big 30-foot Long Line

Now for some outdoor stuff. Attach your dog to the 30-foot long line and let her roam free as you keep a watchful eye. Engage her by playing with a stick or ball and investigate your surroundings together. Avoid over-commanding. Just hang out and enjoy some free time with your dog. Every five minutes, position yourself near the line and issue a command enthusiastically.

Sarah Says
Practice in an enclosed area. It only takes one mistake to lose your dog; until she's an off-lead expert, she may get confused.

If it's a stationary command, like "Sit," "Wait," or "Down," stop abruptly and stamp your foot while giving the command and signaling. If it's a motion command, like "Come" or "Heel," run backward as you encourage your dog toward you. If she races over, help her into the proper position and give her a big hug. If your dog ignores your command, quickly step on the line and say "No." Don't scream; just speak sternly. After your correction, give your dog the opportunity to right her reaction before lifting the line to snap it or reel her in. End your session with a favorite game.

Those Nagging Questions about Off-Lead Training

Before I address questions, let me warn you: Practice all initial training in an enclosed area. When you start off-leash, your dog may turn into a little comedian and bound away from you just for fun, so keep it safe until he's reliable. You may be wondering many things at this point. Here are a list of questions I'm asked most often:

When will I know that I can trust my dog off lead? You should feel it. It's never a smooth road in the beginning; some days you'll get a quick and happy response, others will feel more like your first day of training. Stay cool though. Frustration is a sign of weakness and you'll lose your dog's respect. Keep your dog enclosed as you practice so that if she starts to act cocky, you can retreat immediately. And don't hesitate to go back to Long Line or Teaching Lead® exercises for quick review.

It's so frustrating when my dog ignores me. I know I shouldn't, but I really felt like hitting my dog. Feeling like hitting is fine. Hitting your dog isn't. It would erode your relationship and diminish his off-lead trust. If you're really angry, walk away calmly. Remember, a graceful retreat is not a failure.

Can I use treats for the off-lead stuff? I don't recommend it. Treats become very addictive and, as you'd soon find out, dogs taught with food are less responsive when the food's not around. Training should focus your dog on you, so make yourself the treat!

My dog breaks every time I leave him in a "Sit-Stay" on his Flexi-Leash®. Increase your distance slowly. For example, if your dog gets up every time you walk out 15 feet, practice at 10 feet for a week, then 11 feet, 12 feet, and so on. In addition, don't face your dog as you walk out. Walking backward invites a "Come" response. Instead, walk out confidently, back toward your dog, and pivot at your final destination. Remind him to "Stay."

There are times when my dog crouches and barks at me. Don't look at her. She's trying to turn all your hard work into a game. Ignore her until her antics subside. Work her on the Teaching Lead® if she's being impossible.

Don't the lines get caught around trees and doors? Yes they do. Clip all lines to the buckle collar and never leave your dog unsupervised.

When I go to position my dog, she stays just out of reach. Watch that body language and negative eye contact. Being off the Teaching Lead® is nerve-wracking for both of you. Look at the ground as you return to your dog. If she's still out of reach, kneel down and wait. When she approaches, take her collar gently, reposition, and work at close range.

My dog picks the end of the line up in her mouth and prances around me like a show horse. Clever girl. Try soaking the end of the line in Bitter Apple® liquid or Tabasco sauce overnight. If she's still acting cocky, quietly go inside and watch her discreetly from the window.

Sarah Says
No off-lead practice in an unconfined area. Your dog's a fragile jewel you must protect.

When I place my dog on the short lead, I can't get near her. You'll need to work on your 10-foot line for another week or so. When you try the short lead again, place it on *with* your 10-foot line and correct her by stepping on it when she darts away.

Emergency Down

This exercise can be a real lifesaver once your dog learns that when you say "Down," you want him to drop as though he's been shot. In the beginning, it can be a little confusing; so be patient and positive throughout your training process. Don't start practicing this exercise until your dog has mastered the Down command.

1. Stand next to your unsuspecting dog.

2. Suddenly command "Down" in a very life-threatening tone (the type of tone you'd use if a loved one were about to walk off a cliff). Point toward the ground.

3. Kneel down quickly as you bring your dog into position.

4. Act like you're being bombed too!

Soon your dog will catch on and act independently. Once she does, begin extending your distance from her. Eventually, this exercise could save your dog's life if you were ever

Grrr
This exercise is very stressful! Limit your practice to one out-of-the-blue Emergency Down sequence a day.

separated by a road and her life was threatened by an oncoming vehicle. It's true! The Emergency Down really does save lives. Once I was leaving my training classes with my husky, Kyia, when a tennis ball slipped loose and started rolling toward the road. Kyia, sweet thing, wanted to help and ran innocently to collect it. In a panic, I shouted "Down" and she dropped like she'd been shot. What a good girl!

Practicing the Emergency Down.

The Least You Need To Know

➤ It's all a mind game at this stage. You must be positive, structured, and mentally tough. You're the leader; now it's time to show it.

➤ Your dog's anticipating your behavior as you try to anticipate hers.

➤ Getting your dog off leash requires a good plan. Use longer and longer leashes until your dog responds to you from afar.

➤ Stand tall, command confidently, and don't be afraid to have a little fun!

Chapter 15

Beyond the Backyard

> ## In This Chapter
>
> ➤ Going public
>
> ➤ Car manners
>
> ➤ Once you arrive at your destination
>
> ➤ Greeting dogs and people
>
> ➤ Grates and other scary objects
>
> ➤ Impressing your veterinarian

Training's biggest reward is the freedom it gives you to take your dog everywhere! Your dog will be a welcomed social guest, a plus at parades and picnics, and an added fan at after school sporting events.

Dogs don't transfer their lessons from the living room to public appearances. They need to be taught how to behave in social situations. In this chapter, I'll cover this type of training.

Going Public

Before you jump right in, you'll need to prepare yourself. The first trip out can be a real embarrassment. You'll feel self-conscious, your dog will be too distracted to listen, and you'll feel compelled to tell everyone, even those who aren't paying any attention, that your dog's in training. How do I know? I've been there.

Before you hit the streets, you should practice in selective areas so that you can devote all of your attention to your dog. Eventually, it will seem effortless and your dog will truly be welcomed everywhere. But your first trip out may be a real shocker. Are you wondering, "If it's such a nightmare, why bother?" There are three reasons:

➤ It gets easier.

➤ A well-mannered dog is fun to share.

➤ It enhances your dog's focus. You'll be the one looking confident in new, unexplored territories.

The first outing with your perfect-at-home pal may feel more like his first day of training, but don't be discouraged. Think of it as a test to determine if those house rules apply everywhere. Even I had the "first-outing blues" with my dog Calvin. As I was trying to steady his Heel, I walked straight into a light post. Ouch! But that first day passed and Calvin learned his manners were expected everywhere, whether greeting Aunt Carolyn at the door or ten school children in the park. The eventual compliments overshadowed my initial embarrassment, but I didn't start out with perfection and you may not either.

So now that you know going public requires some effort, I'm going to draw you a map that guides you from putting your dog into the car to the ride home. I'll walk you through step-by-step. But before we begin, there are some universal rules to keep in mind:

Keep your dog on his Teaching Lead®. His leash reminds him of good behavior. No fancy stuff or showing off, please. There are too many dangers!

Use lots of encouragement. Cheerfulness is contagious.

Sarah Says
Bring a bag just in case of accidents!

Paws behind heels! Remember, you lead and he follows.

Keep the communication flowing. Commands provide structure.

No elimination in public. Take care of that activity at home.

Know when to say "No" to both your dog and other people.

I know it sounds like a lot. Once you get the hang of it, though, it'll seem like second nature. It's all about leadership.

Car Manners

The first step in shaping your perfect-public-partner is getting him to the destination with your sanity intact. If some of you are chuckling, it's no wonder. Most dogs are less than cooperative in the car. Jumping from seat to seat and barking at passing strangers is the norm.

Put yourself in your dog's paws. To him, your automobile is a window box with wheels. And while passing cars, pausing for bicycles, and braking for squirrels is part of your normal routine, it pushes his chasing and territorial instincts to the max! Whether he barks or bounces, the predator whizzes away. Conclusion? He's victorious—the champ! Not only do they run away, but they run fast! You haven't even gotten out of the car and your dog's already pumped. See where the problem starts?

Where does it end? Negative corrections don't work. Yelling is perceived as barking—backup, collaboration style. Besides, discipline and driving don't mix. To solve this problem or to train a fresh dog or pup to behave, follow this routine:

1. Lead your dog to the car with the command "Heel."

2. Open the door and command "Wait." Pause.

3. Say "Go to your spot" and direct your dog to a car station.

4. Secure your dog on a car lead and tell him "Stay."

Now you can proceed. Things always go smoother when they're organized. Now it's time to get out of the car. Again, from your dog's paws, the situation is pretty exciting—new sights, smells, and faces. Don't take it personally if he doesn't notice you or listen to commands at first. Getting him focused is the challenge at hand:

1. Before you open the door, instruct "Wait."

2. If he jumps forward, catch the car lead, say "No," and snap it back.

3. Re-instruct "Wait" and pause until he's calm.

4. Put on his Teaching Lead® and say "OK" as you let him exit.

5. Immediately instruct "Heel," bringing him to your side.

6. Instruct "Wait" as you shut the door.

7. Proceed with "Heel." Now you're walking in style!

Sarah Says
Attach the clip to the buckle collar or chin lead. Do not clip the car lead to a training collar.

Car Fear?

Cars really frighten some dogs. It's a worrisome problem. The cause usually goes back to being transported at an early age, but it can result later in life too. If your dog suffers from this, avoid pacifying or being overly forceful. Both reinforce fear. If you must take him somewhere, pick him up if possible or take him to the car while he's napping. Speak or sing softly. Have the car already pulled out with classical music playing on the radio. Equip his area with a familiar blanket and a favorite toy. For further suggestions, see Chapter 27.

Refusal?

Does your dog refuse to hop into the car? Well it's understandable if your dog's a tiny tot, but if you have a 120-pound Great Dane, you're being taken for a ride. You have to make a stand not to lift him ever again. If you do, you're forcing him into a state of learned helplessness. Lead him to the car, taking some of his favorite treats along, and try baiting him in. If this makes little impression, get in the car and, as you bribe him, pull him gently forward. Still no luck? Bring a friend along, pass the lead to her through the car, and have her gently pull as you encourage him forward. If he still resists, physically walk each limb into the automobile one at a time, but under no circumstances lift!

Grrr
Your dog must be vaccinated before taking him out. Many deadly diseases are airborne and vaccinations are your dog's only protection against them.

Once You Get There

Once you get to your destination, the first five minutes is three quarters of the battle. Whatever practice location you've picked—a park, town, friend's house, or building—first impressions really count. If you take control immediately and give understandable directions, the rest will be a tail wag.

Let's pick up where we left off. You've just brought your dog into a Heel after shutting the car door. Instantly, your dog will probably have one of two reactions: he'll become wild or he'll become a scaredy cat.

The Wild One

If your dog is the wild type, his nose will be twitching a mile a minute, he'll pivot toward every new stimulation, and pull to investigate every blade of grass. Here's a way to control your Huck Fin.

➤ Enforce "Heel." Keep his paws behind your ankles at all points.

➤ Tell strangers to back off until your dog's trained. It's embarrassing, I know, but it's a must. You don't want Buddy jumping up and giving someone a scratch, even by accident.

➤ Reinforce your requests. If you ask for a "Sit-Stay," get a Sit-Stay.

Take all commands back to the introductory stage, no matter how well you're doing at home. Initially practice only "Heel" and "Stay" commands.

Scaredy Cat

If you have a passive or scared dog, the experience of arriving at a new place may seem overwhelming. His tail may disappear, his body may lower, and, when stimulated, he'll try to hide behind you. If you bend to soothe your scaredy cat, you'll be reinforcing his reaction. It's so tempting to soothe him, I know. Just keep saying to yourself over and over, soothing reinforces fear, soothing reinforces fear. Instead:

1. Look confident and stand tall like a good leader dog. Soon he'll mimic you!

2. Bring some treats and a favorite toy along to focus his attention on. Withholding them at home makes the new adventure seem really exciting!

3. Use "Heel" and "Stay" commands often; familiar sounds soothe anxiety.

4. If he's too nervous to listen, enforce a response without corrections.

5. Stay calm and positive. Deflect any admirers until he's feeling safe.

Troubleshooting Your Arrival

Having some trouble? Here are some questions I often get:

Heel! Are you joking? He does it great at home, but he's a maniac everywhere else! There are two remedies for an out-of-control Heel:

➤ **The Side-Step.** Whenever your dog is focusing on something to your left, take a giant step to the right, snap the lead, and remind "Heel." The bigger or older the dog, the sharper the snap. Repeat until your dog's alert to you. Praise that!

➤ **The Kick Back.** If you have a charging brut on your hands, lock your left hand to the back of your thigh. The second he moves forward, remind "Heel" as you thrust your left leg back. Don't kick him, though; just move your leg in the opposite direction as you remind "Heel." Repeat until he stays behind your leg.

If you're still having problems, consider a different collar or try holding the lead behind your back.

My dog starts barking the second I let him out of the car! He's obviously a very excited guy. Start practicing in empty parking lots. Bring along a travel mister pump filled with white vinegar or Binaca Mouth Spray®, which you can find at your local pharmacy. If he should start barking, spritz his nose and say "Shhh." You must be sneaky about the spritz though; he can't know where it's coming from.

My dog's so afraid, she freezes and won't move. I've never seen her this bad. If she's terrified, get some help. Try coaxing her forward with her favorite treats or peanut butter and praise.

Greeting People

Stop shaking. This doesn't have to be a hair-raising experience. Just keep your head on straight and remember everything I've taught you. I have faith in you! Before I talk you through this, though, please read over the following disclosures. If you identify with any of them, please follow my specific instructions and skip the rest of this section.

First Disclosure. If you're having aggression problems, the only person you must introduce your dog to is a trainer with a specialty in aggression rehabilitation. How do you find such an expert? Ask your veterinarian. It's better to be safe than sued.

Second Disclosure. If you notice your dog getting nervous or tense around unfamiliar people, join a class or work under private supervision. Don't push the issue alone.

Third Disclosure. If you don't believe it will work, it won't. Hire some extra help to build your own confidence!

If you're still with me, here are five key rules to follow when debuting that dog of yours:

➤ **Rule #1.** Make sure your dog is familiar and comfortable with the setting before attempting to introduce him to anyone. Don't greet people your first day out!

➤ **Rule #2.** Feet ahead of paws! Correct all attempts to scoot forward.

➤ **Rule #3.** Tell admirers what you're doing; "We're in training."

➤ **Rule #4.** Stay more focused on your dog than the admirer. Correct all attempts to break.

➤ **Rule #5.** Put faith in your own knowledge. Just because everyone has advice, that doesn't mean it's right. "I don't mind if he jumps," doesn't hold water. You mind! Period.

Now for the actual greeting. Drum roll please! How you handle the situation will depend on none other than your dog. If your dog is overly enthusiastic, you'll need to tame his expressiveness. Keeping him focused on you is the key.

Dogs are fun to share, but they must greet properly. Even when greeting others, your dog should stay focused on you.

175

Greeting a Wild One

Ask people to wait until your wild one is calm. Enforce a "Sit-Stay," keeping your feet ahead of his paws. Place your left hand, fingers down, along his waist and below the ribs. Using your right thumb to brace his collar, hold him steady in case he jumps. If the person still wants to, he can pet your dog! Remind your dog to "Stay" and don't let up your vigil until the person is gone. Whew—what a work out!

Greeting a Scaredy Cat

Ask your greeter to wait until you and your dog are in position. Place your dog in a "Sit-Stay" and kneel down at his side. Put your left hand on his waist and your right hand on his chest, holding his head up for confidence as the greeter pets him.

Help with Greeting Problems

If your dog is a little cautious when people approach, before you start, place some treats in your pocket. Ask the person to wait until you and your dog are positioned. Enforce a "Sit-Stay," keeping your feet ahead of his paws. Once he's steady, ask the person to give him a fist full of treats without attempting to pet him. If he seems comfortable, pet him together as you hold his head upright with your left hand. If he still seems nervous, quit while you're ahead! You'll get there.

As he gets more confident, wean him off his treat dependency. Use one with every other person, then every third person, and so on.

> **Sarah Says**
> If your dog's nervous, bring along some goodies or, if he likes peanut butter, bring along a jar. Have your greeter give him some to win his approval.

Encountering Other Dogs

Are you shaking again? Envisioning your dog hurling himself at the end of the lead? Well, wake up! You're having a nightmare.

Seriously, though. If you've had some stressful encounters in the past, try to put them behind you. Memories cloud control. Wipe the slate clean and have faith in what I've taught you. If you see a dog when you're out and about, don't approach it immediately. First, get control of your situation:

1. If your dog acts excited, snap the lead firmly and remind "Heel."

2. Continue in your original direction and pick up your pace.

3. Don't look toward, approach, or follow the other dog.

4. If your dog continues acting wild, speed up and keep snapping.

5. Praise him for focusing on you.

6. Never give in or let up!

Letting Your Dog Greet Other Dogs

Once you have your dog under control, you can permit a greeting by saying "OK, Go play!" Before you do, though, make certain the other dog is friendly and the other owner is respectful of your training efforts. When playtime is over, instruct your dog to "Heel" and move on.

If your friend has dogs and you want to get the dogs together to play, let them meet each other on neutral ground, such as an empty playground or field. This prevents a fierce territorial reaction. When they first meet, you should expect a lot of bluffs, such as growling, mouthiness, and mounting. Don't choke up on the leads. It's natural. Interference might prompt a fight. Stay calm, but observe closely. The dogs must determine a hierarchy. Once that's accomplished, they'll settle down. If you're certain a fight has begun, separate them with the leashes. Don't handle fighting dogs.

If You're Approached

If you're not in the mood or your dog's too hyped, just say no. If you're game, however, get your dog in control behind you and then release with an "OK, Go play!" Call him back to "Heel" when playtime is over.

If You're Approached by an Off-Lead Dog

If you're approached by an off-lead dog, don't hesitate, don't look at the dog, and don't let your dog look at the dog. Just walk quickly away from the area. Discourage any confrontational attempts your dog makes by snapping the leash and walking faster. Both of you should avoid eye contact. An off-lead dog defends his territory. If you leave without confrontation, he'll stop the chase immediately to harbor his fighting reserves for a more threatening foe.

Entering Buildings

Pick a building you might visit with your dog: the veterinarian's office, hardware store, pet shop, or your kids' school. Your dog's behavior in those buildings will depend on who enters the building first. Yup, that's it. If your dog leads you, then he's in charge. If you lead your dog, then you're the head honcho. Whoever *starts* in charge *stays* in charge.

Sarah Says

Some dogs are nervous when they enter new buildings. If your dog is, don't reinforce his anxiety. If your dog's showing fear, show confidence. Don't pet him or reassure him things will be okay. Instead, take along some treats to encourage him as you approach the building. Stand tall and ignore his caution. If he puts on the brakes, kneel down and encourage him inside.

1. Bring your dog to a "Heel" as you exit the car.

2. As you get to the threshold, brace your arm behind your back. (Dogs sense when they're going somewhere new!)

3. Say "Sshh" if he starts getting excited.

4. Pause before you open the door and command "Wait."

5. Don't open the door until he's settled down.

6. Re-command "Wait" as you open the door.

7. If your dog lunges, snap him back sternly and say "No!"

8. Pause again until your dog is calm.

9. Say "OK" as you lead him through!

Curb Etiquette

Whether you live in a city or not, eventually you'll run across a curb. Applying our usual psychology, some restraint is in order here!

1. As you approach the curb, your dog should be in a "Heel."

2. At the curb, instruct "Wait."

3. If your dog continues, snap the lead and say "No, Wait," pulling him behind your ankles.

4. Say "OK" as you lead him across.

5. Remind "Heel."

To keep your dog behind you, hold the leash behind your thigh.

Grates and Other Scary Objects

When you go out, you may run into objects or obstacles that are pretty scary to your dog. How you handle the situation will determine his reaction. Take a grate, for example. If your dog's nervous and you soothe him, you'll be communicating fear and he'll grow more cautious.

On the other hand, if you act confident by investigating the new object on your own, you'll highlight your courage and impress your dog. He'll follow your lead and, after seeing no harm came to you, he'll grow more confident. Follow this approach.

*Grates can be
a formidable
obstacle.*

Take you dog's favorite treats and go sit on a grate. Encourage him to the perimeter. Slowly encourage him forward and praise him as he attempts to take his first steps. It may take weeks to see him walk over a grate calmly.

Other Common Fears

One of the cutest miracles I get to perform is teaching pups to handle stairs. I'll tell you my secret. Once your puppy is large enough to handle stairs, avoid carrying him. Instead, brace his rib cage securely in your hands and help him to manipulate his body to do the action. Don't forget to praise him while you do. If yours is really frightened by the whole flight, carry him to the bottom few steps and ask someone to kneel below to coach him forward.

Some dogs fear people in uniform. To help him overcome his fear, act very friendly toward uniformed people. Ask them to help you socialize your puppy as you give them some treats to offer to him. If they're willing, ask them to kneel and avoid eye contact until he's sniffed them out. Another great trick is to rent a uniform from a costume shop and dress up in one yourself!

Some dogs fear people of a particular sex. This problem results from any number of circumstances. Generally, they all fall under either inappropriate or lack of socialization with a particular sex. If this happens at home, place your dog on his Teaching Lead® during arrivals and follow the directions given for uniformed people. If the problem doesn't improve or if you notice any aggression, seek professional help.

Whatever the cause, make sure that you use your dog's favorite treats for the introduction. Try this approach (we'll use a man for the example):

> ➤ Instruct the man to avoid direct eye contact with your dog.

> ➤ Do not force the situation. Act cheerful and cordial to the man, setting a good example.

> ➤ Casually place a treat on the man's foot and praise your dog if he takes it, or ask the man to hold out a jar of peanut butter and let the dog approach. No staring allowed!

> ➤ Eventually, when your dog initiates the interaction, try petting him together.

Grrr
If your dog tenses up, his eyes grow cold, or he starts to growl, do not work him around children until you are under the supervision of a professional trainer. Don't become another statistic. Dogs that bite children are often forcibly euthanized.

If your dog is afraid of children and the problem doesn't improve with the following suggestions, find a private trainer who has experience with this problem. Practice your "Heel" and "Sit-Stay" commands around the perimeter of a playground. Do not let the children approach.

Act like a child with your dog. For example, poke him or pull his ear like a child would do, squeal in a high-pitched voice, and stare at him at his level by kneeling or crawling. Once he's socialized to these patterns, he'll be more accepting when the children do it. If your dog's nervous around babies, borrow a friend's blanket (for the aroma) and wrap a doll in it to carry around the house, including your dog in all the fuss!

Condition your dog to the sound of his treat cup. Allow kids to take the cup and toss treats to your dog. If he's enthusiastic, let the children toss treats toward him. You can let him take treats gently from the children.

Impressing Your Veterinarian

I'll let you in on a secret. Veterinarians love a well-behaved dog. It makes their job a lot easier. To impress yours:

1. Bring your dog's favorite chew in case you have to wait.

2. When you get to the office, your dog will probably be excited or afraid.

3. Instruct him to "Heel" at the car and enforce a "Wait" at the entrance.

4. Say "OK" and remind "Heel" as you check in.

5. If you must wait, place him in a "Town Down" under your legs and give him his favorite chew.

6. Instruct "Wait" as you go into the examination room to keep him calm and focused!

Some dogs aren't wild about receptionists and aren't too impressed by the DVM. Set up a practice run and ask the receptionist to meet you outside. Give her your dog's treat cup and ask her to avoid making eye contact with your dog. If your dog is tense, avoid confrontation. If your dog wants to approach, have the receptionist reward him with treats.

A client told me her male German Shepherd gets on the waiting room bench next to her and looks threateningly at everyone who passes. She wondered why. What is he doing on the bench? He's not a person. By letting him sit at your level, you're encouraging him to assume a protective role. Instead, instruct a "Town Down" and ignore him. If he growls, tell him "No." If you're still having problems, refer to Chapter 11.

Going for an Overnight Visit

Taking your dog with you on an overnight visit can be a lot of fun or it can be a disaster. It all depends on how you handle the situation. Do some predeparture planning; pack a bed, a crate, chew toys, treats, leads, and a small portable radio. Yes, a radio; it drowns out any unfamiliar sounds and soothes his anxiety while you're gone.

Sarah Says
Find an easy listening station. Heavy metal can be a little jarring!

When you arrive, greet everyone calmly or leave your dog in the car with the radio playing. Enforce a "Sit" for greetings and a "Wait" at all thresholds. When you go to your room, set up the crate or sleeping station. Offer your dog his treats and toys. Set up the radio next to his area.

If possible, avoid crating immediately. After setting up the bedroom, lead him around the outside perimeters and play a familiar game. If you must go, place your dog in his area with a chew toy and turn on the radio. Make sure you depart and arrive calmly. No overly theatrical guilt-trip scenes, please.

If there are children in the household where you'll be staying, before you go, take a box of Cheerios, shake it, and toss your dog a handful. Repeat this activity until your dog recognizes the sound. Tell your friends to have an identical box waiting for your arrival. Let your dog check the place out when you first get there. Then encourage the children (or the parent and the child) to shake the box and offer fists full of cereal as your dog is first introduced to the new smells and stimulations involved with kids.

Grrr
If you anticipate or sense any aggression, leave your dog at home or, if he must come, keep him apart from the children. Get professional help immediately!

The Least You Need To Know

➤ Keep your dog on his Teaching Lead® when he's out and about.

➤ Good social manners start the moment you enter the car.

➤ Leaders lead. You should lead down the street, crossing the curb, approaching strangers, and into buildings. Feet ahead of paws.

➤ If your dog is aggressive in public, stop and seek help immediately.

➤ Your behavior must be tailor-fit for your dog's personality: is he a wild creature or a scaredy cat?

➤ Harsh discipline will only frighten your dog or make him more rambunctious. Be stern and serious with your commands and happy with your praise!

Functions for the More Adventurous

Is your dog training getting stale? Well, your fun doesn't have to stop here. In this chapter, I'll give summaries of trials and events you and your well-mannered dog can take part in.

Agility Competitions

Agility is the up-and-coming sporting event in the dog world. It is similar to the equestrian Grand Prix, with a few canine twists. The concept originated in England and was demonstrated at the Crufts International Dog Show in 1978. Although it took the United

States nearly a decade to catch on, the United States Dog Agility Association (USDAA) was incorporated in 1986 and events and training classes have been popping up across the country ever since.

Agility is a blast for you and your dog!

At first sight, an agility course looks like a gigantic playground! The course obstacles include:

➤ **The Open Tunnel.** A long, open tube; often bent in competition.

➤ **The Closed Tunnel.** A tube with a rigid opening that has a collapsible canvas or nylon tunnel that the dog must push through.

➤ **The Tire Frame.** A raised tire, secured in a frame, for the dog to jump through.

➤ **A-Frame.** Two eight- or nine-foot ramps, leaned against and secured to one another, making a frame to navigate across.

➤ **Dog Walk.** Three narrow eight- or 12-foot planks arranged like a catwalk. The dog must go up, cross over, and descend.

➤ **Cross Over.** Similar to the dog walk, this obstacle presents a square table four-feet high with four narrow ramps on each side. The handler must direct the dog both up and down a specified ramp.

➤ **See-saw.** A see-saw! The dog must ascend and descend in a controlled fashion.

Bet You Didn't Know

The Cross Over and See-saw events are known as the *go-ups*. Each entry and exit point has a special paneled area 36 inches by 42 inches that the dog must touch as he approaches and descends each obstacle. These areas are known as the *contact zones*.

➤ **Pause Table.** A three-foot raised platform that the dog must go to, sit or lie down, and stay at as the judge counts down from five: "5, 4, 3, 2, 1, Go!"

➤ **Pause Box.** A similar challenge, although the box is a four-foot low platform or marked area.

➤ **Weave Poles.** A row of poles, spaced 20–24 inches apart, which the dog must weave through slalom style. This is no easy task!

➤ **Jumps.** The jumps compose a major part of the competition. There are hurdle jumps with brush underneath or wings on each side, single bar jumps, solid walls, spread jumps, and long jumps. The height of each is determined by the dog's height class.

As you can imagine, the teamwork required to get through one of these courses is tremendous. The handler must act as the navigator and strategist, while the dog does all the physical stuff. Each agility event presents a different sequence of obstacles and sets a Standard Course Time (SCT) according to the length and difficulty of the course. The SCT is the maximum number of seconds a team has to complete the course without penalty. Scores are given based on performance and time. Teams are disqualified if they exceed the Maximum Course Time (MCT), refuse an obstacle three times, take an improper route, act aggressively, soil on the course, leave the arena, or if the handler gives excessive assistance or shows poor sportsmanship. The AKC awards titles including Novice Agility Dog (NAD), Open Agility Dog (OAD), Agility Excellent (ADX), and Master Agility (MAX).

Agility fever is *very* catchy! To find a dog or Agility Club in your area, call or write to the American Kennel Club (add "Attn: Agility" to the address) or the U.S. Dog Agility Association, Inc. (see the "Contact Listings" section at the end of this chapter).

AKC Obedience Trials

Obedience trials don't take a dog's physical appearance into account. Although the dogs must be purebred to enter this ring, the only thing that wins brownie points is good temperament and mindful behavior. Competition in the obedience ring is divided into four levels. The initialized AKC obedience titles are earned after a dog completes three "legs" in competition. To achieve a "leg," a dog must score at least 170 points out of a possible 200 and get more than 50 percent of the points on each exercise. The exercises vary for each class:

Bet You Didn't Know

Although mixed-breeds are barred from AKC competitions, they do have their own activity club with similar rules and certifications. For more information, write to the Mixed Breed Dog Club of America (see the section "Contact Listings" at the end of this chapter).

➤ **The Companion Dog or Novice Class (C.D. title).** To achieve a C.D. title, a dog must heel on leash, stand to be examined by a judge, heel free, recall (come), and do a group long sit and long down.

➤ **The Companion Dog Excellent or Open Class (C.D.X. title).** To achieve a C.D.X. title, a dog must heel free, drop on recall, retrieve on a flat, retrieve over the high jump, and do a broad jump, long sit, and long down.

➤ **Utility Dog or Utility Class (U.D. title).** To achieve a U.D. title, a dog must respond to a signal exercise, two scent discrimination tests, a directed retrieve, directed jump, and group examination.

➤ **Utility Dog Excellent (U.D.X. title).** To achieve a U.D.X. title, your dog must earn qualifying scores in both Open B and Utility B classes at the same obedience trial on 10 different occasions (and under 10 different judges.)

To become Obedience Trial Champion, a dog must win 100 points, first place in a Utility competition, first place in an Open B competition, another first place ribbon in either Open or Utility classes, and have first place finishes under three different judges.

Though the instructions for this type of training are beyond the scope of this book, many other books have been written specifically about preparing for the obedience ring. If you have a well-mannered, friendly, obedient dog resting nearby and your eyes are lighting up at the thought of a little friendly competition, this might be just the challenge for you! For more information regarding obedience regulations, write to the American Kennel Club and include "Attn: Obedience Regulations" in the address (see the section "Contact Listings" at the end of this chapter).

Canine Good Citizenship Test

The Canine Good Citizenship Program (CGC) is a noncompetitive training and acceptance test designed in 1989 to recognize and certify dogs and their owners as responsible citizens of their community. Although this test is promoted by the American Kennel Club, it is not limited to purebred dogs. Mixed breeds are encouraged to gain certification as well. Presented as more of a program than a competition, this test measures a dog's social skills and public manners. The goal of the CGC test is not to eliminate participants, but to encourage pet owners to learn the skills necessary to train their dogs to be safe members of our society.

The commands a dog must respond to take part in this test are "Heel," "Sit," "Down," and "Stay." The test is comprised of 10 evaluations:

1. **Accepting a Friendly Stranger.** To pass this test, the dog must allow a non-threatening person to approach and speak to the handler.

2. **Sitting Politely for Petting.** The dog must allow a friendly stranger to pet him while sitting at his handler's side.

3. **Appearance and Grooming.** The dog must allow a stranger (representing a veterinarian or groomer) to handle and groom him without suspicion.

4. **Out for a Walk (Walking on a loose leash).** The dog must walk attentively at the handler's side. To pass this evaluation, the dog does not have to heel perfectly or sit when the handler is instructed to stop.

5. **Walking Through a Crowd.** The dog must be attentive to the owner and in control as he is led through a crowd of people.

6. **Sit and Down on Command/Staying in Place.** The dog must respond to the handler's commands.

7. **Coming When Called.** The dog must come when called by the handler from a distance of 10 feet. The handler can encourage the dog using body language or "Stay" or "Wait" commands.

8. **Reaction to Another Dog.** The dog must be controlled and focused on the handler while passing another dog.

9. **Reactions to Distractions.** The dog must remain calm and confident when faced with everyday distractions. The distraction at an evaluation might include a child running, a person riding a bike, or a person on crutches or in a wheelchair.

10. **Supervised Separation.** For this test, the dog is fastened to a six-foot line and expected to wait calmly while the handler disappears for three minutes.

I am a certified CGC evaluator and give this test to my college (dog college) graduates. It's a fun way for everyone to measure their success. If you think you and your dog are ready for this evaluation, you can contact the American Kennel Club in North Carolina (see the section "Contact Listings" at the end of this chapter; refer to the address that includes "Attn: CGC").

Earth Trials

Do you have a Terrier whose instincts are driving you crazy? If so, these trials might be the perfect outlet for all his natural instincts. The breeds allowed to compete include all purebred dogs from the Terrier group, as well as Dachshunds.

At the test sight, a tunnel is rigged with a caged hooded rat to serve as bait. The dogs are tested in three classes:

Novice. This trial presents the dog with a ten-foot tunnel and allows one minute for a response. The dog may enter and leave during the allotted time. Although encouragement may be given by the handler, it does lower the overall score.

Open. This presents each entry with a 30-foot tunnel and allows 30 seconds for a response. No encouragement is permitted.

"Certification of Gameness." This certification is given to dogs who score 100 percent of the points in the open entry.

Dogs are scored on (what else?) their spirit, which is measured by their barking, lunging, and biting capabilities. Poor rat! If you think this is something you and your dog would be interested in, you can write to Patricia Adams, the Entry Trial Secretary (see the "Contact Listings" section at the end of this chapter).

The Sport of Flyball®

Here's a real heart pounder. This game is quite unlike anything else in the dog world. Although the majority of enthusiasts remain in Canada and the north midwestern United States, I have a strong feeling its popularity will be growing!

To play the sport of Flyball®, you need a team of four spirited dogs with a slight obsession for tennis balls. The team will race together on a relay-type system. The goal of each individual dog is to run 51 inches, over four jumps to the Flyball box, pick up a tennis ball, and run back over the jumps to the start-finish line. As one dog returns, another is sent until all four dogs have run. Sounds pretty simple, huh? Well I thought so too, until I talked to an expert.

Glen Hamilton, one of Canada's chief Flyball® enthusiasts, filled me in on a little of the behind-the-scenes strategy. At a Flyball® competition, two teams race against one another simultaneously. At the start of the race, a lighting system is the equivalent of "On your mark, get set, go!" Instead of a voice ringing out, however, a light flashes yellow-yellow-green. One of the goals is to get the first dog racing over the start-finish line at maximum speed when the light flashes green. So how can this be accomplished? Strategy! Each handler knows his dog's speed well enough to measure how far back he must stand when releasing the dog on the second yellow so that he will cross the start-finish line full tilt when the green light flashes. Dogs can hit speeds up to 30 kilometers per hour as they race down to the Flyball box, which is painted black to highlight the ball that awaits their retrieval. After the dog gets the ball, the handler must coach him back as quickly as possible. As dog #1 is nearing the start-finish line, the handler and dog #2 are timing their release so that dog #2 will cross the start-finish line within inches of dog #1.

The winning team's score is the cumulative time of all four contestant dogs. Suppose Glen's winning team finished in 21.40 seconds. Each dog would get a score of 21.40 added to his scorecard. To be considered a Flyball Champion, a dog must earn 500 points. Out of the 3,500 dogs registered in the North American Flyball Association, Inc., 1,000 have earned this honor. (Note that the NAFA is not recognized by the AKC.)

What dog breeds make the best competitors? No breed taller than 8 inches is barred from competition, although the breeds most frequently seen include Border Collies, Doberman Pinschers, Jack Russells, Shelties, Miniature Poodles, and mixed breeds.

If the idea of such heart-stopping fun is raising your eyebrows, you'll want to contact the NAFA and get their rule book and information about their training and competition locations (see the section "Contact Listings" at the end of this chapter). Good luck!

Herding Trials

Though there are still farms that utilize the instincts of the traditional herding, guarding, or all-purpose farm dog, most of the dogs from the Herding group are coveted as cherished pets and family members. However, some of these dogs still take their genes very seriously. You'd notice them in a minute. They're the ones herding their owners from the kitchen, rounding up the schoolchildren as they get off the bus, and staring longingly as the Discovery channel airs a special about the sheep of the Scottish highlands. It's not that they don't appreciate luxury, it's just that they'd like to work a little for it. If you find yourself feeling woeful for your little herder, read on. Perhaps this activity will be for you!

Herders have true concentration.

There are four different classifications of Herding dogs:

The Shepherd. These dogs work in front of their sheep and are known as the "headers." They use a gaze, known as the "eye," to control their herd. The Border Collie and Bearded Collie are two breeds that are known to possess this quality.

Drover. This dog works behind sheep or cattle herds and drives them forward. They are known as "Heelers." Both the Pembroke and Cardigan Corgis fall into this category. Their low bodies are perfect for flattening to avoid being kicked.

Livestock Guarding. These sheepdogs guard flocks, but they don't move them. Bred to work independently, they are raised with the flock and are expected to guard it from wolves, bears, and thieves. Massive and placid in temperament, the Komondor, Great Pyrenees, and the Kuvasz are some examples.

All-around Farm Dog. These versatile dogs are bred to stay around the farm and respond to tasks that come up. The Collie, German Shepherd, and Australian Shepherd are in this group.

The American Kennel Club sponsors competitions and awards titles for Herding Tested (HT) and Pre-trial Tested (PT) for beginners and Herding Started (HS), Herding Intermediate (HI), Herding Excellent (HX), and Herding Champion (HCh.) to more experienced contestants.

Training a herding dog does not have to start in puppyhood. Although many instincts appear in a young dog, some don't show any talent until they're older. If you are interested in pursuing this activity, it's important to remember that you are encouraging your dog's instinct to herd or guard, not to chase or kill. When the herding dog was bred from the wolf, those instincts were suppressed. Rough handling or tugging games can spoil a good herding dog. To get more information about Herding Trials, you can write to the American Kennel Club (include "Attn: Herding" in the address), the American Herding Breed Association, or the Livestock Guarding Dog Project (see the section "Contact Listings" at the end of this chapter).

Field Trials

If you're a hunting enthusiast and you have a dog that fits the bill, then these events might be for you. The AKC sponsors separate Field Trials for Basset Hounds, Beagles, Dachshunds, Pointing breeds, Retrievers, and Spaniels. Each one brings man and dog back together for the task that the dog was originally bred to do.

Hounds. Each breed is tested in the pursuit of a cottontail rabbit or hare and vies for the title of Field Champion. Beagles and Basset Hounds work in packs and are judged by how well they work together and follow a trail. Dachshunds work in braces (pairs) and are judged on their ability to run the rabbit into the ground. The AKC also sponsors Coonhound trials for raccoon hunting and awards Field Championship (FCh.), Grand Field Champion (GFCh.), and AKC Nite Field Champion.

Pointing breeds. These dogs were originally bred to traverse fields far ahead of their owners and stop and point if they found a bird. Trials are often run with the man on horseback. Pointing breeds include the English, Gordon, and Irish Setter, the German Shorthair and Wiredhaired Pointer, the Pointer, Wirehaired Pointing Griffon, Weimaraner, Vizsla, and the Brittany.

Retrievers. Retrievers retrieve game shot by man. In these trials, a hunter may fall two or more birds and the dog must take direction as to the order of the retrieve. All sporting dogs with the word Retriever in their name fall under this heading. While Weimaraners and Vizslas are known as versatile hunting dogs, they can be used in Retrieval Trials as well.

Spaniels. Spaniels were bred to search close to man and flush out birds within gunshot range. They are also expected to retrieve the game after it is shot. Although the Cocker Spaniels are no longer worked in Field Trials, the English Springer, Field, Sussex, Clumber, and Irish Water Spaniels are used in competition. (Cocker and English Cockers are eligible if owners want to train and enter them.)

The AKC offers titles of Junior Hunter (JH), Senior Hunter (SH), Master Hunter (MH), Field Champion (FCh.), and Amateur Field Champion (AFCh.) to the three categories of the Sporting group.

If you are interested in finding out more information regarding these trials, be sure to specify your breed when you write the AKC for their Trial Rules and Standard Procedures. Make sure to include "Attn: Registration and Field Trial Rules and Standard Procedures for Pointing Breeds/Retrievers/Spaniels/Dachshunds (specify breed)" or "Attn: Beagle/Basset Hound Field Trial Rules and Standard Procedures" in the address. You can also write to the United Kennel Club. (See the section "Contact Listings" at the end of this chapter.)

Lure Coursing

The sport of Lure Coursing was set up in 1972 by the American Sighthound Association. Its goal was to "preserve and further develop the natural beauty, grace, speed, and coursing skill of the Sighthound." The breeds involved include the Afghan Hound, Basenji, Borzoi, Greyhound, Ibizan Hound, Irish Wolfhound, Pharaoh Hound, Saluki, Scottish Deerhound, and Whippet. These dogs all have one thing in common. They love to run after game and they love to run fast!

To enter a dog in competition, he must be registered in a recognized organization such as the AKC or the National Greyhound Association. When events are held, the dogs run in trios after a lure, which is usually a white bag with or without fur covering it. Judges score the dogs on speed, agility, skill, enthusiasm, and endurance. The dogs chase the lure 1,000 to 1,500 yards across an open course. The AKC offers the title of Junior Courser (JC), Senior Courser (SC), and Field Champion (FCh.).

As anyone who has witnessed a competition could tell you, the dogs are responding to pure instinct. They do what they were bred for, which is to chase movement. To train young dogs for competition, you can drag a lure in front of them; however, if you have an older dog, you won't be disadvantaged. As long as you have a Sighthound with a love for pursuit, you have what it takes. For more information, write to the American Kennel Club (include "Attn: Lure Coursing" in the address) or the American Sighthound Field Association (see the section "Contact Listings" at the end of this chapter).

Therapy Dogs

Using dogs in therapeutic situations is an activity very close to my heart. Much like music or art therapy, dogs can be used to ease interactions between two or more uncommon people in a variety of situations, such as long-term care facilities and institutions. It is now proven that interacting with animals lowers blood pressure and facilitates interpersonal relationships.

Pets are therapeutic for folks who need special therapy or long-term care.

I remember the first Pet Therapy class I took in 1989 from Micky Niego at the A.S.P.C.A. in New York City. I brought my Husky, Kyia, and together we were exposed to many of the unfamiliar situations that we would eventually encounter on our therapy visits. Kyia and I got used to wheelchairs, walkers, crutches, elevators, different speech patterns, kids, and people with diminished muscle coordination. Later, on visits to nursing homes, disability centers, and mental institutions, I was touched by how much the people appreciated the unconditional affection that only a dog can offer.

If you have a dog who is social and loving, yet calm and well-mannered, you may find this activity very rewarding. Although many facilities welcome volunteers, it is best to take a class or work with someone who is familiar with the rigors of the therapeutic situations before committing yourself. Even the most even-tempered dogs can startle or feel stressed when they are faced with an unfamiliar experience. By exposing your dog to every possible situation that might occur, he'll be better able to cope with unexpected predicaments.

I have taken two pet therapy classes. I am certified with Therapy Dogs International and am planning to hold my own classes to certify dogs in my community. The effect of Therapy Dogs is sentimental and touching. Everyone around can't help but smile. To get more information about outreach programs and certifications in your area, contact your local shelter or write the Delta Society, which has a national center researching Pet Assisted Therapy and a certification test for trained dogs (see the section "Contact Listings" at the end of this chapter).

Sled Dogs

When most people think of sledding, they think of a husky-type dog with a thick coat and curly tail. This sport, however, is not restricted to any breed. When I was five, I went to a local nature preserve to witness a sledding event and saw a sled pulled by two Poodles and another with a trio of Doberman Pinschers. So, for all you snow enthusiasts who have dogs who get a charge out of taking you for a walk, grab a pencil and read closely. Dog sledding is a blast and, although I wouldn't encourage any of you toy owners to hitch up, it's not limited by breed.

OOOH...

Doglish
The big teams even have special names for the dogs. A *lead dog(s)* is the one (or two) dog(s) in front. The *point dogs* follow the lead dogs, the *swing dogs* are the series of pairs in the middle, and the *wheel dogs* are the pair closest to the sled.

Believe it or not, the 1,040 mile Iditarod race from Anchorage to Nome, Alaska, is not the only competition in town. There are also sprint race competitions that vary in number of dogs and distances run.

When I was growing up, I had a thing for dogsleds. I bought one and trained my Husky, Shawbee, and my Collie, Meghan, to pull it. They made quite a pair; Shawbee wanted to pull the sled while Meghan wanted to herd it. Serious advocates start training their puppies at three months. However, if you have an interest, don't be discouraged if you have an adult dog. Most dogs love to learn new tricks and most are more than willing to pull you! For information about competition and training programs, write to the International Sled Dog Racing Association (see the section "Contact Listings" at the end of this chapter).

Tracking

Dogs' noses are analogous to our eyes. Tracking to them is like a land survey to us. However, to train your dog to follow a specified trail is no simple feat. Tracking is advanced obedience work and requires a lot of encouragement and patient repetition.

Anyone who has trained a tracking dog will tell you, however, that the final result is worth the effort. A rapport between a handler and good tracking dog is built on solid trust. Tracking dogs have been used by the police and individual persons to find lost people when all other modern technological techniques have failed.

Training must start with good communication. *Positive retrieves*, where the article is within sight, are the best starting point. As a dog's ability and enthusiasm increase, articles can be hidden from sight in tall grass or around corners. This is known as a *Positive blind retrieve*. Exposing a dog to different weather conditions and locations is important in creating a reliable tracking dog. To find out more about training a tracking dog, please refer to specific training books.

The American Kennel Club offers two titles, Tracking Dog (T.D.) and Tracking Dog Excellent (T.D.X.). Contact the AKC for more information about the test and the courses. Be sure to include "Attn: Tracking" in the address (see the section "Contact Listings" at the end of this chapter).

Breed-Specific Working Titles

Many national breed clubs have designated individual working titles for activities for which their breed was originally bred. For example, the Newfoundland Club of America sponsors clinics and competitions where dogs can earn Water Dog (WD) and Water Rescue Dog (WRD) titles. They also award drafting (cart pulling) titles—Draft Dog (DD) and Team Draft Dog (TDD)—for a team of Newfoundlands.

Many other breed clubs sponsor events not yet recognized by the American Kennel Club. The Dalmatian Club of America offers road titles. The Alaskan Malamute offers titles for weight pulls. To discover what your breed club has to offer, write your National Club, which you can find through your breeder or by contacting the American Kennel Club (see the next section for the AKC address)!

Contact Listings

American Kennel Club (AKC)
51 Madison Ave.
New York, NY 10010
(212) 696-8200

U.S. Dog Agility Association, Inc.
P.O. Box 850955
Richardson, TX 75085-0955
(214) 231-9700

American Herding Breed Association
Linda Rorem
1548 Victoria Way
Pacifica, CA 94044

Livestock Guarding Dog Project
Livestock Guard Dog Assoc.
Hampshire College
P.O. Box FC
Amherst, MA 01002

Mixed Breed Dog Club of America
Attn: Phyllis Massa
1937 Seven Pines Dr.
St. Louis, MO 63146-3717

The American Kennel Club
Attn: CGC
5580 Centerview Drive, Suite 200
Raleigh, NC 27606-3390
(919) 233-9780

Patricia Adams/Entry Trial Secretary
Dogwood Cottage RD2
Box 38A
Franklinton, NC 27525

North American Flyball® Association
Mike Randell
1342 Jeff Street
Ypsilanti, MI 48198

United Kennel Club
100 E. Kilgore Road
Kalamazoo, MI 49001-5593

American Sighthound Field Association
Lester Pekarski
P.O. Box 1293-M
Woodstock, GA 30188

Delta Society
P.O. Box 1080
Renton, WA 98057-9906

International Sled Dog Racing Association
460 S. 43rd St.
Boulder, CO 80303

The Least You Need To Know

➤ Once your dog learns the basics, he'll be ready to take on additional, more advanced challenges!

➤ Pick an activity that both you and your dog will have an interest in. If you own a slow sniffer, tracking wouldn't be your best option, even though you might want to get involved.

➤ Getting a title is a great honor, but it's only a small piece of the pie. Working with your dog should be your #1 incentive, whether or not you're ever recognized. Fun and sportsmanship are the biggest perks.

➤ Seek out a group of professionals to guide you. Advanced training cannot be learned from a book. Though reading helps, it cannot replace experience.

Part 5
Inside-Out

There is more to a happy dog than training. There is the dog's health to worry about. You need to learn about good nutrition and exercise. You also need to know how to take care of your dog when he's feeling fine and what to do if he gets sick. Dogs can get a cold-like bug or have an upset stomach or headache just like you and me, only they can't talk to you about it. You'll need to recognize the symptoms and be sensitive when your dog's under the weather.

There are also emergencies you'll need to prepare for. Hopefully, you'll never be faced with such unpleasant situations, but you should know what to do if your dog gets hit by a car, poisoned, or cut. The time that lapses between the accident and getting him to the hospital can make the difference between life and death. This part of the book explores all the ins and outs of keeping your dog healthy, from nutrition and exercise to what to do if he's ailing or hurt.

Chapter 17

Let's Talk Nutrition

In This Chapter

➤ Food essentials

➤ Interpreting the labels

➤ Does your dog have allergies?

➤ Cooking for your dog

I have to admit, I was fairly ignorant about dog foods before I started working in my profession. After all, broken down, aren't they all basically the same? Some of this chemical, some of that. I had a hard time reading the labels and I studied chemistry! Over the years, I've learned a lot more about *dog nutrition*. And I tell you, it's been a major revelation!

All dog foods are not the same. Just like books, you can't judge the contents by the pretty design of the packaging. To pick the right food, you'll need to think about your dog's activity level. Find a diet with ingredients to complement his lifestyle. As you learn about dog food in this chapter and check into a variety of the brands, you'll find that the food that costs the most isn't necessarily the best.

Grrr
If you feed your dog the wrong diet, it will affect his health and his behavior. The wrong diet can increase your dog's susceptibility to disease, infection, and possibly nervous/aggressive disorders.

Start off your training regime by balancing your dog's nutrition. Finding a good diet before you start training a dog is like setting a sturdy foundation before you build your house. If you don't do it, you could have the finest training regime in history, but it won't live up to its fullest potential. Before we jump into training, let's take a closer look in this chapter at this four letter word—diet!

Bet You Didn't Know

Ever hear of the Food and Drug Administration agency (FDA)? It's the government agency that researches and controls what goes into all that food you buy at the supermarket. There are regulatory agencies for dog foods, too: the National Research council (NRC) and *the Association of American Feed Control Officials (AAFCO)*. Make sure the food you purchase has the AAFCO statement of approval!

Look for a statement of approval from AAFCO on the dog food you purchase.

> **AAFCO STATEMENT**
> Animal feeding tests using AAFCO procedures substantiate that Science Diet® Canine Maintenance® provides complete and balanced nutrition for maintenance of adult dogs.

The Basic Components

All dog foods have certain things in common. To pass regulatory standards, they must contain six essential elements: *protein, fat, carbohydrates, vitamins, minerals,* and *water.* But that's where the similarities usually end. They diverge on what ingredients are used to reach the *minimum daily requirement (MDR)*.

Grrr
More protein is not better. High protein diets are used for show or working dogs. If you have a sworn couch potato or a dog who must spend hours alone, feeding her a high protein diet (which, broken down, equals energy) will make her jittery and hyper.

For example, some foods use soy to meet the daily protein requirement, whereas other foods use animal protein. It's like the difference between eating ten hot dogs to get my daily requirement of protein versus a good wholesome piece of chicken. Well, perhaps I'm exaggerating, but you catch my drift. For dogs, animal protein beats soy hands down. Let's look at the essentials one at a time.

Proteins

Protein is the most costly ingredient in dog foods. Its source often determines the quality of the dog food. Animal sources are superior.

"Why Grandma, what big teeth you have!" For Little Red Riding Hood, it should have been a dead give-away. The wolf and its brethren, the dog, are carni-vores. Meat eaters have teeth designed to tear flesh from the bone. This is all their digestive system is cut out for: ingesting meat. Unfortunately, in today's world, there's not enough meat around to satisfy all the pet dogs in the world, so we have come up with substitute food. To meet the minimum daily protein requirement, many dog food companies use veg-etable proteins. The difference between vegetable and animal protein? Vegetable is often harder to digest and more of it has to be consumed to meet the quota. More food equals more stool. Moral of this story? Find a dog food that uses more animal protein and requires smaller rations to meet the MDR.

Grrr
Many dogs are allergic to grains found in dog food. The most common allergies are to corn, wheat, and soy. Certain grains also may contain fertilizer residue, which can cause an allergic reaction. If your dog refuses to eat his food or his digestion seems abnormal in any way, consult your veterinarian. Save the labels from your dog's food. This will help in identifying possible aggravating ingredients.

Bet You Didn't Know

The need for protein changes throughout your dog's life stages and when-ever there is temperature or emotional stress on his system. When stress occurs, your dog will utilize more protein.

Price, unfortunately, will tell you nothing about protein content and source; you must read the label.

Carbohydrates

Some dog food manufacturers meet the MDR for protein by using primarily vegetable matter. Vegetable sources of protein also contain high levels of carbohydrates. The problem is that dogs don't digest this the way we do. Ours is a much more complicated system. We start digestion in our mouths, where we chew and savor our food. Dogs chew and gulp; their digestion starts in their stomachs. Why is this important? Because carbo-hydrate digestion is a slow process that's not cut out for gulping. Foods high in carbos can cause digestive problems in dogs, such as bloating, upset stomach, constipation, and too much stool. Make sure you pick a diet that contains more animal protein than vegetable protein. How? Pick a food that has two or more animal sources of protein listed in the first five ingredients.

Bet You Didn't Know

Even dog food has ethnic traits! Make sure your dog's food has cereals and grains—such as rice, potato, and corn—from countries near where your dog's breed was developed.

Fats and Preservatives

If you see a "Fat Free" dog food, please run the other way. Dogs need fat to keep their skin and coats healthy and to keep things mobile on the inside. Used in the proper moderation, fat will give your dog energy and keep him cool when it's warm and warm when it's cool. However, fat can be a funny thing. For one, it spoils quickly. If you're feeding your dog a natural diet, make sure you respect the expiration date. Rancid fat can lead to a whole slew of health problems.

Vitamins

Have you ever wondered what vitamins do exactly and why they're necessary for good health? Vitamins do two things:

➤ They unlock nutrients from food.

➤ They provide energy.

Sarah Says
Supplementing fat in your dog's diet is usually unnecessary. If your vet encourages you to increase fat content, use pressed safflower oil—approximately 1 teaspoon for small dogs; one tablespoon for large dogs. This oil has a high concentration of linoleic acid and is least likely to cause an allergic reaction.

That's it in a nutshell. There are two types of vitamins: fat soluble and water soluble. The fat solubles include vitamins A, D, E, and K. These vitamins are stored in fatty tissue and the liver. Water solubles include vitamins B and C; they're flushed through the body daily—either used up or excreted.

The need for vitamins varies depending on your dog and his lifestyle. The average bag of dog food, however, won't point these factors out. Once again, the suggested rations to meet the MDR is averaged for all dogs. The truth is, the MDR was set using beagle-sized dogs living a sedentary life in a laboratory. Take that into account and the fact that vitamins are a rather unstable lot, easily destroyed by light and heat, and you'd be wise to invest in a good vitamin supplement. Ask your veterinarian for suggestions. Vitamin deficiencies can lead to poor growth, digestive disorders, elimination problems, stool eating, a weak immune system, greasy, stinky coats, Addison's Disease, thyroid malfunction, aggression, timidity, and sterility.

Minerals

Minerals are a lot like their cohorts, the vitamins. They help the body in its normal daily activities like circulation, energy production, and cell regeneration. Minerals come in two varieties: elemental and chelated. Elementals come from the earth; they're less easy to digest because they can't be broken down. Chelated are found within organic matter and break down easily. Though mineral deficiencies are more common than vitamin deficiencies, do not supplement your dog's diet unless directed by your veterinarian. Adding minerals to your dog's/puppy's diet can cause an imbalance that will be harmful to his health.

To discover more about how specific minerals affect your dog's health, please refer to *The Holistic Guide for a Healthy Dog* by Wendy Volhard and Kerry Brown, DVM, Macmillan Publishing, 1995.

Sarah Says
I highly recommend the book *The Holistic Guide for a Healthy Dog* by Wendy Volhard and Kerry Brown, DVM, Macmillan Publishing, 1995. It's my nutrition handbook and I recommend it to all my clients whenever I'm fielded health questions I can't answer. In my opinion, the best dog owners are the educated ones!

Grrr
In commercial dog foods, check the label to see what preservatives are used. Ethoxyquin is a recognized carcinogen.

Bet You Didn't Know
The absorption of iron, a mineral necessary for good circulation, is aggravated when feeding a diet high in soy protein.

Water

Did you know that your dog can live three weeks without food, but will die within days without water? Water is necessary for all digestive processes, as well as temperature regulation, nutrient absorption, and as a transportation medium, shipping things between organs and out the body.

Grrr
Cushing's Disease (hyperactive adrenal glands) can be caused by drinking too much chlorinated water.

How much water your dog will need depends on her physical activities and the type of food she eats. Panting is your dog's means of sweating. If your dog is panting, she needs a drink. Dry food also encourages thirst. Because it contains only 10 percent moisture, your dog will need about a quart of water for every pound of dry food. On the other hand, canned dog food or home-cooked diets contain more water and require less rinse to wash down.

Allergies

Sarah Says
If you're using water from the faucet, have it tested or do it yourself to ensure it's free of harmful contaminants. Faucet water has been known to contain bacteria, viruses, lead, gasoline, radioactive gases, and carcinogenic industrial components that can cause chronic health problems. Wal-mart department stores carry a $4.00 water testing kit that tests hardness and measures chlorine, pH, nitrate, and iron levels.

I suffer big time in this arena. I think I'm allergic to more things than I'm not. Funniest allergies? Dogs and cats. As I write, I'm being kept company by my beautiful five-year-old cat, Kashina, who's fascinated with my typing. While monthly shots have salvaged my career, dogs are less fortunate. Canine allergens include wool, dust, molds, pollen, cedar chips, propylene glycol (a rawhide treat preservative), pesticide chemicals, house and garden plants, weeds, and food products. I've owned dogs with allergies and I feel awful for them. They suffer from swollen paws, itchy gums, sneezing, and ecxema. The worst part of it is they can't articulate what's wrong, so pinning down the culprit is a lot harder. If you suspect your dog has allergies, talk to your veterinarian. She can test to determine what's bugging your dog and give him medication to relieve his symptoms.

Bet You Didn't Know

Dieting allergies are being recognized with increased frequency. Hypoallergenic diets utilize a single protein and a single carbohydrate source. The protein chosen is usually one that is not in other types of dog food (such as lamb, venison, rabbit, or duck). Rice is often the carbohydrate of choice for hypoallergenic diets.

Here's a checklist to follow if you suspect your dog suffers from allergies:

➤ Use detergent soap designed for babies' diapers when washing your dog's bedding.

➤ Check out the sprays used in your home, yard, and garden. Do not use any products toxic to your pet.

➤ Use bleach and water (¹/₄ cup per gallon) to clean your dog's areas. Many dogs are allergic to commercial disinfectants.

➤ Don't overuse cleaning or parasite products. Flea sprays, powders, and dips are very toxic.

Grr
Even dogs' dishes may contain allergens! To be on the safe side, use stainless steel dishes for your dog's food and water.

Choosing Your Dog's Diet

Deciding on a diet for your dog is no small order. First, you must decide if you want to go natural or commercial. Natural diets take time to prepare and ingredients must be balanced for your dog's individual needs. Commercialized dog foods can provide a balanced diet, but every food will not suit every dog, so you must be a conscientious shopper. Let's take a look at each option.

Commercial Foods

Here are four constants I can give you when you're making your selection:

➤ Look for the AAFCO's stamp of approval.

➤ Note the suggested daily ration. Is it realistic?

➤ Eliminate foods causing weight loss, loose, smelly stools, or poor coat condition.

➤ Respect your dog's judgment. Refusal to touch the food can be attributed to stubbornness, though it's often a sign of spoiled ingredients or allergies.

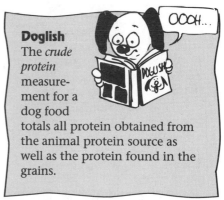

Doglish
The *crude protein* measurement for a dog food totals all protein obtained from the animal protein source as well as the protein found in the grains.

Sarah Says
A good diet should help your dog produce two to three compact, inoffensive-smelling stools a day.

Next you'll need to consider your lifestyle. Are you a high energy person bent on a dog who can keep up with you or do you like to watch movies and sit in front of the fireplace? Performance foods with high levels of *crude protein* provide lots of energy to burn. A food with more cereal grains is ideal for a more sedentary lifestyle.

Now that you've been exposed to what goes into these foods, you should feel more comfortable reading the label. The ingredients are listed by weight. If you can decipher the information, you'll be able to select a good food for your dog. Look for breakdowns in terms of crude protein, fat, fiber, moisture, ash, and often calcium and phosphorus levels.

The Homemade Diet

There are many pros to making your dog's diet yourself. Followed responsibly, the home diet can be modified for your dog's age, breed distinctions, and individual needs. Personalized diets will enhance your dog's health and vitality. Some dogs, regardless of breed, suffer from commercialized dog foods; the natural diet can solve problems related to this condition. The drawbacks of feeding your dog naturally is that it cannot be fudged. You *must* commit yourself to prepare balanced meals and to shop for products regularly to ensure freshness. If you want to try a homemade diet, please refer to *The Holistic Guide For A Healthy Dog* by Wendy Volhard and Kerry Brown, DVM, Macmillan Publishing, 1995.

Dry versus Wet

What's the big difference between dry and wet food? Cost in shipping…and cost to the consumer. Wet food contains 65–78 percent water; the weight of the can and water increases the cost of shipping. No studies have proven either wet or dry to be nutritionally superior. So what it boils down to is that the choice is up to you. Many of the veterinarians I consulted suggest a combination of the two. Mix them up. When searching for the right diet, pay close attention to your dog: how's his digestion? Foods with low quality ingredients don't absorb as well and can give your dog loose stools. Check the nutritional label to ensure you get a blend of high quality proteins (from dairy and meats) and low quality (from vegetables and grains).

Grrr
Dry food requires careful storage. If you let it sit around too long, the vitamins may start degrading or the whole bag will acquire mold or pantry moths.

Lamb and Rice Diets

These diets are becoming increasingly more and more prevalent. The reason? Some dogs have food allergies. These dogs have gastrointestinal reactions that are less than lovely—vomiting, diarrhea, and gas. If you suspect your dog might fall into this category, speak to your veterinarian.

Special Situations

As your dog ages, he'll need a different balance of nutrition to keep him going. Like us, older dogs need fewer calories. Speak to your veterinarian regarding an appropriate diet for your aging pal.

Some dogs have specific ailments that will require a prescription diet. Your veterinarian will guide you in your selections and provide an appropriate food to keep your dog well. These diets will have a guaranteed analysis that breaks down each ingredient to ensure you're getting the identical food sources in every bag/can.

The Least You Need To Know

➤ Buy food with the AAFCO blessing.

➤ More protein is not better; protein equals energy. Only use high protein diets for high performance dogs.

➤ Your dog's needs change throughout his life. Stress also affects his nutritional needs.

➤ Water is necessary for survival. Provide water in a stainless steel dish and change it regularly. Test your tap water for bacteria or chemicals that could be harmful to your dog's health.

➤ Many dogs have allergies. If your dog suffers from food allergies, work with your vet to pin-point the aggravating ingredient and regulate his diet. If the allergens are environmental, speak to your veterinarian.

Chapter 18

Run, Joe, Run

In This Chapter

➤ How you can get involved in your dog's exercise program!

➤ A puppy plan

➤ Age and breed factors

➤ Do dogs always play like that?

➤ Exercise for dogs with injuries or skeletal disorders

➤ Aging dogs

There is a common misconception that leaving a dog outside all day is good for him. "He needs fresh air" couldn't be further from the truth. If you leave your dog out all day, you'll end up with a neurotic creature digging in the yard and barking until the neighbors complain. It's true that proper exercise outside will lead to a calmer dog inside, but "proper exercise" is the key phrase. Proper exercise involves you.

Get Involved!

Dogs don't like to exercise alone. They need a companion to frolic and play with. Unless you have a couple of dogs, you'll need to exercise your dog 2–4 times a day for 5–20 minutes, depending on her age and breed. I know it sounds like a lot, but once you get into it, it will feel like recess in the third grade. Remember the bell? Yes!

Play with your dog 2–4 times per day. It's fun!

When you bring a young puppy home, she has five needs: food and water, elimination, sleep, and *exercise*. Exercise is a need! When it's time to play, you have no choice: you must get involved! Because a walk down the street can be frightening to a new puppy (cars, big dogs, and so on), games like these are the best way tire her out:

Grrr
Avoid games like tug-of-war, wrestling, chasing, or teasing. These games frustrate pups, encourage nipping (especially on clothing), and make you look more like a playmate than a leader.

➤ **Kick the plastic soda bottle.** Get three going at once. Pick up the bottle after it's been punctured.

➤ **Fishing for Fido.** Tie a squeaky toy or bone to a rope and tie the rope to a stick. Now start fishing until you catch your puppy.

➤ **Multiple ball toss.** Never challenge a puppy for what he has in his mouth. Puppies are not into sharing. Play fetch with three balls, bouncing them against walls and trees. When the pup brings one back, praise him and toss another!

As your puppy grows up, you'll want to play more structured games:

➤ **Have a ball toss.** Teach him to release the ball on command.

➤ **Extended rope toy.** Tie a toy onto a 20-foot piece of line. Toss it about and watch your dog's predatory instincts come alive. Don't tug, though! You don't want him to know you're controlling the show!

➤ **Go for a walk.** Dogs love to walk around, seeing new faces and smelling new ground. Keep him under control and behind you.

➤ **Play the obedience games outlined in this chapter.** Training can be a fun way to exercise too!

Up Close: A Puppy Plan

A puppy's tissues are soft. His bones are growing. He's as awkward as an infant trying to take his first step. Stairs frighten him. It would be nice if you could take your brand-new companion with you on your five mile jog, but it wouldn't be safe. Your puppy would quit after the first mile and demand to be carried. Too much exercise would stress your puppy's growing body. You'd notice a limp. Sure, you want to keep your puppy in shape—an obese puppy is an unhealthy puppy—but puppies aren't born ready to run endless miles. Let yours develop first.

Until a puppy is four months old, you should play with him instead of walking him. Any of the games mentioned in the preceding section will do!

Sizing Your Dog Up

Size is another factor. Breed is too. A German Short-haired Pointer—a large dog bred to run around in fields looking for birds—will need more exercise than a teacup-sized Poodle. Yes, common sense would tell most people that, but I'm surprised how many people buy a breed for its looks without realizing the amount of exercise their new dog will need.

Sarah Says
Play on grass or dirt surfaces. Keep pups off the pavement, except if you're going out to potty them; it's too stressful on their bones and tissues. Do you have tile floors? They can be a real nightmare for puppies; they're too slippery. Lay carpet strips down for them until they get older.

Grrr
Remember, if your dog doesn't work off his energy outside, he'll work it off inside. If you don't run him, he may demolish your couch. Is it spite? No, just energy and boredom.

If you flip back to Chapter 1, you'll find a list of breed groupings. Table 18.1 repeats this information to help you understand the energy level of different breeds.

Table 18.1   Different Breeds and Their Energy Levels

Breed	Bred To	Energy Level*
Pointers	Course fields all day, point, and retrieve	Very High
Retrievers	Stay by master's side, retrieve on command	High
Spaniels	Flush and retrieve birds	High
Setters	Run field, point, flush, retrieve fowl	High
Sighthounds	Pursue fast-moving game	High in spurts, then low
Scent Hounds	Follow and trail game	High
Large Game Hunters	Challenge large game	Medium
Sled/Draft	Pull sleds long distances/ pull carts to market	High/medium
Guarding	Guard territory	Medium
Personal Protection	Protect home and master	Medium
Rescue/Water Dogs	Rescue man	Low (Portuguese Water Dog = High)
Sheep Herders	Herd sheep	Medium to High
Livestock Driving	Move sheep and cattle from field to field	High
Terriers	Hunt barn pest	Medium to High
Fighting Breeds	Originally bred to fight each other, or other species	Medium
Non-Sporting	All vary historically	Medium
Dalmatian	Currently bred for companionship	Very high
Toy Group	Companionship	Low

* Energy Level	Amount of Interaction Needed	How Often
Very High	20 minutes	2–4 times daily
High	15–20 minutes	2–3 times daily
Medium	10–15 minutes	2 times daily
Low	5 minutes	1–2 times daily

Dog Play

If you're taking your dog on a play date, get ready for some wild mouthing and jumping action. I know it looks viscious, but it's how dogs play. Have you ever seen a dog swing another around by his scruff? As long as it's in the spirit of fun, it's fair game. The question is how can you tell? Here are some tell-tail signs:

➤ Fights usually start during the introduction. If two dominant dogs meet (usually same sex, though not always), they'll do a lot of "bluffing"—hackles raised, chest out, head up, throaty vocalizations, tail just above the rump, eyes locked. If one dog doesn't back down (by breaking the stare, lowering his head, or doing a play bow), a fight may start to determine dominance.

➤ If two dominant dogs are playing and one gets too rough, the other may not back down. The vocalization will turn from a roughhousing tone to an aggressive one quickly.

➤ Some dogs fight off their playmate when they've had enough. If your dog looks tired and bothered, separate him from other dogs.

➤ If you have a dominant dog, leave a nylon lead on his collar while he plays. This way, if things get out of hand, you have something to grab. Encourage the other dog owner to do the same.

➤ If a fight starts with an unleashed dog, grab the base of one dog's tail while another person grabs the other dog. Back away from each other simultaneously to separate them. Don't reach for their collars; either dog may unintentionally bite you.

An alternative means of separating a fight is to pour/spray water (hoses work wonders) or Bitter Apple® spray on the dogs' heads.

➤ More often than not, people create dog fights. Yes, people. Left alone, dogs usually work out their differences and establish a hierarchy. All out fights occur when people step in screaming and yelling. Dogs respond to the added tension and go for blood. Sometimes, the best way to settle a dispute is to leave the room.

> **Grrr**
> Never correct a Top Dog who's in a fight with another dog. Confrontational play helps them decide who's King (or Queen) of the Mountain! You cannot balance their play. Remember, dogs respect a hierarchy; mess with it and you're asking for trouble.

Puppy Kindergarten

If it's not too late, enroll in a Puppy Kindergarten class today. It's a fun way to socialize your puppy and ensure that he learns how to get along with and be controlled around other dogs.

If your class allows off-lead playtime like I do in my classes, you'll notice that even puppies establish a hierarchy. Size doesn't seem to make too much difference, either. Little dogs can be very bossy. I've seen a Yorkshire Terrier bring a Saint Bernard to her knees!

Bet You Didn't Know

Dogs know the difference between another grown dog and a puppy. Everyone is more tolerant of puppies! Don't be surprised, however, if a grown dog pins a pup or growls a warning. It's nature. Don't interfere. The grown dog is teaching the pup a lesson on respect and self-control.

Exercising Dogs with Genetic Skeletal Disorders

Let's take a closer look at *hip dysplasia*. Normally, the femoral bone's head grows into the joint socket and rotates freely as your dog moves around. Hip dysplasia affects many

Doglish

Genetic disorders are passed from parent dogs to puppies on blueprints known as a genes.

dogs, both pure-bred and mixed. In a moderately dysplasitic dog, the femoral head angles outward and the bone thickens, leaving a gap in the joint. This creates slips in motion, discomfort, and instability. When hip dysplasia is severe, it's extremely painful. The X-rays will make you cringe. With the femoral head degenerated and practically dislocated, motion is crippled and pain is constant. Your veterinarian will inform you of surgical options.

Normal hip joints on the left and severe hip dysplasia on the right.

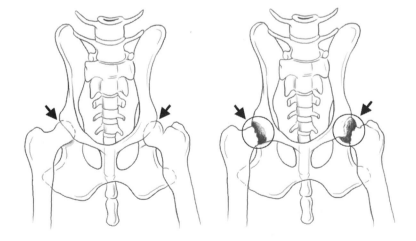

If your dog has a skeletal disorder, like hip or elbow dysplasia, you must deal with it. Begin by following this check list:

✓ Neuter your dog. Don't pass on your dog's problem.

✓ Feed your dog a balanced diet.

✓ Avoid high calorie, rapid-growth diets. They can aggravate the disorder. The tissues, bones, and muscles must grow together evenly.

✓ Avoid supplementing the diet, especially with calcium. Ask for your veterinarian's suggestion.

✓ Keep your dog's weight down. Too many pounds on a stressed joint is a bad thing.

✓ Talk to your breeder. He should know of your heartache. If he's responsible, he'll eliminate that breeding combination.

✓ Avoid all contributing environmental factors. Long jogs are no good. Correct jumping habits. Are stairs stressful? Talk to your veterinarian.

✓ Buy cozy bedding. Buy heating pads too.

✓ Carpet any area your dog travels frequently. Slippery floors don't provide good traction.

✓ Avoid leaving your dog out in the cold. Keep him in a warm, dry environment, especially at night.

✓ And last, but not least, massage that joint. (Avoid putting pressure on the joint itself.) Get blood flowing to the muscles, especially if your dog's on bed rest.

There is a wonderful exercise for dogs with these conditions. Swimming. Not everyone is fortunate to have a pond or pool in the backyard, but if you look hard enough, you may be able to find one. Long swims and leash walks on turf (no cement) can build the muscles up and build your dog's strength slowly.

If you have a setback and the limping starts again, talk to your veterinarian, ease off exercise, and start back slowly when you're given the go ahead. Your dog is physically handicapped. He needs you to take care of him.

Bet You Didn't Know

A dog can be born with a predisposition for dysplastic disorders, but you can avoid the worst effects by controlling your dog's diet and avoiding stressful exercise.

Exercise for Your Injured Dog

Some dogs are under doctor's orders to keep still. A spinal injury, a broken bone, a bad cut may all require what, in veterinarian circles, is known as "strict cage rest." I can tell you from experience that this will be a bigger problem for you than your dog. He can't understand the doctor; as he heals, he'll want to move about as usual. It's your job to keep him immobile until he gets his doctor's clearance. You can wreck a good surgical job or bone realignment by giving your dog too much freedom too fast. Here are a few ideas to keep your dog's mind busy when his body must be still:

➤ Provide him with his favorite chews—pig's ears, hooves, bones, a rope toy. Go ahead, spoil him rotten!

➤ Buy a Kong toy or hollowed out bone and stuff it with peanut butter.

➤ Massage his muscles. It increases blood flow to his muscles and keeps them healthy. It feels good, too!

➤ Play calming music to help relieve the stress of being confined from outside activities.

➤ Talk to your dog. He'll love the attention and the distraction of listening to your voice.

Remember, you're going to have to be the strong one. Your dog will want to run around before it's safe. Follow your veterinarian's orders to the letter.

Exercise and Aging Dogs

Old dogs like to play too. Sure, they're not as rambunctious as pups and they may walk a little slower, but they love the attention and the time you spend together. If your dog suddenly loses interest in a game or refuses a walk, bring it to the attention of your veterinarian. Though it's understandable to chalk it up to old age, in most cases, it's a sign of illness.

The Least You Need To Know

➤ Exercise is as important to good health as eating and eliminating. Exercise your dog 2–4 times per day for up to 20 minutes at a time.

➤ Puppies need more exercise and interactive play than adult dogs.

➤ Size, breed, and personality also determine how much exercise your dog will need.

➤ Dogs love to play with other dogs. Though their mock fights may startle you, it's their version of fun.

➤ Socialize your pup with other puppies. Join a Puppy Kindergarten today!

➤ If your dog is on strict bed rest, stock up on favorite chews and massage his muscles to keep them healthy until he's back on his paws!

Chapter 19

Keeping Your Dog Healthy

In This Chapter

➤ Surviving the brush-n-bath

➤ Toenail clipping

➤ Facial necessities: eyes, ears, nose, and mouth

➤ Neutering, vaccinations, and pet insurance

➤ Sniffing out a good veterinarian

A lot can be said for good doggie hygiene. Staying on top of good health can prevent a lot of disease and heartache. Not only will your dog look good, but you'll also be able to discover any ailments before they get serious. Brushes, nail clippers, toothpaste, cotton swabs...these are just some of the paraphernalia you'll use to keep your dog in tip-top shape!

Brushing

For some people, grooming is a complete nightmare. Here's what usually happens: Puppy's hair finally starts growing. Owner buys a brush, usually a wire slicker. Owner proudly pulls the pup aside for her first groom. Wire bristles hurt puppy's tender skin—

after all, there's not too much hair yet. Puppy mouths owner. Owner gets upset. Pup sees this experience as terrifying, painful, and confrontational. Puppy mouths harder and squirms. First impression? Brushing stinks!

So now what do you do? Or how can you prevent this? Here are some suggestions:

1. Use a soft bristle human brush.

2. Spread peanut butter, margarine, or chicken broth on a section of clean flooring.

3. Bring your dog in on a leash or short lead.

Grrr
If your dog growls at any point while you're brushing him, stop everything. Call a professional right away!

4. As she's standing and licking, brush softly as you say "Stand still" and praise.

5. If your dog gets agitated, tug the leash downward and say "Shhh" without staring at her or getting too tense. Staring and tension create stand-offs.

6. Eventually work towards using a brush of choice. Talk to a groomer to decide what brush is best for your dog's needs.

Bathing

I remember dog baths back when I was a kid. I had a big Husky-Shepherd mix named Shawbee. To say she hated her bath is an understatement. She dug her heals in the minute we'd turn her down the hall. Restraining her in the tub was no picnic either. Four hands had to be on her or else she was hall bound, shaking suds as she ran down the stairs and out the door. It was quite entertaining.

There is a way to prevent this, and the trick works so well, your dog might start jumping into the tub on command!

1. Make Tub a command.

2. Say "Tub," run to the tub, and treat your dog. Repeat, repeat.

3. Next, teach your dog to climb into the tub/or be lifted in without water. Place a mat down in the tub for footing and have plenty of favorite chews waiting. Treat her upon tub entry. Play for five minutes and take her out. No bath.

4. Repeat this step until your dog looks forward to tub togetherness.

5. Next, run the water as you're playing. Let it drain.

6. Once your dog allows this, let the tub fill to hock (ankle) depth. If your dog squirms, bring in some peanut butter to rub along the edge of the tub while the water fills.

7. Proceed gradually until you're able to tub and bathe peacefully.

I know it sounds like a lot, but think of it as one week's adventure. After all, it's a training exercise and a small effort for a lifetime of easy bathing.

Stick with one bath a month at most. I never bathe my dogs more than a few times a year, although I water my dog down if he needs a mud-rinse. The reason? Dogs don't have pores to produce oil. If you bath them constantly, their coats will become dry, dull, full of dandruff, and brittle.

Skunked?

My dog, Shawbee, loved skunks. She never did learn to avoid them. And we never learned a good remedy for getting rid of the smell. Sure we tried tomato juice, spaghetti sauce, ketchup, V8, but to no avail. We had to wait it out. Now, there's a product on the market called Snuck Off® (by Thornell Coop) that you dilute in water. It is an improvement on the age old tomato remedy and a lot less messy. The one time I used it, it worked better than tomato juice, but I could still depict skunk on my Labrador, Calvin, for a week. Here's one remedy I haven't tried, but which I've heard works wonders. It's an odd concoction, but from my client to you, "it's miraculous!"

> 1 quart of three-percent hydrogen peroxide
>
> $^1/4$ cup baking soda
>
> 1 teaspoon liquid soap
>
> follow bath with water rinse

I also hear Massingil® douche works miracles. Just don't stock up all at once—they might commit you!

Manicure, Doggie Style

Dogs take no pride in their nails. None. I'm not sure they even think about them until you try to cut them. Then there's the big sob story. If you have a dog that struggles every time you take the clippers out, you know what I'm talking about. If you have a pup who hasn't seen the clippers yet, lucky you. You can prevent this problem before it begins.

Cut on the dotted line.

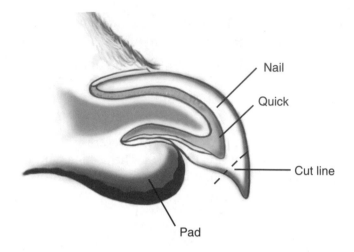

Nail

Quick

Cut line

Pad

The best kind of clipper looks like a guillotine. Seriously. I can't explain it any better than that. When you're clipping your dog's nail, you want to clip the very tip just at the point it starts to curl. Front nails grow faster than hind ones. If you have a dog with a dew claw (a nail that rides high on the hock), don't overlook it. If nails grow too long, they can crack, break, or become ingrown. Nails need to be clipped about once a month.

Handle your dog's paws every time you pet or treat her. Just handle them, nothing fancy. If you're in the car and come to a red light, turn to your dog, handle her paws, and tell her "Good girl." Have as much hand-on-paw contact as possible for one week. No clipping.

Grrr
God forbid you cut into your dog's *quick* (the tissue part of the nail). Aside from being excruciatingly painful, it will bleed for hours. There are lots of veins and nerves down there. To prevent excess bleeding, purchase a clotting solution from your veterinarian. It works like magic.

Take out your peanut butter, margarine, or broth and swipe some across the refrigerator at your dog's eye level. As she licks, rub her paws with the clipper. Don't cut the nails just yet. Open and shut the clippers to acquaint her with the sound.

Now try one cut—just one. Place the edge of the clippers over the top of the nail and squeeze the handle quickly. The next day, try two nails, and then three. Do not correct your dog if she protests. Be understanding and slow down. Again, it sounds like a production, but it's worth it in the long run. Anyone who has cut his dog or frightened her by being too rough can tell you having a "clipper phobic" dog is a disaster.

Facial Concerns

Dogs don't spend as much time worrying over their looks as we do, but that doesn't mean their facial features should go unnoticed.

Eyes

Soulful, sweet, comic…your dog's eyes express it all. It's up to you to keep them healthy, bright, and clear. Do not let your dog hang her head out the car window. Sure it looks refreshing, but one pebble could knock out an eye. Leave the windows open a crack if you must or station your dog far enough away to keep her face clear of open windows. Be careful! Watch your dog's head when playing interactive games like stick toss and soccer. Eyes are very tender! If you have a long-haired breed, clip the hair surrounding the eye.

Don't squeeze shampoo on your dog's head or spray flea repellent directly at your dog's face. Cover her eyes as you apply any products with your fingertips. Does your dog have morning eye crust? It's not so bad as long as you wipe it clear everyday. Use warm water and a soft rag or tissue. Built-up crust can be painful, irritating, and a pretty gruesome sight.

Avoid dogs/cats with mange, ringworm, or other skin irritations. How do you know? Sometimes, it's hard to tell. Make sure that the pets your dog hangs out with are healthy.

Eyes are very precious. Take care of them. If you notice your dog's eyes are tearful, full of mucous, swollen, or itchy, see your veterinarian. She could be suffering from conjunctivitis (which is very contagious), a cold, internal parasites, or an allergy.

If your veterinarian prescribes eye medication, you'll need to administer it carefully. To apply drops, swipe something tasty on the refrigerator (peanut butter or margarine) 30 degrees above your dog's eye level. Pull back the upper lid until you see the white of your dog's eye and administer the medication.

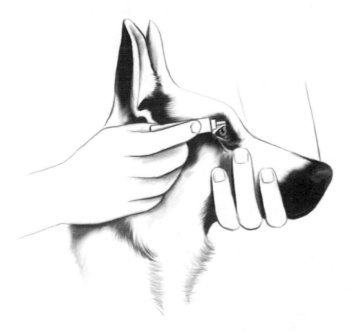

Pull back the upper eyelid to apply eye drops.

To apply ointment, set up the same situation, but pull the lower lid down and squeeze in the medication along the lower lid. Eyes are tricky; you don't want to poke them. Stay very calm and positive to help your dog relax. If your dog puts up a big fuss, ask for drops so that you can keep the applicator further from your dog's face.

Ears

I'm mesmerized by this body part. I can literally lull myself into a trance petting ears. And it doesn't seem to matter what shape—uprights, floppy, short, cropped. Dogs seem to love the ear massage as well. Ahh, bliss.

But ears need more than massaging to keep them healthy. The ear can play host to all sorts of bacteria, mites, and yeast infections. You must take good care of that flap to prevent these microscopic suckers from moving in and settling down. Since they do best in moist, damp, waxy environments, you'll need to keep the ear dry and clean. Different dogs will require different cleaning schedules (from every couple weeks to daily). It's a general rule that floppy ears require more care than uprights because of limited air circulation.

Bet You Didn't Know

Ears don't always follow the same pattern. One ear can have good air circulation and the other can have poor air flow and be perpetually dirty. My lab was this way. In the warmer months especially, I cleaned one ear daily and the other only weekly.

If you have a hairy-eared breed, you may be instructed to pluck the hair out of the way. Talk to your veterinarian or groomer for personal instructions. Excess hair can trap wax and make one big mess that cries out for parasites. (Refer to Chapter 20 for information regarding ear mites.)

Grrr
Do not use Q-Tips® or poke into your dog's ear canal. You can do irreparable damage.

Clean the outer ear flap. Ask your veterinarian to recommend a commercial ear solution that will help prevent infection. Soak it in a cotton swab and swipe the outer flap (don't go too deep; it's very tender and can be painful). Repeat this process until the cotton comes up clean.

Prevent water from entering the ear. If you're bathing or taking your dog for a swim, put a large piece of cotton in the opening ahead of time, and wipe the ears out with a dry piece when you're finished.

Ear infections are quite common. Signs of infection include a red/swollen ear, discharge, head shaking, ear itching, or a bad odor. What a drag. Get your dog to her doctor immediately. Left untreated, infections can cause fever, depression, irritability, and loss of balance. Your veterinarian will prescribe an ointment you'll administer at home. Here's how:

1. Wait until your dog's a little sleepy.

2. Bring her to the refrigerator and swipe some peanut butter or margarine at her eye level.

3. As she's licking it, gently squeeze the amount of ointment specified by your veterinarian into her ear canal.

4. Massage her ear as you praise her warmly.

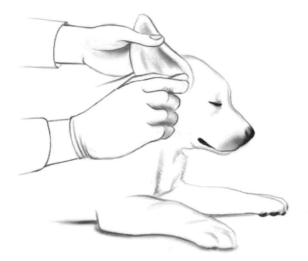

Clean your dog's ears regularly to prevent infection.

Nose

There's not too much to say about the nose. Back when I was growing up, you used to feel it to determine how your dog was feeling. If it was too hot, the dog had a fever. If it was too dry, the dog was depressed. It may sound crazy, but that's what I was told. The truth is, dog's noses can heat up in a warm environment and can get dry when the air lacks humidity. If you want to know whether your dog's running a fever, take his temperature, rectal style.

Dog's noses can get discolored. How? Sometimes from the sun. Other times it can be an allergic reaction to a food dish or household detergent. In such a case, use a stainless steel bowl and clean with environmentally safe products. And when your dog goes out into the sun, protect that nose with Sunblock 45!

Mouth

I have one obsession. It's my teeth. I love brushing, flossing, going to the dentist for my bi-annual cleaning—odd, I know. But hey, it could be worse. Based on this, you probably know what I'm going to suggest before I even write it. You must take care of your dog's teeth. Though dogs are less prone to tartar build-up than we are, they're not immune. Sure, they have more concentrated saliva and they chew bones and things, but this doesn't take the place of dental care. Without a little help from "friends" (that's us), they'll suffer from tooth decay, cavities, abscesses, periodontal disease, and tooth loss.

Sarah Says
Do you have a puppy? Good. Acquaint her with this procedure early on. Rub your fingers along her gums throughout the week and praise her calmly as you brush.

To keep your dog's teeth healthy:

> ➤ Feed dry food. Crunchy is better.

➤ Brush your dog's teeth once a week. Use special dog toothpaste. (Avoid human toothpaste; fluoride and dogs don't mix.) Read the label for instructions. If your dog is adverse to the brush, use your fingers. If your dog growls, quit immediately and call a professional.

➤ As your dog gets older, you may opt for a yearly professional cleaning. Your veterinarian will need to sedate your dog, scale each tooth separately, and then polish. Good dental care prevents disease and decay.

Bet You Didn't Know

Some dogs put up an enormous struggle. For these dogs, your veterinarian may suggest an oral spray that breaks down tartar.

Sniffing Out a Good Vet

Choosing a veterinarian is one of the most important decisions of your dog's life. And unless you live in rural America, you'll have several to choose from. Here are some concrete guidelines to make the process easier:

➤ Ask other pet owners.

➤ Visit the vet with/without your pet. Call first to let them know you'll be arriving to check the place out and meet them. If you bring your dog, take along some favorite treats and encourage the staff to feed her. Her first recollections will be very good!

➤ Look around. Is it clean? Well organized? How does it smell? Will they let you tour the hospital? That's a good sign.

➤ Ask the doctor some questions: Where did he study? How long has he been practicing? Are there certain diseases he won't handle? Does he have references for serious ailments or procedures, such as total hip replacement or ultrasound?

➤ Do you get good vibes? Trust your opinion.

➤ Finally, trust your dog. Does her personality do a 360 when you enter the door? If she's miserable, try a different doctor. If she's still miserable, you'll know it's all in her head.

The Yearly Vaccinations

I used to tutor biology in college, explaining concepts that were sometimes hard to visualize. Let me give this a crack.

When your dog's getting a vaccine, she's actually getting a small portion of the disease against which she's being protected. It sounds dangerous. However, what usually happens is a special defense system in her body, called *antibodies*, rally together to shoot down these foreign travelers. Since the vaccine injects only a small portion of the disease, your dog's antibodies can cope with it. Conversely, if your dog got the full-blown disease, it would overwhelm the antibodies and make her sick or even kill her. Once the antibodies have conquered the vaccine, they've built up enough of an army to handle the disease should your dog get it.

Vaccines are given in one of three ways: intramuscular (IM), subcutaneous (SC), and intranasal (IN). IM vaccines are injected into the muscle and create a stronger, faster immune reaction. It may make your dog sore for a couple of days. SC vaccines are injected into skin. Though it may be itchy, it won't be too sore. IN vaccines are administered through the nose, via drops or a spray. Pretty tricky!

First vaccines should be given as puppies are weaned off their mother's milk. When they're nursing, they're protected under maternal immunity. After

Grrr
Vaccines aren't guaranteed 100 percent. Some dogs are allergic to them. Others antibodies don't build up enough of a defense. Post-vaccine illnesses are tragic. Keep your puppy at the animal hospital for a half hour after initial vaccines and learn the signs and symptoms of each in case she should get ill.

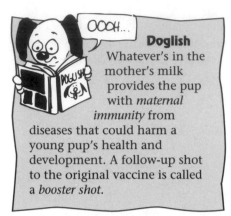

Doglish
Whatever's in the mother's milk provides the pup with *maternal immunity* from diseases that could harm a young pup's health and development. A follow-up shot to the original vaccine is called a *booster shot*.

the puppy reaches doghood, vaccines will need to be given annually, in general.

Maternal immunity protection, however, fades off soon after pups are weaned. This is where vaccines come in. Unless a puppy is orphaned, a puppy's first vaccine should begin at six weeks. If a series is recommended, follow-up shots will be given two to three weeks later. These shots are called boosters.

Table 19.1 reviews dog vaccines and when your dog needs them. (The shot packages offered by your vet may differ.)

Table 19.1 Keeping Your Dog's Vaccinations Up-to-Date

Vaccine	Disease	Symptoms	Age	Boosters
Canine Distemper (CDV)	Upper respiratory viral infection	Fever, vomiting, diarrhea	3–4 doses/ 6–16 weeks	weeks/ annual
Canine Adenovirus		Abdominal pain, jaundice, "Blue Eye" (clouded cornea)		
Type 1 (CAV-1)				
Canine Infectious Hepatitis	Liver virus	Fever, loss of appetite, vomiting	Same as CDV	Same as CDV
Type 2 (CAV-2)				
1. Canine para-influenza	Flu virus for dogs			
2. Infectious Tracheo-bronchitis	Respiratory virus	All three viruses cause kennel cough, reaction: runny	2 doses before 12 weeks	Annual booster
3. Bordetella bronchiseptica	Respiratory virus	nose and eyes, coughing, sneezing, and wheezing.		
Leptospirosis*	A spirochete bacteria entering through mucus membranes	Invades liver, kidney, and bladder; aches fever, no appetite, vomiting, nose bleeds, abdominal pain, eye inflammation, liver enlargement, blood in stool, jaundice	Included with distemper and hepatitis vaccine	

Vaccine	Disease	Symptoms	Age	Boosters
Canine Parvovirus	A new and possibly deadly gastrointestinal virus	Watery foul diarrhea, high fever, acute stomach pain, vomiting	3–4 doses in puppies, from 6–20 weeks	Annual boosters
Canine Coronavirus	Intestinal virus; less serious than parvo	Vomiting, diarrhea, fever	2 doses in pups before 12 wks; vaccine is optional	Annual booster
Lyme Borreliosis Vaccine	Spirochete bacteria	Lameness, fever, loss of appetite, swollen joints	Optional, 2 inoculations initially	Yearly booster
Rabies*	FATAL virus spread through saliva	Neurological: aggression, lock jaw (cause foaming) uncoordination, seizures	Vaccine at 3–4 months	Yearly booster

* Can be transmitted to humans

A Word about Rabies

Rabies is a very serious virus. I cannot stress proper vaccination enough. The following story brought it home to me.

A Tribute to Crash

Crash wasn't a dog. He was a kitten. A tiny creature whose black-and-white coloring looked more like a surrealistic painting than any sort of genetic code. He was a young animal, killed by a mysterious virus that is still far too rampant in our country. In his story, there is a lesson for all animal lovers.

Crash was rescued from the roadside by a good friend of mine named Mo. At approximately six weeks, his jaw had been smashed and his paws torn apart by what, at first, seemed like a car. Today we're still unsure.

With his jaw pieced together and his feet wrapped and stitched, Crash was sent home with Mo, who nursed him patiently back to health over the next month. Crash updates were given every few days. He went from a drowsy, shell-shocked, frightened animal to a lively, humorous, and otherwise normal little kitten. But for every step forward, Crash seemed to have something pulling him back. First there was a fever, then a cold, and then mysteriously everything fell apart. He had trouble walking, his head jerked and pulled to one side, and he no longer responded to the liquid antibiotics he had been on since he was rescued. Mo and Crash made their last trip to the hospital.

Crash did not make it through the night. When he died, his head was severed and sent in to be analyzed. It was confirmed, Crash had rabies. It was a sorry ending for a creature who already had shared and experienced so much love.

Grrr

Yes there are a lot of us animal lovers out there, but even I learned a big lesson from Crash. In the future, when I find a stray with noticable erratic behavior, I'll call the animal authorities and let them make the rescue.

Unfortunately, there is no test to determine rabies in an already infected, but symptom-free animal. If you pick up a stray, early precautionary measures and a six-week quarantine are advisable to avoid possible infection. With your own pets, prevention is the key. Yearly or tri-yearly vaccines must be updated to prevent pointless deaths and the spread of this deadly disease. Though nothing could have been done to save Crash once the disease entered his system, a loving home and early veterinarian care could have prevented this trauma. Responsible pet ownership is the only way to prevent the disease from entering our pet population.

To Breed or Not To Breed, That Is the Question

Doglish

A female dog is prevented from reproducing by an operation commonly called *spaying*. Her ovaries (those egg-producing sacs) are removed. This operation requires your gal to be anesthetized. It takes 5–14 days to recover. A male dog is prevented from fathering puppies through an operation called *neutering*. Basically, his testicles will be popped out of a small incision and his sacs sewn up before you can say, "Boo." Your dog will be anesthetized and back on his feet in 5–10 days.

If you're not planning to breed your dog, have your dog spayed or neutered. Here's my argument: wild dogs have three needs. They need to eat, driving them to hunt and kill for survival. They need shelter; it's the den thing. And they need to reproduce. Hormonal drives can override all else; a hungry lost dog can block out all other concerns when presented with an opportunity to mate.

Now let's take a look at the domesticated dog. Two needs are taken care of immediately by offering your dog food and shelter. But there's that third need to reproduce that, when left unsatisfied, can be quite frustrating. A dog will leave the warm, safe perimeters of home to go out and look for a mate.

Therefore, you should either enter a responsible breeding program if you've decided to breed your dog or alter him.

I've loved every dog who lived under my roof, but none of them were picture perfect and consequently all were either spayed or neutered. It didn't change their personalities. They didn't get fat. Trust me, it's not like a lobotomy. Altering simply removes the need to scope and fight for mates. Here's a list of some other, more scientific arguments for altering your dog:

➤ According to the Adoption Option, approximately 4–6 million dogs are euthanized in animal shelters each year. Think about it. Don't add to the problem. If you're not breeding your dog responsibly, have him altered.

➤ Having your dog fixed reduces the chance of breast, ovarian, uterine, or cervical cancer for females and testicular cancer or prostrate infection for males.

➤ Male dogs are less likely to mark the home or fight with other male dogs and are more likely to stay close to home.

> **Sarah Says**
> If you adopt your dog from a shelter, you'll be required to neuter him. Some shelters offer to do it for you; others recommend you to a low-cost facility. Neutering can cost anywhere from $50–250, depending on the individual dog's sex and health.

Doggy Health Insurance?

Just when you thought everything was insured! Now you can get a plan for your dog. Be very careful in selecting your carrier, however, or you might get stuck paying for ailments you thought would be covered. Here are some questions to ask when you're out shopping for a good policy:

➤ How long has your company been in business?

➤ Are you licensed within your state?

➤ Is your policy accepted by the state commissioner's office?

➤ Will I be able to choose my own veterinarian?

➤ Will you cover care if my veterinarian refers me to a specialist?

➤ What's the yearly deductible? Is there a cap on specific illnesses/accidents?

➤ What does the policy not include (worms, check-ups, dental care, heartworm tests, and so on)?

➤ Are there any conditions/diseases not covered by your policy?

➤ Do you cover ultrasounds, CAT scans, bone scans, intensive care, reconstructive surgery, or medications?

➤ Do you cover preexisting conditions?

➤ How do I pay the premium? Monthly, bi-annually, annually?

➤ Will you cover my dog throughout her lifetime, or is your policy limited by age?

➤ Are there any situations when you've terminated a policy?

➤ What is involved in signing on?

Make sure you read the fine print before you sign anything. No plan will cover 100 percent of everything. Health insurance for your dog can be a real lifesaver in an emergency or if your dog gets extremely sick, but you don't want to pay for a policy only to find it doesn't cover all services necessary for her recovery. Please ask your veterinarian to recommend a good carrier.

Bet You Didn't Know

Some western states offer HMOs, which provide a whole range of services for a monthly fee and a small co-payment. Operating on the philosophy that preventive care is the best guarantee against illness, these plans cover routine check-ups, lab testing, medicine, and hospital care. Ask your veterinarian for more information.

The Least You Need To Know

➤ What do brushing, bathing, nail clipping, and medicating have in common? They're no fun! But they're a necessary evil, canine style. Stay calm, use goodies and praise to make the process more positive, and never lose your cool!

➤ Selecting a veterinarian is a major life decision. Make sure you and your dog jive with whomever you choose.

➤ Vaccines ward off life-threatening illnesses by exposing your dog to small portions of a specified disease. Vaccinate your dog from the start!

➤ Give spaying or neutering serious consideration. Unless you plan to breed, fix your dog.

Bug-mania

Gee-whiz...how can I make this chapter fun? It's a hard task considering the fact that I'm completely bug phobic. It really gives me the creeps to think about any bug—flea, worm, tick, or otherwise—nesting on or in my dog. Visualization is definitely not advisable.

In this chapter, you'll learn how to recognize and get rid of parasites and prevent them from coming back.

A creature that lives off another animal is called a *parasite*. Parasites can feast on skin and blood or can leach on inside, eating your dog's leftovers. If your dog itches one spot too much and starts to pull her hair out, she may get a *hot spot* (acute pyotraumatic dermatitis that is not due to a single underlying cause). Go to the doctor immediately and treat it before it becomes infected.

External Parasites

External parasites live for blood—your dog's, to be precise, although some will settle for a human snack if the mood strikes them. Let's go through them one at a time.

Fleas

Fleas generally hang out in the lower portion of your dog's body, behind the shoulder blades. One sure fire way to detect a problem is to buy a flea comb and brush your dog's rear with it. If you pull out some "dirt," put it in your hand and add a few drops of water. If the dirt turns a reddish color, you're holding flea excrement. Oh joy!

Fleas are an age old problem. Contrary to popular belief, they don't live on dogs; they feed on them. Fleas live in carpets and grass, so treating the problem involves all-out war.

When getting rid of fleas, be sure to select a product that kills all life stages and repeat the treatment every three to four weeks.

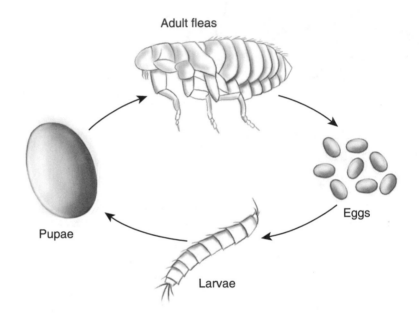

I'm obsessive about flea prevention. I use every home-spun herbal remedy known to man—from brewer's yeast and garlic, to menthol, eucalyptus, and citronella—and I've never had an out-of-control flea problem. (If you don't feel like pressing your own garlic, there are commercial pills for brewer's yeast and garlic that work just as well.)

Treat your dog with sprays, collars, oil pouches, or other products recommended by your veterinarian during flea season. Use only as frequently as the label instructs.

Insect growth regulators are not new, but their internal (systemic) use is. They have extraordinarily low toxicity and are useful in preventing house and bedding infestations. Ask your veterinarian about flea tablets or Preventative powder. The pills sterilize fleas, putting a cramp in their reproductive cycle.

Dogs can be allergic to flea saliva. Veterinarians call it *Flea Allergy Dermatitis*. Itching is intense and can lead to hair loss and self-mutilation. Sometimes it gets so bad that your dog creates a "hot spot" and a bacterial infection develops.

Home isn't so sweet when you share it with these critters. A full-blown flea infestation is like a scene from a horror show—bugs hopping onto your skin from every direction faster than you can bat them away. My suggestion? Treat your home the second you discover a flea problem.

➤ Ask your veterinarian for advice.

➤ Vacuum, vacuum, vacuum. You'll not only pick up the adults, but you'll scoop the eggs and larva from their nests too. Make sure you toss the bag, though; adult fleas are wonderful acrobats.

➤ Treat your dog's bedding or throw it out.

➤ Check the flea product label; it should be FDA approved. Follow instruction for personal safety.

➤ Treat all rooms in your house. Fleas love to travel.

➤ If your treatment's toxic, make sure all creatures, two-legged and four, are out of the house for the day. It's a good time to take your pets in for a flea dip.

➤ Open all windows when you get home.

➤ Vacuum again and toss the bag.

➤ Select a product that treats all life stages and repeat treatment in three to four weeks.

Grrr
Do not spray, rub, or squeeze flea prevention products near your dog's face or scrotum! Most products are toxic.

Grrr
Flea products are very toxic. If you have a pup, talk to your veterinarian first and discuss safe treatments.

Yards are very tricky and can be expensive to exterminate. A good freeze will take care of all parties involved, but if you can't wait, talk to your veterinarian about your options.

Ticks

Ticks are another blood sucking parasite, as if one wasn't enough. Like fleas, ticks prefer furry creatures, but they'll settle for humans in a pinch. Unfortunately, they're found all over the world and can carry airborne diseases.

Ticks, like fleas, develop in stages: eggs, larva, nymph, and adult. Eggs are laid in a damp shady environment. As they develop from stage to stage, they have several hosts and can pick up a bacterial infection from any one of them. Adults feed on blood.

Ticks love to climb. Their favorite area is around your dog's head. Removing a tick is no picnic. When they feed, they insert barbs into the skin like fish hooks. If you try to pull them out, you'll end up with a headless blood-filled sac and your dog will have a nasty bump on her head. To remove a tick:

Grrr
Do not spray around your dog's eyes. To treat your dog's forehead and ears, place the product onto a glove and massage in those hard to reach areas. Don't forget your dog's paws! Tick products are very toxic. To prevent your dog from licking himself after treatment, keep him occupied with his favorite game until the product dries. If you have a pup, discuss safe treatments with your veterinarian.

1. Stun the tick with a cotton ball soaked in mineral oil for 30 seconds.

2. With special tick-removing tweezers you can buy from a pet store, press down on the skin on either side of the tick.

3. Squeeze the skin surrounding the tick tightly and grasp the head.

4. Lift up and out. This can be painful. Give your dog a spoonful of peanut butter or some biscuits while you take care of the removal business. Make sure you wash your hands when you are done.

Stabilize the skin surrounding the tick, grab as close to the skin as possible, and use a steady pull instead of a sharp tug.

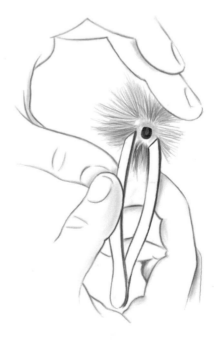

A lot can be done to prevent ticks from feasting on your dog:

➤ Ask your veterinarian to recommend a tick collar. Secure it snugly around your dog's neck. Also, ask your veterinarian to recommend a repellent.

➤ Walk your dog in the open sunshine. Ticks love to hang out in shaded woody areas.

➤ Inspect yourself and your dog after every walk. Run a flea comb, which can be purchased at any pet store, over your dog's coat after every outing. Ticks take a while to burrow and a flea comb will pick them up.

➤ To protect yourself, wear light colors and tuck your pant legs into your socks. To protect your head, wear a cap.

Bet You Didn't Know

It's hard to kill these (blood) suckers. They're drown-proof, squish-proof, and squeeze-proof. I find the best way to kill a tick is to burn them or drop them into a jar of bleach, rubbing alcohol, or vodka (for lower toxicity). (Please keep the jar out of the reach of the kids.)

Tick Diseases

Ticks often have many hosts throughout their life stages. Believe it or not, an adult can live up to two years! Cold won't kill them either; they hibernate, insect style. Feasting on blood from birds on up through the food chain, they often carry diseases. Here are the four most common:

➤ **Rocky Mountain Spotted Fever.** Ticks carrying this disease (Dermacentor ticks) are most common in the southeast, although RMSF has been diagnosed as far north as Long Island. Dogs who have been bitten can become symptomatic within two weeks. Symptoms include:

➤ Blood clotting mechanisms fail

➤ A rash may develop

➤ A fever

➤ Their urine and stools may be loose and bloody

➤ They may have nose bleeds and respiratory difficulty

Your veterinarian will run a *titer* (measures level of antibodies or immunity) to determine if your dog has been infected and needs treatment.

➤ **Canine Ehrlichiosis.** This nasty condition is transmitted by a Rhipiecphalus tick (although deer ticks are also in question). It causes severe anemia, fever, bruises, and bleeding disorders by attacking the white blood cells. Your veterinarian will do a blood titer to determine if your dog's infected. Early detection is necessary; the prognosis is poor once the condition has progressed.

➤ **Canine Babesiosus.** This disease is more common in Europe than the United States. This organism attacks the red blood cells causing severe anemia. Symptoms include fever, pale mucous membranes, and a yellowing of the skin. The infection is detected through a blood titer and the prognosis is good if detected early.

➤ **Lyme Disease (Canine Borreliosis).** This little spirochete was first diagnosed in Lyme, CT in 1977. In two decades, it has spread to over 47 states. It can affect most mammals and is transmitted through the common deer tick. This tick is so small, it looks like a speck of dirt with legs. These ticks pick up the disease in their nymph stage and continue to transmit it as adults. (Nearly 50 percent of all adult deer ticks carry the disease.) Like their relatives, these ticks enjoy a damp cool environment, so one of the best safeguards is to avoid shaded areas.

Sarah Says
Check your dog twice a day! It takes 24 hours to transmit the disease, so early removal is your best bet!

Once the organism gets into your dog's system (or yours, for that matter), it seeks out joints, causing painful inflammation, fever, loss of appetite, and lameness. Left untreated, your dog's kidneys, heart, and neurological processes may be in danger. Once it reaches your dog's major organs, the prognosis is poor.

Your veterinarian will take a Lyme titer to determine if your dog is infected. Sometimes the accuracy of this test is cloudy because it takes weeks to months for the disease to become symptomatic. Your doctor may recommend two or three titers for an accurate diagnosis. All tests are compared to note a rising number in your dog's anti-body level. Your veterinarian will also ask for any and all clinical signs of illness. When possible, create a symptom log with dates and durations. Your efforts and concern will be appreciated.

There are vaccines for this disease, though there's a lot of controversy as to their effectiveness. Vaccines are more effective with dogs who have not contracted the disease. (See Chapter 19 for more information on this vaccine.)

Mites, Mange, and Lice, Oh My!

These bugs are quite content hanging around on or in the skin or coat of your dog, living on skin, hair, or blood. Before treating, it is recommended that your vet accurately diagnoses your dog.

➤ **Ear Mites.** Ear mites nestle in your dog's ear and feed on the outer layer of skin. The first sign is your dog's behavior; she'll scratch her ear intently, shake her head, and walk funny. You can check for ear mites by examining your dog's ear canal; is it filled with brown wax and crusty around the edge? Your veterinarian can make a quick and certain diagnosis and get her on the road to recovery. After she gets a professional flushing from her doctor, you'll need to follow up with daily drops and cleaning procedures.

➤ **Lice.** Lice live on hair shafts. It's a species-specific, contagious condition that's common in shelters, pet stores, or any other crowded area. These bugs secure themselves to your dog's hair shaft and hold on for dear life. Symptoms include itching and hair loss. Left unchecked, anemia can occur. Fortunately, treatment is easy.

➤ **Mange Mites.** These nasty creatures are related to ear mites although they're more free-ranging, often localizing along the spine, legs, head, or underside. There are three different types of mange mites:

> ➤ **Cheyetiella or "Walking Dandruff."** These critters hang out along your dog's spine and create a lot of flaking as they munch the skin. The surest sign? Intense scratching and nibble-biting along the spine. Your veterinarian can confirm suspicions by skin scrapings and micro-scopic observation. The situation is brought under control by a pyrethrin-based dip. All bedding and frequented rugs should be cleaned or discarded. Three dips must given at weekly intervals. Long haired dogs must be shaved (especially their mats) before treatment.

Grrr
Cheyetiella can affect humans, though it happens infrequently. The symptoms include red, itchy bites that leave a yellow crusty lesion. If the situation persists, see a dermatologist.

> ➤ **Demodectoc Mange.** Demodex mites are usually transferred from a mother dog to her pups during nursing. Under normal conditions, they exist at a harmonious level; however, if a puppy gets stressed or is malnourished, they can multiply and create an infection. There are two types of invasions:

> *Localized Demodex* like to stay in one area, usually around the face or legs. The infected area loses hair and becomes itchy, red, and bald. Treatment involves daily application of a specified ointment.

> *Generalized Demodex* involves a more serious infection that can be wide-spread over the entire body, creating large, inflamed, bald patches. A reaction can be severe, causing fever and enlarged lymph nodes. Left unchecked, this

241

can develop into a secondary bacterial infection. Should that go unnoticed, the area may abscess in the skin. This condition, called deep pyoderma, can threaten your puppy's life. Treatment is difficult and is more effective when diagnosed early. Dips must be performed at the veterinarian because it involves a strong chemical. If a secondary infection has occurred, your pup will need to take special antibiotics.

➤ **Sarcoptic Mange.** Otherwise known as scabies, these crab-shaped bugs burrow into your dog's skin and tunnel around laying eggs and sipping blood. Their favorite spots are the head region, legs, and underside. The surest sign is a dog that literally can't stop itching all over. It can lead to hair loss, yellow crusty skin, and bacterial infections. These bugs are hard to find under a microscope; only 50 percent of the scrapings locate the actual mite. Often the condition is misdiagnosed. Treatment comes in the form of several dips or a double-dose injection.

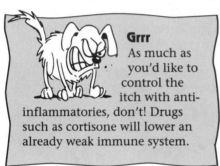

Grrr
As much as you'd like to control the itch with anti-inflammatories, don't! Drugs such as cortisone will lower an already weak immune system.

Scabies like humans, too! Although they prefer hosts with fur, they'll settle for our skin in a pinch. Symptoms are small red dots that itch and become crusty and yellow. Consult your dermatologist.

Internal Parasites

Internal parasites are much more of a health hazard to dogs than external parasites, especially puppies.

Roundworm (Ascariasis)

These worms are big and long, measuring up to 20 centimeters in length. As they develop into adults, they float inside a dog's body—in the liver, through the heart, and onto the lungs. In their final stage, they settle in the small intestine where they feast on your dog's dinner.

Dogs who have a case of roundworms are plagued with:

➤ An insatiable appetite

➤ A chronic cough

➤ Loose, smelly diarrhea

➤ Dry, brittle coat

➤ Gas

➤ Uncomfortable and difficult elimination

➤ Bloating

➤ Inflammation of the eye

Roundworms are brought under control through oral medication. Because it only kills adult worms, your veterinarian will repeat the worming in three weeks to ensure the worms are killed at every stage.

Roundworms aren't strangers to humans. The larva can penetrate skin from the soil. Another way to transmit this parasite is through fecal-oral contact. It's not unheard of for a responsible owner to forget to wash his hands after cleaning up stool or for a child to play with a dog's elimination. Once they get into your body, these worms can end up in the liver, kidney, brain, or eye, which can be hazardous to your health to say the least. If you suspect you or a child has roundworms, call your doctor immediately. To prevent this problem, clean up after your dog (and cat!), wash your hands after cleaning, and check your child's play area twice a day.

> **Sarah Says**
> If you suspect your dog has round-worms, observe your dog's stool and vomit. If you see a spaghetti-like organism, get your dog to her doctor immediately!

Hookworms (Ancylostoma Caninum)

These corkscrew-shaped creatures cluster together in large numbers and measure only a few millimeters in length. They not only feed off your dog's food, they suck her blood. In young pups, especially, this can lead to severe anemia. Other symptoms include:

➤ Bloating

➤ Excessive gas

➤ Smelly, loose stools

➤ A skinny dog who has a large appetite

➤ Bloody stools

➤ Dry, brittle coat

Dogs pick up hookworms by eating the feces of infected animals. A young pup can become infected nursing on mom or even coming in contact with worms who creep through their tender skin. Treatment involves a double dose of oral medication given three weeks apart. To prevent this parasitic problem, keep your dog's environment free from stools.

> **Grrr**
> This parasite can affect humans; children often fall victim if their play area is frequented by free-ranging pets (cats as well as dogs). Not only can it be transmitted fecal-oral, but the worms can enter through the skin.

Whipworms (Trichuris Vulpis)

These worms live and reproduce in your dog's large intestine, causing inflammation and the following symptoms:

➤ Bloating and cramps

➤ Bloody or mucous-coated stools

➤ A dry, brittle coat

➤ Smelly diarrhea

➤ Major appetite

Dogs become infected by eating worm-ridden stools (an especially popular activity for pups!) or by stepping in feces and licking their paws. Whipworms are difficult to find in a fecal sample. Treatment is often given based on clinical signs in the form of a powder and repeated again in three months.

Tapeworms

I remember asking my brother why there was a piece of rice crawling out my dog's rear end. Turns out it wasn't rice; it was a tapeworm. Truth is, that's how most people discover their dog is infected: the "white rice" diagnosis. Other tell-tail signs include:

➤ Incredible appetite and noticeable weight loss

➤ Rectal itching

➤ Abdominal pain and indigestion

Dogs pick up this parasite by eating fleas that serve as the tapeworms' intermediate host. Treatment involves medication, flea control, and environmental clean-up.

Heartworm

I can close my eyes right now and see the preserved heart that sits in my veterinarian's office with long spaghetti strands hanging out of it. The dog with that heart died from heartworm disease. This nasty worm is transmitted by mosquitoes (and, therefore, is more prevalent in warmer climates) and lives in the chambers of the heart and the lungs. Left unnoticed, heartworm disease is fatal. Actually, once the adult worm develops in the heart, treatment is slow and dangerous. This is one parasite that's better to prevent than cure. You have two preventative options:

➤ **Daily preventative pills.** These pills are less expensive than the monthly version and come as chewables or tablets. They must be given consistently to be effective. (Daily preventatives are also available as a syrup.)

➤ **Once a month preventative pills.** These medications are prescribed according to weight. If you have a pup, be sure to ask your veterinarian how to accommodate for his growth. Though it's more expensive, it's often the preference for the busy crowd.

Follow your veterinarian's prescription. If he says to use the heartworm prevention year round, do. You must have an annual test done; prevention's never 100 percent.

> **Grrr**
> If you forget to give a daily for more than a week, or one monthly pill, have your dog tested before you resume medication. Pills can be dangerous, even fatal, if given after the worm has entered the heart.

Coccidia

Coccidia lay their eggs in stools. Dogs become infected by eating other dogs' stools. These internal pests are not from the worm family. They're protozoans, one-celled microscopic organisms that line the intestinal track. Intestines playing hotel to these creatures become inflamed, which leads to loose, watery stools, bloating, vomiting, weight loss, and strained elimination. Fortunately, diagnosis is easy and treatment is quick and effective.

Giardia

Another protozoan, these are water loving creatures found in most outdoor water sources. Once ingested, they feast on the inner lining of the small intestine. This creates inflammation, which leads to loose, mucous-coated stools, bloating, and weight loss. Dogs pick up this parasite by drinking infected water or by digesting stools of other infected animals. Easy to detect, early prognosis is key. Treatment involves the use of a drug that can have side-effects over long-term use.

> **Sarah Says**
> If you're going to picnic by the pond, bring along some fresh water and a bowl for your dog. Keep his tongue wet with the fresh water and encourage him to leave all protozoans in the pond!

The Least You Need To Know

➤ Keep your dog parasite-free. Take every possible precaution and check his stool sample with your veterinarian three times a year.

➤ If your dog has fleas, it's all-out war to exterminate them!

➤ Ticks have many hosts throughout their life cycle: dogs, cats, birds, mice, deer—even humans! They can carry disease from one host to the next. Check your dog for ticks every day.

➤ Mites and lice are microscopic bugs that dine on your dog's skin and coat. If you notice a bald patch that gets bigger, see your veterinarian.

➤ Clean your dog's yard and discourage him from investigating questionable stools or decomposing tidbits.

➤ Heartworms can be fatal. You can prevent this mosquito-transmitted disease with medication from your veterinarian.

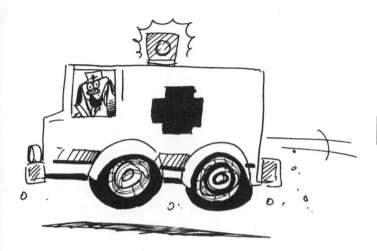

Emergency

Nobody wants an accident to happen. No one wants to see his dog get hit, cut, be poisoned, or suffer from the heat. But, the reality is these things can happen and you need to be prepared. Learning what steps to take before you get your dog to the animal hospital can save your dog's life. This chapter covers all the steps you need to follow in an emergency. None of the suggestions in this chapter takes the place of seeing your veterinarian immediately. Familiarizing yourself with canine first aid, however, may keep your pet safe as you are transporting him to the vet.

Dog-proofing Your Home

Try to prevent as many emergencies as possible. Dogs, especially puppies, are curious creatures. Let's take a look at your house from your dog's point of view: "Plants, dirt, leaves that go pop when I pull them from their stalks. This gets a giant reaction from my parents if they're within hearing distance. What fun!" Inside or out, plants can entertain your dog for hours, but not all plants are dog-friendly. Some are deadly.

Indoor plants that are harmful to your dog include:

➤ Cactus

➤ Dumb Cane

➤ Marijuana

➤ Mistletoe

➤ Philodendron

➤ Poinsettia sap

➤ Tobacco

Outdoor plants that are harmful to your dog include:

➤ Azalea bush

➤ Daffodil flower bud

➤ Honeysuckle

➤ Horse Chestnut

➤ Lily of the Valley

➤ Morning Glory flower

➤ Rhododendron shrub

➤ Rhubarb

➤ Skunk Cabbage

➤ Tulip bulb

➤ Wild Mushroom

Plants aren't the only edibles that can poison your dog. Though many would argue that gasoline isn't too tasty, you'd be surprised at what a dog finds tempting. Rat poison, acids and alkalis, poisonous plants, and anti-freeze are just a few of the substances that will cause a reaction with your dog. Put all dangerous substances out of the reach of your pet, just as you would put them out of the reach of children. See the "Poisons" section later in this chapter to learn what to do if your dog swallows something harmful.

Grrr

If your dog is carrying a plant in his mouth, do not race toward him. This is perceived as prize envy and may encourage him to gulp the evidence. Approach calmly and stare at the floor, not into his eyes.

Walking through your house, I see one dangerous temptation in every room. Take, for example, the infamous lamp cord. Hanging there like a snake, it can be quite tempting to attack and chew. The damage can range from a sharp to lethal shock to a mild to third-degree burn.

If you notice a severed cord, check your dog's mouth for burns. If your dog is in pain, apply ice to the burns and give him ice water. If the burns are severe, get him to his veterinarian who'll prescribe antibiotic oral gel to prevent infection and may recommend a dietary change until his mouth is back to normal.

Severe electrocution is often life-threatening. Your dog will show signs of shock and may need CPR to resuscitate him on the way to the animal hospital.

Progressing through your home, I see a lot of small ingestibles for the dog who's so inclined. Though it may seem odd to you, some dogs love to swallow what they chew. Problem is, not all things pass through a dog's intestines. Some get stuck in the intestines, initially causing vomiting, gagging, dry heaves, and coughing. This can go on for days. If that's not cause enough for alarm, the dog will stop eating and drinking. When blocked, the intestine will rupture if nothing is done.

Treatment depends on how soon you get your dog to the veterinarian. If the object is large enough, it may be identified on the exam table; otherwise, an X-ray will be needed. To remove the foreign objcct, the doctor may order a mineral oil laxative or surgery. The sooner you get your dog to the doctor, the better the prognosis!

Sarah Says
Prevent lamp cord electrocution! Tape all cords hanging four feet from the ground to the wall and pin floor cords to the baseboard!

Sarah Says
Pick up! Dogs love to carry things in their mouths. If you chase them or get uptight, they often swallow their find to hide the evidence. Keep all rooms free from swallowables!

A Crash Course in Canine First Aid

If your dog has an accident, stay cool. If you lose it, he'll get nervous and go to pieces. Be a rock of confidence. Be mentally tough. Organize. Think. Get him to the hospital as quickly and efficiently as possible. I'll go over how to handle possible situations later, but for now, let's take a quick look at how dogs experience pain.

Dogs can't articulate pain. They can't intellectualize it, meditate on it, or seperate themselves from it. Pain is pain. An emotion. A state of being. Pain puts dogs in a vulnerable state. It confuses their thought process and their organization. Their only drive is to protect themselves and alleviate their distress. Add that state of mind to your dog's natural temperament and what you'll get is a fairly predictable reaction. For example, suppose my dog is a big baby. Sure he looks ferocious, but heaven forbid a Yorkshire Terrier barks—my dog dives for my legs in a flash. When in pain, he'll seek me out desperately looking to me for help. Another more dominant, independent dog may bite his owner when she tries to help. A really shy dog might pee on his own leg. Though dogs experience pain in the same way, they deal with it differently.

The key in an emergency is to relax. Keep your head on straight. If you have done the proper preparation, you'll be fine.

Restraining Techniques

Even the most beloved pet may bite when he's in pain or confused. If he doesn't bite you, he'll probably go for the vet or one of the technicians, so restrain your dog for their sake. The simplest restraining technique requires a bandanna or a rope (the bandanna being more comfortable). To restrain your dog, follow these steps:

1. Fold the bandanna into a long band.

2. Drape the center of the band across the top of your dog's nose.

3. Cross the two ends underneath your dog's chin.

4. Tie the ends securely behind your dog's ears.

5. Check the crossing point underneath. If it's too loose, your dog will paw it off; if it's too tight, you'll choke your dog.

Restrain your dog to prevent him from biting out of pain or confusion.

Transporting an Injured Dog

Transporting a dog who has internal injuries is tricky business. He'll be restless and want to move. It's your job to make sure he doesn't. If you suspect a broken bone, spinal injury, or internal bleeding, transport your dog on a firm surface such as metal or ply-wood. Otherwise, placing your dog on a sheet or towel is acceptable. Don't cover his face or he may panic.

Be ready! Place a dog-sized board aside for emergencies.

Artificial Respiration and CPR

It's a horrible thought. Imagine seeing your dog lying there after a fire, a car accident, choking, ingesting poison, or electrocution. However, it may not be too late to save him, so be quick and think clearly when performing the following steps:

1. Check for a heartbeat (see instructions that follow for administering CPR).

2. Check for any obstructions in the mouth. Clear his mouth of any blood or mucous.

3. Pull out his tongue to make sure the airway is clear.

4. Shut his mouth gently.

5. Pull his lips over his mouth and secure them by wrapping one hand under his chin.

> **Sarah Says**
> If your dog is in cardiac arrest, it's ideal to have two people working: one pumping the heart and one breathing.

Give your dog mouth-to-muzzle respiration when you can feel a heartbeat, but no breathing.

6. For breeds who have pushed-in noses, wrap your mouth around the nose.

7. Create an airtight funnel to his nose with your free hand.

8. Inhale and then exhale air smoothly into your dog's nose.

9. Repeat every five to six seconds.

If you cannot feel your dog's heartbeat, you must pump his heart for him by performing CPR (cardio pulmonary resuscitation). To give CPR, follow these steps:

1. If you have a large dog, lay him on his right side. If you have a small dog, place a hand on either side of his chest.

2. Compress the heart area of the chest in short bursts, 70 times per minute.

You'll know when you've saved your dog. He'll come back to life!

Stopping Bleeding

Bleeding comes in three forms:

➤ **The everyday cut and scrape.** This is no big deal. Wipe it with some hydrogen peroxide to keep it safe from infection twice a day and it'll heal just fine.

➤ **A continuous or oozing stream.** This requires medical attention immediately. Raise the body part above the heart if possible and apply bandages one on top of the other to soak the blood as you press down on the area to slow the flow.

➤ **A gushing spurt and flow.** This type of bleeding is serious—very serious. Your dog can go into shock quickly and die if too much blood is lost. Unfortunately, applying hand pressure will not be enough. You'll need to apply a tourniquet (only for limbs or tail). Sound scary? A tourniquet must be tied between the wound and the heart to stop circulation. Use whatever is available to make your tourniquet: a rope, cloth strip, or belt. It must be tied tight enough to prevent circulation. READ THIS! Tourniquets cannot stay on longer than ten minutes. If it takes you longer than that to get your dog to a veterinarian, loosen the tourniquet to allow blood to get to the limb. While blood is re-entering the area, apply hand pressure to the cut. Loosen the tourniquet every ten minutes for three to four minutes.

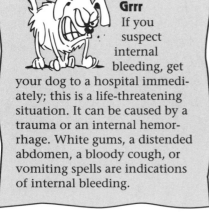

Grrr
If you suspect internal bleeding, get your dog to a hospital immediately; this is a life-threatening situation. It can be caused by a trauma or an internal hemorrhage. White gums, a distended abdomen, a bloody cough, or vomiting spells are indications of internal bleeding.

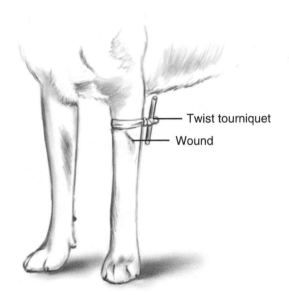

Twist tourniquet

Wound

Use a tourniquet to slow severe bleeding. Don't leave it on for more than ten minutes and get to the vet quickly!

Tourniquets can be very dangerous. A limb may die without circulation and need to be amputated. Use only in an emergency and remember to loosen it every ten minutes while applying pressure to the wound. Dogs with severe wounds should also be treated for shock (refer to the next section).

Sarah Says
Ice packs can also slow the flow of blood. Only use ice packs for oozing cuts and scrapes.

Shock

A dog in shock will show the following symptoms:

➤ A fast heart rate (the heart tries to make up for a drop in blood pressure)

➤ Rapid breathing pattern (trying to increase oxygen flow to the body)

➤ Dilated pupils and glaring stare

➤ Unconscious or semi-conscious behavior

A dog can go into shock if he experiences a sudden loss in blood, a trauma, or electrocution. Shock is life-threatening; it causes blood pressure to drop dramatically, which prevents oxygen from circulating in the body. Without oxygen, your dog will die quickly. If you suspect your dog has gone into shock, stay calm, keep him still, and get to the nearest veterinarian immediately.

Bites and Stings

Outdoor dogs run the risk of meeting creatures who aren't all that friendly. Insects sting, snakes bite, porcupines quill, and life goes on. However, for the concerned dog owner, the suffering that's involved can be heartbreaking.

Most bug bites are no more of an annoyance for a dog than they are for us. A bump, scratch, and a bit of swelling doesn't alter the day too dramatically. But if a dog is allergic, the reaction can be severe or even life-threatening. Symptoms of a mildly allergic dog include:

➤ Fever

➤ Joint pain

➤ Muscle ache

➤ Swelling

➤ Vomiting and diarrhea

A severely allergic dog will go into respiratory failure that can be fatal within minutes. This reaction is called *Anaphylaxis* and requires immediate veterinary attention.

Though most snakes will bite when they feel threatened, most aren't poisonous. How can you tell? Poisonous snakes have fangs that make holes in the skin! Also, most native North American snakes that are solid colored or have stripes running the length of the body are non-venomous. Be careful of snakes with diamond backs, stripes running around the body, or those with blotch patterns. In North America, poisonous snakes include rattlesnakes, water moccasins, cottonmouths, coral snakes, and copperheads.

Sarah Says
If you know your dog is sensitive to insect bites, ask your veterinarian to prescribe a bee sting kit that can counteract the reaction in an emergency.

A dog who tangles with a poisonous snake usually doesn't have long to live. The first thing that will happen is he'll swell up like a balloon. Within hours, he'll go into seizures, fall into a coma, and die. If you suspect your dog has been bitten, follow these steps and get him to the nearest animal hospital immediately:

1. Stay calm. Don't stress your dog. Get him to an animal hospital immediately! Bring the dead snake, if possible.

2. Limit his movement. Movement circulates the venom.

3. If possible place a tourniquet above the wound. Suction via a snakebite kit, if available.

4. Flush the wound with hydrogen peroxide or water.

If your dog runs into a porcupine, he'll end up with a face full of quills. These nasty darts are hooked on the end and should be removed by a veterinarian.

Burns

Curiosity strikes again! Dogs can get burned from a variety of chemicals and household appliances. As with human burns, dog burns have three degrees: first, second, and third. All involve layers of tissue destruction. First-degree burns are superficial; the top layer of the skin peels and gets red and sore. Second-degree burns go deeper, damaging many layers of skin. This can result in bleeding, blistering, or oozing. Your veterinarian will prescribe medications and ointment to lessen the pain. Third-degree burns are really nasty. They burn away every layer of skin right down to the tissue. These burns can be life-threatening if more than 50 percent of the body has been harmed. Third-degree burns often cause shock and require immediate veterinarian care.

Grrr
Do not try to pull porcupine quills out yourself. The end of the quill hooks into your dog's tissue. Aside from being painful, ripping out the quill can cause a serious infection.

Burns come in three varieties: thermal, chemical, and electrical.

Type of Burn	Caused by
Thermal	Candles, car mufflers and tailpipes, fireplaces, flames, furnaces, heating pads, hot water pipes, hot plates, ovens, radiators, scalding water, and stoves
Chemical	Acetone, ammonia, asphalt, bathroom cleaners, battery acid, bleach, flooring adhesive, gasoline, kerosene, lime, liquid drain cleaners, lye, paint thinners, phenol cleaner, and road salt
Electrical	Car batteries, extension cords, hobby batteries, lamp cords, and wall outlets

From *Puppy Owner's Veterinary Care Book*, James DeBitetto, DVM, Howell 1995.

To treat burns:

1. Remove your dog from the area.

2. If the burn is from a chemical source, flush it with a lot of water. Apply ice if swelling occurs.

255

3. Run water in a gentle, but steady stream over the area.

4. If the burn is superficial, apply an ointment such as bacitracin twice a day and keep the area clean.

5. If it's more serious (second- or third-degree burns), see your veterinarian.

Choking

Choking usually occurs when your dog is chewing or playing with a toy and is suddenly startled or takes a deep breath. If you're not around or you don't react quickly, it could be fatal. Don't give your dog toys smaller than his face. If your dog chokes on something, keep calm and stay focused when following these steps:

1. Stand your dog.

2. Try to reach in and dislodge the object. Be careful—you could jam it in further or get bitten if your dog's panicking.

3. If you can't dislodge the object, try a modified version of the Heimlich maneuver.

   Clasp your hands together underneath your dog and pull up into your dog's abdomen (just behind the sternum). Repeat this five times vigorously.

4. If all else fails, get your dog to the veterinarian immediately.

Use the Heimlich maneuver if your dog is choking.

Poisons

Dogs, especially puppies, love to investigate everything with their mouths. Are they naughty? No, they're just curious. Sometimes, however, what they put in their mouths can be poisonous; if they swallow it, they could be in big trouble.

Bet You Didn't Know

Household garbage is one of the most common sources of inedible ingestions (toxins) for dogs. Keep a lid on it!

If your dog has something bad in his mouth, don't race toward him angrily. You'll look like you want the prize and he may gulp it to hide the evidence. Walk into the next room calmly and start shaking biscuits or gathering your car keys—anything to get his mind on something else fast!

You can't always be there to watch your dog and there's so much for him to investigate outdoors. You can, however, watch for signs of intake, which include:

Sarah Says
Ask your veterinarian how to induce vomiting in an emergency. If your dog swallows something harmful (but non-corrosive), get him to throw it up quickly.

➤ Vomiting

➤ Bowel discharge

➤ Muscle trembling

➤ Increased salivation

Table 21.1 is a list of common household poisons and what to do if your dog gets into one.

Table 21.1 Poisons and How To Treat Your Dog if He Ingests One

Poison	What To Do
Acetone	IV, VI
Ammonia	V, VO, VI
Anti-freeze	IV, VI
Bleach	IV, VA

continues

Table 21.1 Continued

Poison	What To Do
Carbon Monoxide	M2M, VI
Charcoal Lighter Fluid	IV, L
Chocolate	IV
Deodorants	IV, VI
Soap	IV, VA
Furniture Polish	IV, L, VI
Gasoline	IV, VO, VI
Ibuprofen	IV, VI
Kerosene	IV, L, VO, VI
Lead	IV, L
Lime	W
Insecticides	W, VI
Paint Thinner	IV, W, VI
Phenol Cleaners	W
Rat Poison	IV, VI
Rubbing Alcohol	IV
Strychnine	IV, VI
Turpentine	IV, VO, VI
Tylenol	IV, VA

From *Puppy Owner's Veterinary Care Book*, James DeBitetto, DVM, Howell 1995.

IV = Induce vomiting (if the dog swallowed the poison in the preceding two hours) by giving hydrogen peroxide (several teaspoons for a small dog or tablespoons for a large dog) or syrup of ipecac (1 teaspoon or 1 tablespoon, depending on dog's size).

L = Use a laxative (if it's been more than two hours since the poison was swallowed). Give mineral oil (1 teaspoon for dogs under 25 lbs., 1 tablespoon for 25-50 lbs., and 2 tablespoons for dogs 50 lbs. and up).

W = Wash off skin with water and vinegar.

M2M = Give mouth-to-muzzle resuscitation, as described earlier in this chapter.

VI = Take dog to vet immediately.

VA = Schedule an appointment with the vet some time in the next week.

VO = Give a dose of vegetable oil and water to block absorption.

Bet You Didn't Know

Did you know that chocolate is toxic to dogs? I don't know whether that's a blessing or a curse!

Anti-freeze, chocolate, lead, and rat poison are especially big hazards to your dog.

If you have to take your dog to the vet for poison treatment, try to find the substance and bring it with you to the animal hospital. If your dog should get a topical substance stuck on his fur, do not try to remove it with turpentine or gasoline. Vegetable oil works best.

Bet You Didn't Know

There's a 24-hour poison center that can be reached if your dog has swallowed something poisonous: 1-900-680-0000. With this 900 number, your phone bill will be charged.

Heatstroke

Dogs don't have pores. They can't sweat. The only way they can release heat is through the pads in their feet and by panting. Dogs can suffer from heatstroke if left in poorly ventilated areas, such as a car, kennel, or tied out, or if over-exercised on a humid day. If you notice shallow breathing, a rapid heart rate, and high temperature, cool him gradually with wet towels, a cool bath, or ice around the neck, head, and groin and take him to the veterinarian.

Heatstroke is preventable; never leave your dog in a poorly ventilated environment and make sure water is available on warm days. If the dog must be left in the car, leave the windows open or the air conditioning on.

Grrr
Please don't take your dog with you on hot days. A car, even with all the windows down, can overheat within an hour. What a horrible way for a dog to die—locked in a hot automobile, just wanting and waiting for his caretaker to come back.

Your First Aid Kit

Here's a first aid kit for dogs! Please set these things aside in a safe place or take them with you when you travel with your dog.

➤ Strip of cloth to use as a muzzle

➤ Gauze pads

➤ A sheet or towel that can be used to carry your dog in a supine position

➤ A rope or bandanna to muzzle your dog

➤ A few strips of cloth to tie around a bleeding wound

➤ A tourniquet rod (use only in severe emergencies)

➤ Hydrogen peroxide

➤ The poison hotline number and a list of all poisonous plants

➤ Bacitracen

➤ Ice packs

➤ Snakebite kit if you're in snake country

➤ Towels to wet in case of heatstroke

➤ A rectal thermometer

➤ A towel and water jug (to be kept in your car) in case you get stuck

Trusting Your Veterinarian

You've done all you can do. Now the situation is in more experienced hands. If you insist on observing procedures, do it quietly. Stand back in a corner of the room, stay out of the way, and be quiet. Honestly, I'd prefer the waiting room. Getting emotional not only distracts your veterinarian, it upsets your dog. If your veterinarian asks for your help, do exactly what she says; no more, no less.

The Least You Need To Know

➤ The first thing to do in an emergency is RELAX!

➤ With a dog, anything can happen. Learn each emergency technique backwards and forwards until you can run through them in your sleep.

➤ If your dog has a serious bleeding wound, get him to the doctor immediately. If it's a gusher, you may need to apply a tourniquet with a strip of cloth and short stick, which you twist to tighten the tourniquet. Tourniquets must be loosened every ten minutes.

➤ Your dog can choke while playing with objects smaller than his muzzle. If your dog does choke, you may need to use the Heimlich maneuver for dogs. From behind, grasp your hands under your dog's stomach and pull up to dislodge the object.

➤ Dogs and heat don't mix; dogs can't sweat. I know you'd love your dog's company while you run an errand or pick up the kids, but for her sake, leave her home with a big bowl of water!

Part 6
Extra Stuffing

This section is a hodge podge of material that includes such topics as good neighborhood manners, handling life changes (babies, roommates, a move, and so on), traveling with your dog, coping with serious faux-paws like aggression and separation anxiety, harmonizing relationships between the dog and the kids, and dealing with the loss of your pet (and friend).

Things affect different dogs in different ways. One dog may show his frustration or anxiety by returning to puppy-like behaviors or becoming aggressive, while another may fall to pieces and start eating your underwear! So explore your options, be sympathetic, and do your best to ease the pressure.

Chapter 22

Won't You Be My Neighbor?

> **In This Chapter**
>
> ➤ Keeping your dog and your neighbors happy when you must leave home
>
> ➤ Handling other dogs on the block
>
> ➤ Cat and car chasing, and other fun pastimes

"It's a beautiful day in the neighborhood…," except for the pounding rhythm of a barking dog! I love my neighborhood dearly, but on a quiet summer day when my neighbors leave for the beach and tie out their Beagle, Basil (bless her little soul), I'd like to move to Barbados. It's not Basil's fault. Once I went over after three hours of the street dog serenade, only to find her water bowl empty. I gave her a fresh bowl of water and a chew bone, which kept her busy the rest of the afternoon. Ahhh…peace and quiet.

To be a good dog neighbor, there's a lot you need to keep in mind, which you'll learn about in this chapter.

Leaving Your Dog Alone

To be a good neighbor, you'll need to keep your dog quiet when you're away from home. Your dog won't like being left alone; she's sociable by nature. Don't be surprised if she thinks of some activities to pass those lonely hours—digging, chewing destructively, or *barking*. Is there anything you can do?

Yes! You have a lot of options when you leave your dog alone. She can stay inside or outside. You can confine your dog in a room or let her roam around. You can tie her up or fence her in. What's best? Put yourself in your dog's paws. Outside is okay; there's fresh air and sunshine. But being confined outdoors can be stressful because there is so much activity that the dog can't get to. Most dogs would rather remain inside with a cozy blanket and bone to chew. You'll have to decide. Preparing your dog for your departure will have lasting benefits.

Fido in a sit-stay while Mom is out.

Grrr
If your dog suffers from separation anxiety and is a gulper (eating things she shouldn't), enclose her in a small space with a large bone and no bedding. She might eat the bedding otherwise.

Before you leave:

➤ Exercise your dog for ten minutes.

➤ Follow play time with a two minute training session.

➤ Leave a special chew toy and scent it by rubbing it in your palms.

➤ If indoors, leave your dog in a dimly lit, confined space with an old shirt or blanket and a radio playing some soothing tunes.

➤ If outdoors, provide her with access to a shaded area and plenty of fresh water.

The High-Class Neighbor

High-class neighbors get along. They know when to accept what won't change and make the best of it. Low-class neighbors bicker and fight. They make a mess. They're loud and intimidating. The question is, what do you want you and your dog to be? The choice is yours, but if it's high class you want, it's high class you'll get—just follow these steps.

Good Neighbor Dog Manners 101:

➤ Instruct "Heel," as you parade around the neighborhood; teach your dog to follow your lead.

➤ Teach your dog to "Wait" at curbs and while you visit or window shop.

➤ Teach "No" to discourage your dog from everyday temptations like cars, joggers, and other animals.

➤ Have your dog eliminate on your own property. Dogs recognize boundary limits with their noses. Help your dog learn where her territory ends. In case of an accident, carry a bag with you to remove the evidence from your neighbor's lawn and dispose of it properly.

Uh-Oh! Have some of you already slipped into the bad neighbor status? Don't worry. There's hope. You'll just need to rearrange things and do some set-ups. First, learn a good "Heel," which was covered in Part 4. You should also go over the "Wait" and "No" exercises covered in Part 4. You'll need to toilet your dog on your own property, too. I know, she's used to peeing and pooping as you walk, but there are new rules now. Next, you'll need to do some set-ups to retrain your pooch if she's aggravating other animals in the neighborhood or chasing anything that moves. See the end of this chapter for instructions.

Other Dogs on the Block

Most dogs like to think they own their neighborhood. The problem is, there's usually more than one dog on the block. Left to their own devices—free ranging, so to speak—they'd establish a hierarchy and get along fine. But they're not free. Leashes and other confinements cause territorial frustrations.

The leash *should* be used to communicate leadership—human leadership, that is. Dogs, however, don't always get that message. Some dogs think they walk their owners. A dog leading its owner wants to investigate other dogs. When this dog is suddenly restricted by a choking feeling around the neck or chest, he gets very defensive. He pulls harder, growls, and barks; he threatens from afar.

To correct this situation, follow the Good Neighbor Dog Manners listed in the preceding section and remember:

➤ Do not look at the other dog.

➤ Walk by the dog at a brisk pace.

➤ Keep your dog behind you at all times.

What if you want to let the dogs play? Keep your dog at heel while you cross the street or they approach each other. Then release your dog on a loose lead with "OK!"

Bet You Didn't Know

Do you know what to do if you and your on-lead dog are approached by an angry off-leash dog? Walk swiftly from the scene, correcting your dog from facing off to the aggressor. If either of you makes eye contact, you may be attacked.

Cat Chasing

Chasing is an instinctive behavior that goes back to wolf times when dogs had to hunt for a living. Even though we have given them all the luxuries of retirement, they still think it's a great pastime to chase cats (squirrels, lizards, and bunnies count, too)!

Some dogs just can't resist a small moving tidbit. Heaven forbid you should get dragged along for the ride as you're shouting for control. You've become the perfect backup. To solve this dilemma, you'll need to focus on your dog's ears. Ear perk is preliminary to the chase. You must correct the thought process.

Bet You Didn't Know

Dogs ears act like built-in radars. They can pick up sound in every direction. Unfortunately, if your dog's ears are alert to every distraction, she's not focused on you. Some training is definitely in order!

➤ If your dog's radar picks up a temptation, snap the lead and say, "No!"

➤ Do not look at the temptation! Eye contact means interest.

➤ Walk away from the object confidently. Remind "Heel."

➤ Continue to snap, and say, "No" until your dog focuses on you.

➤ Do not drag your dog away from the object. Snap and release.

Car Chasing

To solve the classic problem of car chasing, you'll need to think a few steps ahead of your dog:

1. The second you hear a car, tell your dog, "To the side," and run to the curb quickly!

2. Next, tell her to "Wait" and bring her behind your heels.

3. If she looks at the car, say, "No!" very sternly and snap the lead.

4. Spritz her with Binaca Mouth Spray® if you need extra reinforcement.

Use this same technique with bikers and joggers. Correct your dog the second she *thinks* about chasing them. Once she's in motion, it's too late.

Child Chasing

They dart, they spin, they stare, they bark…wow! Those little two-legged creatures are just like puppies. This set-up requires a few volunteers—little volunteers, that is. If you don't have kids, you'll need to borrow some. Then practice these steps:

Practice set-ups like this to teach your dog to behave around children.

1. Place your dog on her Teaching Lead®. Keep her behind your heels.

2. Ask the children to run in front of you. Watch your dog.

3. As she prepares to bound after them, say, "No!" sternly and snap back on the lead. *Correct the thought process!*

Now for distance control. Place your dog on her Flexi-Leash®. Tell your little volunteers to race around in front of you. Correct all thoughts of a chase by snapping back on the lead, saying "No," and calling her into a "Heel" position.

The Least You Need To Know

➤ Most dogs get frustrated when you leave. Keep your dog in a cool, confined area when you leave, turn on some music, and scent a chew toy by rubbing your palms against it to help him pass the time.

➤ Good neighbor dogs focus on their owners for direction. Help your dog learn this by using the commands "Heel," "Wait," and "No."

➤ If your dog sees another dog, keep her at your side and correct her each time she tries to face off. If you want to let her play, release her after she calms down.

➤ Many dogs love to chase anything that moves. When correcting your dog, correct the thought process; once he's in pursuit, it's too late.

Life Changes

Change is a part of life. Though most changes are for the best, all changes are stressful. I'm not just talking about humans; dogs experience stress, too. The difference between their stress and ours is how they display it. Sure, I may pack in some extra calories when I'm feeling anxious, but I won't destroy the couch; your dog might. Do you know what happens if you correct an anxious dog? He'll get more stressed and destroy other things—perhaps your rug or bed, for example. Is he a bad dog? No! He's just confused. He'll need your help to adjust. Other signs of stress are aggression, barking, hyperactivity, or extreme withdrawal.

Moving and Your Dog

Moving is one of life's most stressful changes. First there's the financial decisions, which may bring about more theatrical conversations than on the average day. Then there's the packing, shipping, and traveling back and forth. When the big day finally arrives, your energy is spent; you've reached a new peak of exhaustion. My heart aches for you, but it bleeds for your dog. Chaos really throws him. Due to his biological nature, he depends on predictability to ensure his safety. Through this change, you may notice your dog getting increasingly more puppy-like; he may become hyper, demand attention, nip, jump, or chew. Forgive him now and help him cope. Following are some suggestions that you can use to help him.

Play some classical music while you debate and discuss your big move. It'll calm your dog and may have side benefits for you and your loved one! Include your dog in your packing activities. Don't isolate him in the backyard. If he gets in the way, station him with a bone to chew and pet him when he settles down.

If you're traveling back and forth to the new house, bring your dog on his Teaching Lead®. Lead him around the new house and bring along some favorite chews and a familiar bed or blanket to settle him. If you're spending the day at your new house, don't forget to pack some dog food and water. Bring his familiar bowls.

Keep your dog with you while you're unpacking. Let him sniff the collectibles as you remove them; he identifies objects with his nose and will feel happy to recognize something!

Sarah Says
Are you moving to a new climate? Going from extreme cold to hot or vice versa can be alarming for your dog. Perhaps a sweater will be in order in colder climates or a big bowl of water if the weather is suddenly blistering.

The first time you leave your dog in your new home, he may stress out, resulting in destructive chewing or excessive barking. Confine your dog in a small room or crate with one of your old shirts and a favorite chew. Do not correct your dog if he demolishes something. Your corrections will only increase the anxiety and destruction.

Do not let your dog off leash in your new environment unless it's fenced in. He'll be disoriented for a few weeks and may get lost if he wanders off. Was your old place fenced in? If your dog was accustomed to running free in a yard, but can't now, you'll need to make up for the loss. Buy a Flexi-Leash® and discover some good games to burn off that energy.

Bringing Home Baby!

This can be one of the coolest changes of a lifetime—for people, that is. Dogs often feel shafted and shoved to the back burner at first. After all, your dog was your first baby! To ensure this doesn't happen to your four-legged pal, start planning for the new arrival before you're running to the hospital.

Pre-Birthing Preparations

Imagine you have the baby, a cute little creature, just weeks old. Your parenting instincts will be in full throttle. Now enters your beloved dog. Is he used to lounging on the furniture or jumping up for attention? Can he order up a back rub by pawing, barking, or nudging you? Can you see a problem developing? He won't stop this behavior just because you're holding a newborn. Heaven forbid you shout at or isolate him; he'll grow very jealous of your new fancy. Fortunately, there are steps you can take ahead of time to ensure that nobody gets left in the doghouse.

Socialize your dog with small children. Put some Cheerios (Cheerios have less calories than dog biscuits; kids can be very generous) in a cup, and shake and treat until your dog associates the sound with a reward. Invite some friends who have children over and ask them to shake and treat. Stay calm while they visit; keep your dog on a leash if you're uneasy. Dogs are very telepathic; your emotions come across loud and clear.

➤ Bring your dog to a playground. Keep him at heel and ask the kids to take a break and shake the Cheerio cup.

➤ If your dog is showing any signs of aggression, call a professional. Your reaction can make the problem worse. Petting or soothing reinforces the behavior; disciplining will make your dog feel more threatened.

➤ Establish an exercise schedule that will be realistic with your new responsibilities. Mornings may be rough—get your dog used to afternoon romps.

➤ Establish a station in or just outside your baby's room and get your dog accustomed to settling on command. Tell him "Settle down," and secure him on a three foot lead if he seems restless.

➤ Walk through your daily routine with a stuffed doll. Allow your dog to sniff it regularly. When changing your baby (both the doll and the real thing), put your dog in a "Sit-stay." When putting your kid down for a nap, send your dog to his station with a "Settle down." When nursing your baby, tell your dog to "Down, stay" under your legs (similar to the Town Down).

➤ Watch your words. Phrases like "What a good boy" must be changed to "What a great dog!" If the phrases you use for baby and dog are too familiar, it'll be confusing.

➤ New furniture rules! Dogs shouldn't be allowed on the furniture near a new infant. If you wait to spring this on your dog after the baby's home, the dog might feel shafted. Lay down the law now. Keep a short leash on your dog's buckle collar; if he hops up, snap him off with the lead handle and say, "No." Remember, pushing is interactive and suggestive of a game.

Get your dog used to one hour of the cold shoulder every day. Yes, I want you to ignore your dog completely. You can break it up into two 30-minute or three 20-minute segments, but get your dog accustomed to life without your doting. If your dog can get your attention wherever and whenever he wants it, he'll be upset when you're focused on the baby.

Stop all confrontational games, like tug-of-war and wrestling, and eliminate all in-home chasing matches. Teach your dog calm household manners.

Consider your child's toys and how they might compare to your dog's favorites. Give your dog one object to chew or play with and discourage him from picking up everything on the floor. Mark all the child's toys with Scope® mouth wash. Just a dot will do. If he goes for it anyway, pick it up and shout at the toy (not the dog). Soon he'll avoid everything that smells like Scope®. Lead him to his object and praise him.

Sarah Says

If you must have your dog on the furniture, give him the luxury on command only. Tell him "Up" and pat the cushion when you want him there, and "No" with a leash correction if he comes up uninvited.

Babies like to grab and pull, and your dog may be startled if their tug is the first. Grab and tug on your dog's coat as you treat and praise him. Pull that tail. Hug him tight. What a wonderful dog! Isn't this great? Don't forget to make some baby sounds too—go for the full effect.

Don't give your dog shoes, socks, rags, plastic, or stuffed toys. He'll think anything in that category is fair game.

Honey, It's Time!

The day will come. Your baby will break into the world and your life will never be the same. To help your dog adjust, follow these steps:

1. Ask the nurse if you can bring home some bed sheets from the nursery. It may seem like a strange request, but I'm sure yours won't be the first. Place them in the baby's new room and around the area you plan to nurse. Praise your dog for sniffing them, but discourage chewing or tearing. (Keep your dog on leash if necessary.)

2. Brush up on obedience lessons while mom's in the hospital. Dogs love structure.

3. Hire a dog walker if the house is empty. Isolation is stressful.

4. Introduce dog and baby on neutral ground. The hospital parking lot will do if the weather cooperates. Exercise your dog before the meeting and bring along some peanut butter to distract your dog's interest if you're nervous. DO NOT choke up on the lead or shout at your dog to stay calm. That's unsettling and will make a bad first impression.

5. If your dog's too boisterous, give his leash a quick snap and say, "Ep, Ep." Spread some peanut butter on your hand and say, "Kisses."

6. Plan your homecoming. Keep your dog on leash and let him welcome the baby, too. Use the same techniques as the first meeting to ensure a smooth arrival.

7. Let your dog drag a leash and use it to correct all mouthing or jumping behavior. Look at and praise your dog when he's calm.

8. If your dog is restless at his designated stations, secure three foot leads and hook him up while you direct him to "Settle down."

Grrr
Sometimes it doesn't work out. Your dog may be too used to being the only child. If your dog growls at the baby, call in a professional to assess the situation.

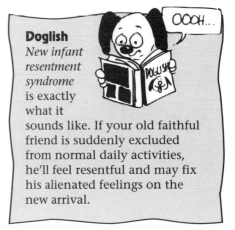

Doglish
New infant resentment syndrome is exactly what it sounds like. If your old faithful friend is suddenly excluded from normal daily activities, he'll feel resentful and may fix his alienated feelings on the new arrival.

Dogs like diapers, so don't be surprised if you find your dog nibbling on one. My suggestion? Get a super secure diaper bin and spray a little Bitter Apple® outside the diaper bin to discourage his interest. Last, but not least, correct *it* when your dog goes near: "Bad, bad diaper bin!"

The Addition or Loss of a Human Companion

Whether you're inviting someone in, shipping someone out, or mourning the loss of a loved one, it's a life-altering experience—one your dog will feel almost as much as you.

Moving Them In

Getting a new roommate has a lot of perks. Expenses are cut in half, chores are split, and company is permanently installed. It probably won't take you too long to adjust. Your dog may be another story, especially if your new companion's sharing that sacred spot on the couch or your bed. To help your dog adjust:

1. Think ahead! Limit your dog's bed or couch time to invitation only. If he jumps up uninvited, say, "No" and snap him down. (Keep a short lead attached to his buckle collar.)

Sarah Says
If your dog just won't stay off your bed, secure him on a short lead until he's accepted his new sleeping quarters.

2. Create a special sleeping area next to your bed. Place an old shirt there to keep your pal cozy.

3. Limit your attention when your new companion is around. Encourage your dog to seek out the new arrival for some love.

4. Ask your new companion to feed your dog.

Your roommate and dog will soon be the best of pals, especially if your roommate feeds the dog from time to time!

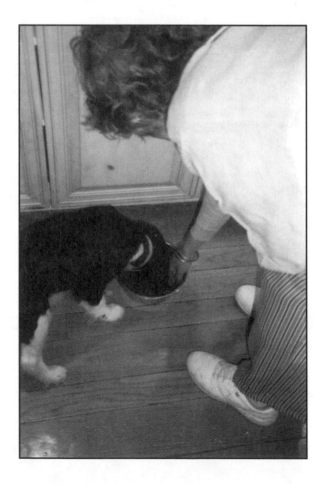

5. Let your companion know your house rules: no jumping, barking, pawing, or begging at the table allowed. If he/she is a spoiler, your dog will be confused, you'll be angry, and you'll need to refer to the next section!

Shipping Them Out

There are many reasons to ship someone out: relationships don't always work out; kids grow up and move out of the house; kids grow up and take the dog with them. Dogs, however, grow very accustomed to a pack and may suffer the loss of an extra companion, especially if that companion is a major care giver. To help your dog adjust:

➤ You'll need to fill in the extra spaces. If your dog was used to a walk at 4 p.m., you'll need to be there or hire someone a few times a week until your dog's adjusted to your schedule.

➤ Avoid spoiling your dog to make up for the loss. More structure is in order, not less.

➤ Enroll in a training class. It's fun and will give you both something to focus on.

➤ If your dog loved to play a certain game with his missing companion, play it with him.

Losing a Loved One

I've lost two people very close to me in my lifetime. In both cases, I was in a trance for weeks. Emotionally, I had to drag myself out of bed. I lost my zest. Sure, my dogs felt confused by the passing, but I think they were more confused by my mental state. Here are some things I did to help them out:

➤ I asked a friend to walk them in the morning and had the neighbor's kid come by in the afternoon.

➤ I set my alarm clock to ring at their meal times.

➤ I set aside five minutes per day for an obedience lesson.

➤ I bought them new chews and tried to play kick the bottle (their favorite game) with them in the afternoon.

Dog Plus One

Getting another dog may seem really exciting to you, but your dog may be less than thrilled. Some take to new paws on the carpet, others don't. To make the transition as smooth as possible:

Two dogs equal twice the fun!

1. Introduce the dogs in a neutral place, like a park or parking lot.

2. Stay cool. If you tighten the leashes and start shouting every command in the book, your old pal will be a nervous wreck. Nervous dogs are likely to attack.

3. Put 20 foot leashes on both dogs and stand back as they check each other out.

4. Dogs do a lot of body and vocal bluffing when they first meet. Their hair will stand up and they may even growl. They're trying to establish rank. If you interfere, they may fight. Just stand back and ignore them.

Having two dogs can be twice the fun! Or it can be double the trouble. It's up to you. Here are some hints for making it easier.

Grrr
Some dogs just won't get along. If you're bringing together two dogs of the same sex or dogs who got used to being an "only child," they may fight. Be prepared. Have two people handy to take the leads and run in the opposite direction.

A dog is a dog is a dog. Truer words were never spoken. Certain similarities string them all together. However, like us, each dog has his own unique personality and temperament that will affect the way he relates to his world. In a multi-dog household, everyone must be sensitive to the needs of each individual dog.

Hierarchy. Personality also affects the way dogs relate to one another. Groups of two or more dogs form a hierarchy, with the most outgoing, assertive dog assuming the Top Dog rank.

Who's your Top Dog? To determine who your Top Dog is, observe your group's behavior. The Top Dog is the one who insists on being the first through the door, pushes the others out of the way for attention, and ends up with all the toys in his lap. There is no sexism in dogland, so don't be surprised if your female is running the show!

Royalties. Once your dogs develop a hierarchy, you must support it by giving all the household royalties to your Top Dog. He should be fed, greeted, pet, and allowed out first. If you pay more attention to the subordinate dog, you may cause discontent among the ranks, which can lead to fighting.

Same Age. Raising two dogs of the same age can be quite a challenge. Resolving housebreaking, chewing, nipping, or jumping habits can be double the work load. You'll have to pay close attention and be very consistent. On the other hand, raising two dogs can also be twice the fun if you're considerate of their individual needs and train them to be more focused on you than each other. Often, when raised together, puppies will develop opposite personalities. The more outgoing one assumes Top Dog rank, while the other is more passive.

Although it's tempting to console the introvert, remember the Laws of Nature, which instruct you to defer all royalties to the Top Dog, and the Attention Factor, which reminds you that if you pay attention to an introverted dog, you'll get an introverted dog. Here are some other hints to prevent future problems:

➤ Left alone 24 hours a day, your puppies will form a strong bond to each other, which is good, but they also will be less attached to you. To prevent this, separate them at least twice a day. If possible, let them sleep in separate bedrooms.

➤ Use individual crates for housebreaking, chewing, or sleeping difficulties.

➤ Feed them separately. If fed together, the Top Dog may horde the food.

➤ Support their hierarchy. Feed, pet, and greet the stronger dog first.

Dogs of different ages. "Monkey see, monkey do" could not apply more. Puppies raised with older dogs pick up a lot of their habits, both good and bad. To discourage the younger dog from bad behavior, resolve it in your older dog first. In addition, follow the same suggestions just described.

If you've welcomed a mature dog into your pack, you'll need to observe the new hierarchy and respect it. When I brought my Labrador in, he quickly dominated my eight-year-old Husky. Though it broke my heart initially, once I supported their system, everybody was happy.

Discipline. If you don't know who did it, you can't correct either dog. That's the rule. If you find a mess after the fact, forget it. Disciplining both dogs will only weaken your connection to them and strengthen their resolve to one another. For suggestions on specific problems, see Chapters 9 and 10.

Is wrestling okay? Yes, to a degree. Try to teach your dogs to go to certain areas of the house or outside to play. If they're out of hand, leave their short leashes on in the house and correct them by saying, "Sshh!" as you pull them apart sternly. Instruct "Sit" and refocus them on a chew toy.

The name game. Teach your dogs two names: their personal name and a universal one that you can use when they're together, such as "Dogs!," "Girls!," "Boys!," or "Babies;" whatever works for you. It makes it easier when you have to call them. "Buddy, come!" rolls off a little easier than "Buddy, Fi-Fi, Daisy, Marlo, Come!"

Feedings. Feed your dogs separately. Place your Top Dog's bowl down first. If you're having difficulty keeping them separate, station them apart on their Teaching Leads.

Toy war. I know, you want them both to have a toy. But one dog keeps insisting on having both. You give it back to the other dog, and he takes it away. Give-take-give-take. Remember your Top Dog rule. If the Top Dog wants both, Top Dog has both. Period.

Dog fights. Whatever you do, don't yell! Yelling is perceived as threat barking and will actually make the problem worse. If you have a dog fight, the best thing to do is walk out of the house and slam the door. No words or discipline; just leave abruptly. It's usually your presence that prompts an argument. You can also try breaking up the fight by dumping a bucket of water on their heads or turning a hose on them. Once things are calmed down, review your actions. Were you supporting the Underdog? That's not good. After the fight has settled, you should isolate the subordinate and praise the Top Dog. I know it sounds cruel, but if #1 feels supported, he won't challenge the other dogs. Additionally, if you catch a fight before it begins, shame the Underdog and reward your Top Dog with attention. I know it feels unnatural, but remember that your dogs aren't human and they don't think you are either. If the situation repeats itself, call in a professional.

Introducing Other Animals

Perhaps you want to add another species to your home. A bird, cat, reptile, rabbit, or rodent can be a real eye-opener, especially for your dog, who may see the little addition as more of a snack than a pal.

Set up the cage or confinement system ahead of time. Let your dog get accustomed to the smell of fresh bedding. Have someone walk your dog while you settle your new pet.

Your dog will probably notice the smell immediately. Encourage him to "Settle down" near the cage. Discourage barking with Binaca Mouth Spray®.

Avoid disciplining your dog vocally. It will be perceived as barking or growling and will enhance his stance against "the intruder." If you're welcoming a kitten or other baby creature, keep them separated until the animal is big enough to escape and can defend itself from being snapped at or stepped on.

Grrr

When I was a kid, I got a French lop-eared bunny. Shadow, the bunny, grew to be a whopping 24 pounds. Unfortunately, another favorite pet, Shawbee, my Siberian Husky/ Shepherd mix, decided that was big enough. The inevitable happened; she ate Shadow. It was horrible. Moral? If your dog won't give up his snack vigil, take your new pet back.

The Least You Need To Know

➤ Are you moving? Pay attention to your dog's stress. Use your Teaching Lead® to help your dog adapt to his new environment and set up stations with old blankets and toys to help your dog feel at home.

➤ Are you having a baby? Create a routine ahead of time that you'll be able to keep once the baby comes home. Practice your commands with a baby doll before your baby arrives to help your dog adjust. For example, use a "Sit-stay" while changing the diaper, a "Heel" while you lull baby to sleep, and a "Settle down" while you nurse.

➤ Do you have a new roommate? Let your dog bond, too! Encourage your new roommate to feed and walk your dog and let him/her provide attention when you're all together.

➤ Did you get a new dog or other pet? Congratulations. Your dog may be less than thrilled, however. To encourage harmony from the start, introduce them on neutral ground and don't interfere as they check each other out.

Chapter 24

Kids and Dogs

In This Chapter

➤ Kids and dogs: sibling rivals or constant companions?

➤ Transferring the control

➤ Catch phrases

➤ Kids can help

➤ Cool games

Are dogs and kids the perfect match? Picture Timmy and Lassie frolicking in a field or exploring the backyard stream. Unfortunately, dogs and kids don't always hit it off. More often than not, the dog views the child as another puppy to bite and bully. I've dealt with many situations where the kids don't like playing with the puppy anymore because "she bites too hard." Another situation, the Sibling Rivalry Syndrome, happens when the child becomes jealous of the attention the new addition is getting. In this situation, the child takes out his anger on the dog, which increases rough puppy play and turns what was supposed to be a beautiful relationship into an all out war. Don't worry...I can help.

Constant Companions or Sibling Rivals?

One of the hallmarks of my childhood was my dog, Shawbee, who was a Husky-Shepherd mix. She was my constant companion, waiting for me at the bus stop, hanging outside the church while I took ballet lessons, sharing my ice cream cone on a hot summer day. Unfortunately, it rarely happens this way. First, it's a different world than when I was a child. Most communities have leash laws. Dogs left waiting are stolen. People are more dog phobic. It's a shame, but times have changed and new problems are cropping up. Today, kids, often overstimulated at a young age, have less time to hang out with dogs. Riding bikes and running around is often limited to parks where dogs aren't allowed. Both parents usually work, which limits the amount of quality time a child spends with his parents, and quality time is something some kids don't like to share. This may sound depressing, but these are things you must think about before I can lead you out of these troubled waters.

Classic Signs

Are you worried? Here are some classic scenarios typical of sibling rivalry:

"My dog, Tucker, is a four-month-old Labrador-Doberman Pincher mix. I got him for the kids, but I haven't had a moment's peace since the day we brought him home. Tucker is biting the children and tugging at their clothes. The other day when my son Alex went to take a toy, Tucker snapped at him."

Sarah Says
Know when to ask for help. If your dog is becoming less tolerant of your child, showing signs of aggression, or creating so much havoc that your normal daily tasks and parental responsibilities are stressed, call an animal trainer or behaviorist immediately. They really can help. Ask your veterinarian for a referral.

"Sasha is a great dog when the kids aren't around. But when the kids get home from school, she jumps at them, knocks them down, and tries to make away with their backpacks."

"My dog, Darby, is always stealing the kids' food from their hands. She also snatches their toys from them; the other day when my daughter lifted her doll above her head, Darby jumped up and scratched her in the eye."

"My eight-month-old Pug has taken to mounting my son whenever he comes through the door. It's totally embarrassing."

A Game Plan for Conquering Sibling Rivalry

So the cards are dealt. Suddenly you find yourself in a situation that's less than ideal, full of mayhem and chaos. You love the kids. You love the dog. You want them to love each other. What can you do? Let's take a look:

Step 1: Transferring the Control

Let go of the idea that the kids can communicate leadership. Though you can get your dog to respect the rules, you'll have to be the one to teach him. Young kids can't "train" dogs until they grow tall enough to stare you eye-to-eye (12–14 years of age). They're just too close to the dog for him to take them seriously. They also bend and bark too much. You'll need to teach the dog to respect the children.

Teach your dog some basic commands ("Sit," "Wait," "Excuse Me," "Let's Go") and walk through them with the children, issuing lead corrections if your dog disobeys. Encourage the kids to say the commands clearly. Teach the dog a negative sound for unacceptable behavior, such as nipping, and then use it regularly when you see your dog wind up with the kids.

Bet You Didn't Know

"Monkey see, monkey do." You are your children's best example. If you're calm and structured with your dog or puppy, your child will copy you. If you're frantically confused or encourage rough play, your child will copy that, too.

Step 2: Use Set-Ups

Set up everyday situations, like the kids' running frenzies or building/doll sets, to teach your dog how to handle himself. Use your Teaching Lead®. Here are some examples:

Mouthing/Nipping. Train your dog not to nip you. Pull him away from your body and say, "No!" Next, sit on the floor with your child. Take the child's hand in yours and stroke your dog while you hold the end of the Teaching Lead® in your other hand. If your dog even thinks about mouthing, pull back sharply and say, "No!"

Food Grabbing. With your dog on his Teaching Lead®, walk him by a plate of cookies (placed on the floor). If your dog even looks at the cookies, say, "No!" and continue walking. Catch the thought process. Ask your kids to have a snack. If your dog even twitches a nostril, say, "No!" and continue to interact with the kids. Repeat with the children sitting on the floor.

Teach your dog that all food is not his to have.

Chasing. Dogs love to chase kids. If the play escalates, your dog might bring your kids down. To teach him to hold his horses, ask the kids to run in front of you while you control your dog on his Teaching Lead®. When your dog lowers his head in the crouch-and-pounce state, say, "No!" sharply and snap him back behind your heels. Repeat as often as necessary or until the kids crash out.

Step 3: Teach Catch Phrases

Kids don't respond well to nagging; "Don't do this, don't do that" has a tendency to go in one ear and out the other. Like dogs and puppies, kids like a more positive approach. Catch phrases can be very helpful!

> **OOOH...**
>
> **Doglish**
> When the kids come home from school, ask them to *look for rain.* Tell them to cross their arms in front of their body and look to the sky until Rex has calmed down. The look for rain reaction also works great if Rex jumps on them or if he tries to join them on the couch.

Four Paw Rule. This one helps the kids remember not to pet Rex until all four paws are planted on the floor. It sounds a lot better than, "Stop calling the dog on the couch." (At which point, I would defiantly do exactly what you said not to do, if I were the kid.)

Look for Rain. When the kids come in from school, have them look for rain until Rex has calmed down. Also have them do this when he jumps into their laps for attention.

Peacock Position. This helps the kids remember to stand straight when giving Rex commands. It's a lot less wordy than, "If you bend over, Rex thinks you want to play."

Kids should look for rain until the dog calms down.

Stand like a statue. Ask your kids if they've ever seen a dog chasing a statue. Answer, no. Why? Because statues don't move. When the dog's getting out of hand, encourage the kids to stand still and "stand like a statue."

Those are just some of my all-time favorites. Think hard, add to the list, and keep me informed. I'm always on the lookout for clever ways to help kids and dogs get along together!

Step 4: Get the Kids Involved

Kids like to help, but training exercises can bore them to death. Let's face it, mud wrestling to a five-year-old is more exciting than a two-minute heel. There are ways to get the kids involved, but you must be very upbeat and creative. Staying positive is a plus! Kids like to be involved. But training exercises are just no fun and the phrase, "it's your responsibility to feed Rex" has a negative spin. Here are some ideas:

Peanut Butter Magic. This trick is fabulous. Put some peanut butter on the back of the kids' hands, have them extend their hands, and instruct "Kisses." It not only teaches your dog to kiss a hand that reaches toward him, it also discourages nipping.

Fun Charts. Make a responsibility chart, except think of a better name for it, like "the sticker chart." Every time one of the kids completes a task (feeding, walking, or brushing your dog), he can add a sticker to his column. Be clever! If you have more than one kid, you'll need plenty of column space.

Super Schedule. Kids love to be creative. Ask them to help you write "the SUPER schedule for REX." Include times for everything: feeding, brushing, playing, and napping. Let them decorate around the edges and place it somewhere where all your friends can see what cool kids you have.

Step 5: Cool Games for Kids

You eliminate tug-of-war. You take away the shared stuffed animals and socks. No more wrestling, teasing, or chasing the dog. What's a child suppose to do for fun? Here's a list. The rule of thumb is to encourage games that keep the dog's attention off the kids.

Snoopy Soccer. I play this game with an empty plastic soda bottle or milk jug, removing both the label and the cap. A regulation ball will also do the trick. The rule for this game: *no hands!* This one is great for kids and dogs because it keeps the kids standing up while the dog is focused on the ground. WARNING: Once the plastic container is punctured, discard it.

Bet You Didn't Know

Dogs view humans' hands as mouths. If you're too physical when playing with or training your puppy, you're teaching her that mouthing is a good game.

Ricochet Rover. Fetching is simple. You throw an object and the dog retrieves it. If you have a dog that will release the ball to you immediately, this is the game for you. However, if your dog finds it more amusing to play "keep away," you must teach the Release command before you play or play with several balls to avoid "dog-organized" games.

Hide and Seek. Most dogs don't like to lose sight of their owners. When your dog is sniffing around on her Flexi-Leash® or in an enclosed area, call her name to get her attention. When she looks up, race away and hide behind something (a tree, house corner, and so on). When she finds you, give her a big hug!

Fishing for Fido. I have a lot of fun with this one. Find a stick. This is your "fishing rod." The bait will be a squeak toy. Pick out a favorite toy and tie it to the stick with a four-foot piece of string. When your dog is really hyped, you can wave your rod around and help her burn off all that excess energy! Don't tease her though; let her catch the bait from time to time. Keep the game fun!

Snoopy soccer keeps your dog's attention on something other than your kid's hand.

Bet You Didn't Know

Some dogs mount kids (even adults) when they get too excited. Don't be too embarrassed. Mounting is more a sign of dominance than sexual preference. This makes it no less acceptable, however. Mounting dogs are bossy dogs who get overstimulated in exciting situations. To rehabilitate yours, do the following:

1. Leave a short lead on your dog. Do not face off to a mounting dog. No eye contact or pushing.

2. When the mounting starts, calmly grasp the short lead and snap down firmly.

3. Once your dog is grounded, stand very tall, glare at your dog, and say "Shame on you!" in your most indignant tone. Station your dog for 15 minutes with no attention. Do not storm into the situation.

4. If your dog acts aggressively, terminate the corrections and seek help.

The Least You Need To Know

➤ Kids and dogs don't always blend. Dogs sometime view children's constant attention and rough play as confrontational and use their mouths to interact and control situations.

➤ Parents! You influence your kids by example. Avoid physical discipline or yelling when correcting your dog. Though it may work temporarily, when the kids copy you, it often backfires.

➤ Establish non-negotiable rules like no tug-of-war or chasing games. Both games encourage nipping and tackling. Teach them cool game alternatives.

Chapter 25

Aggression: The Big Faux-Paw

In This Chapter

➤ Dominant aggression

➤ Spatial and object guarding

➤ Territorial and protective aggression

➤ Fear-induced reactions

➤ Psychotic dogs

Though many hesitate to admit it, most dogs show aggression in some situations, whether to their owners, strangers, other dogs, or furry little tidbits running around the backyard. If you're dealing with an aggression problem, you're not alone.

Aggression is a normal form of canine communication, similar to our anger. It is often seen in dogs who as puppies were dominant and bossy and not given enough structure from their owners. Consider the spoiled dog who is given too much attention. This dog

Sarah Says
If you meet up with an aggressive dog, do not run away.
Think about it; have you ever seen a dog attack a post? If you must approach the dog, move in sideways. Frontal approach equals a challenge. You can extend a stick or an arm to distract the dog from your body.

Grrr
WARNING!
Aggression is a serious topic. If you're having a problem, get help. Seek a well-known and respected animal behaviorist or trainer in your area. Your veterinarian may be able to help you find one. My recommendations are just that, recommendations. Do not follow them if you are unsure. Aggression, if approached incorrectly or with caution or fear, can result in a serious bite.

thinks his owner depends on him for leadership; after all, he acts like a servant. When that owner tries to direct or discipline his dog, he is out of line and like a delinquent child, must be reprimanded. Because dogs can't send sassy owners to their rooms, they snap, growl, or bite. Same concept, different communication. This, however, is not the only type of aggression. It comes in many other forms. This chapter examines them all.

Understanding What You Have on Your Hands

One of my specialties is dealing with aggression. It's hard to find words to describe the pleasure I feel when I see a situation resolved. When I enter the situation, both the dog and the people are confused and frustrated. By the time I leave, there is harmony, which is how it should be.

If you have an aggressive dog, the first thing you must do is consult a professional in your area immediately! The world does not need another dog bite on the record books. Next, keep your dog off your bed. This *is* a big deal. If you have an aggressive dog, he thinks it's his duty to protect or keep you in line. The first step in resolving this issue is to take over the high sleeping grounds. Tie your dog to your dresser if you must, but no bed until the aggression is gone. In the meantime, until you contact someone (consult your veterinarian), let me give you some words for thought about identifying and dealing with various types of aggression as you strive to resolve your problems.

When approaching an aggressive dog, move in sideways, not from the front.

Dominant Aggression

The potential for developing dominant aggression can usually be seen in puppyhood. An active pup who steals clothing for fun, barks for attention, leans against his owners when in new environments or around strangers, or who successfully solicits attention whenever the mood strikes is *dominant*. Though the aggression may not surface, all too often it does. When it does, the problem lies not with the dog, who thinks his leadership qualities are appreciated, but with the owner, who must now be assertive to solve the problem.

Let's get something straight. You must stop being your dog's slave. His aggression is a sign; he thinks you're weak and in need of leadership. Your constant attention and dedication to his every need puts you at servant status. When you assert yourself, he has no other choice than to remind you to get back in line. It's his job as leader to be the boss. To regain control, for starters:

➤ Review Chapter 8. Lead your dog to show him who's boss. Do not look at your dog unless he's responding to you. Period.

➤ Create stations and use them.

➤ Use the "Excuse me!" command when your dog gets in your way. This is the most passive way to communicate your leadership.

➤ Ignore all his attempts to get your attention, including but not limited to barking, pawing, head butting, and whining.

➤ Have a command lesson 2–5 times a day for three minutes. Go through all the commands he knows, skipping "Down" if he's growling until you get professional help.

➤ If your dog does the "Down" command willingly, repeat it throughout the day.

➤ No staring matches unless you've initiated them.

➤ Regulate the feeding to twice a day. Do not give food rewards or treats until your problems are gone.

➤ Once a day, do a 30 minute anchoring session without toys or attention.

Grrr
If your dog growls during any of these efforts, such as getting him to move out of your way, don't push it. Stop everything until you get professional help. Your problem is serious.

Spatial Aggression (Object Guarding)

A dog who shows aggression while eating, sleeping, grooming, or being medicated by a family member, stranger, or other dog professional (veterinarian or groomer) is showing *spatial aggression*. It is usually tied in with dominant, territorial, or psychotic aggression.

Proceed with caution. Don't freak out, hit your dog, or scream. These reactions will only reinforce his defensive notion that you've come to steal his prize. In his mind, your dog thinks you have prize envy. To help your dog accept you as less threatening, follow these steps, which use the food dish as an example:

1. Do not make a power struggle out of the feeding ritual. For example, some people make their dog "Sit" and "Wait" before every meal. This is excessive and encourages food frustration. Ask your dog to sit and release your dog as you put the bowl down.

2. Shake a plastic cup with some small dog biscuits and reward your dog with one. We'll call this the *shake cup*. Keep doing this until your dog connects the sound with a reward. The best shake cups contain your dog's favorite treats. If your dog loves

Milk Bones, use them. I like using Cheerios. If your dog's finicky, but loves cheese, cut up some chunks and place them in a party cup with a couple of pennies. Your dog will condition to the rattle of the pennies. Good enough!

3. Approach him once a day with the shake cup while he is eating a meal. If he growls as you approach him during a meal, stop and toss him a few treats before you leave. Continue this step until you can stand over him and drop treats into his bowl.

4. At this point, approach his bowl speaking happy praises, but *without* shaking the cup. When you get to his side, toss a treat into the bowl and leave.

5. Next, try kneeling down as you shake the cup and toss a treat into his bowl.

6. When this passes without tension, try placing the treat into his bowl with your hand.

7. After you've offered your dog a handful of treats, try stirring the kibble with your hand.

8. If you're successful, continue this once every other day for a week. Next, after offering a handful of treats, try lifting the bowl. Give it back immediately and leave. Repeat once a month only.

9. Repeat this process for prized objects, like bones or squeak toys.

To ensure your puppy gets used to occasional interruptions around his bowl, follow the preceding procedure as a precautionary measure. If your puppy thinks your approach means he's getting something, he'll never be concerned!

Grrr
Dogs notice fear. If you're afraid, your dog will know it and be suspicious. Call a professional immediately.

Sarah Says
I cannot guarantee you will not get bitten in the process. Be your own judge; proceed as your dog is comfortable and seek help if necessary.

Territorial Aggression

Dogs who act aggressively when strangers approach their homes are *territorial*. This problem is encouraged by the following:

➤ **When delivery people approach and leave the home territory,** the dog thinks that he drove them away and his aggression is reinforced.

➤ **When the owners are home and react to a territorial response by yelling or physical handling,** the dog perceives their heightened response as back-up. Job well done!

➤ **When a dog reacts aggressively in a car or on a tie out,** he is warning all intruders to stay away. Because they do, he considers himself victorious and his territorial aggression is reinforced.

➤ **When dogs are isolated during greetings or visits** they may develop *Frustrated Territorial Aggression (FTA)*. This is not a good thing. In a normal group of dogs, the leader would permit or deny entry to a visitor, who is then "sniffed out" by the rest of the pack. Isolation frustrates this normal process and will encourage a more aggressive response the next time the doorbell rings.

Sarah Says
While guard and herd dogs are more commonly known for this type of aggression (again detectable in puppyhood), it can be found in any breed.

Grrr
Handling an aggressive dog on a chain collar is like holding an angry man's arms behind his back. It creates fury. Using a chin lead reduces this tension and communicates structure and discipline passively.

You must assert yourself. Stake out your territory. A strict training regime is necessary. Your dog must be led or stationed during arrivals. If he is truly out of hand, I suggest you handle him on the chin lead (see Chapter 7). This collar reduces the negative restraint around the neck and places the dog's body in a submissive posture.

Now for some hard and fast regulations:

➤ No bed privileges.

➤ He must go to the bathroom on your property.

➤ No marking, inside or out.

➤ Instruct "Wait" through all thresholds and doors.

➤ Insist on a "Heel" when walking your dog outside. You may release your dog to go to the bathroom, but make him return to your side.

➤ When people approach, keep your dog behind you and ignore him. If he's impossible to control, use a chin lead. Don't let anyone give him attention until he's calm.

➤ Use a shake cup or peanut butter jar to help your dog associate outsiders with a positive reward.

Peanut butter jar? Yes, peanut butter. Most dogs love it. Get them their own little jar and tape a bell to it to help them associate a special sound. When people come in, encourage them to offer the jar to your dog *after* he has settled down.

➤ Eliminate all yelling or verbose/physical corrections because they add more negative energy to an already tense situation. To calm your dog, you must set the example.

➤ Get help immediately. A territorial dog is a dangerous dog.

Protective Aggression

This dog thinks his job is to protect his owner. Even outside of his territory, this dog will react aggressively if anyone approaches. It is not uncommon for dogs to develop this sort of relationship with a young child or passive, inexperienced owner. The owner—man, woman, or child—is perceived as weak and in need of protection.

"Don't come near my owner, or else!"

Does your dog feel responsible for you? If he's acting like your guard wherever you go, you have a serious identity crisis to deal with. You must let your dog know you're the boss.

Buy a chin lead. Both you and your dog need training. You must learn how to assert dominance over your dog. Train your dog. Keep him behind you at all thresholds and when meeting new people. Call a professional if you need help.

Predatory Aggression

Predatory aggression is another instinctive behavior from ancestral times when dogs were wolves and hunted for survival. Although we have suppressed the drive to kill in most breeds, some (Nordic breeds and terriers especially) still kill instinctively.

Most dogs still possess a chasing instinct. Predatory aggression, however, usually results in a kill. If you have encouraged your dog's behavior by egging him on, stop. It's not funny. Teach your dog the meaning of "No" (see Chapter 12) and use it whenever you notice his desire kindling.

If you have a revved-up Nordic breed or terrier breed, you have your hands full. Their instincts are strong. After one of these dogs kills, their desire becomes stronger. However, this instinct rarely transfers to children. For solutions, please contact a professional.

Fear-Induced Aggression

In every litter, there will be shy puppies, mama's boys or girls who depend on her wisdom for safety. In human homes, these dogs continue being needy. Their timidity, which surfaces in new situations, may turn into overwhelming fear if they're not given proper direction and support from their owners. A dog in this situation may react aggressively.

Although shyness is a temperamental trait, there is also a learned element to the behavior. If an owner attempts to soothe a frightened dog, the attention reinforces the fear.

Does your dog flee every time a stranger enters? Does he approach, and then avoid while barking protectively? This problem demands a lot of understanding and patience. You cannot correct a fearful dog, as it will only increase his fear. You can't soothe him either as your attention will reinforce this behavior. A large part of the problem is that the dog feels no one has control of the situation. To help correct this problem, set the example.

Sarah Says
When strangers or caring professionals back away from a threatening dog, the dog gets the message that aggression works!

Keep your dog on his Teaching Lead® and act confident and secure in new situations. Encourage everyone to ignore your dog until he approaches. Use your shake cup or peanut butter jar to encourage a more positive association to situations. When seeking a professional, find one who uses a soft and positive approach. Threatening this type of dog often creates more fear.

Dog-to-Dog Aggression

Aggression between dogs occurs when they perceive their territories as overlapping (this can happen anywhere because some dogs think their territory is very extensive) or there is a hierarchical struggle in a multi-dog household. It is often exaggerated by well-meaning owners who scream or pull back when their dog is showing aggression. This only adds to the tension.

There are two categories:

➤ **Outside Disputes.** This problem usually results from lack of early socialization. The next time around, enroll in a puppy class immediately. In my Puppy Kindergarten classes, I allow ten minutes of off-lead play. It's a great time for the puppies to socialize with each other and with people. If you have this problem, you must assess how serious it is. A class might be the perfect solution. You must learn to assert yourself and act like a dominant leader when you meet another dog.

➤ **Inside Disputes.** Whenever there are two or more dogs in a home, they will develop a hierarchical relationship. You will notice the leader. He is the one pushing the other dog out of the way when attention is offered and dominating over toys or food. In addition, your leader will be the one racing to be out the door first. Disputes arise when you undermine their organization by paying more attention to the underdog. The lead dog is frustrated and the underdog is confused. To calm things down, pay more attention to the Top Dog. Feed, greet, and play with him first and most. Spend time training him. The other dog will follow. If they fight, praise the Top Dog and ignore the other. I know it sounds cruel and it's hard (I had to do it), but trust me. It works. If you're having difficulty, bring in a professional.

Sarah Says
Aggression is no small problem. There are no guarantees. If your dog has bitten, there is no promise that he won't do it again. Your effort to remedy the problem will only help, however, and this is your only option other than euthanasia. Passing an aggressive dog onto another home or into a shelter would be irresponsible. You'd be responsible if he bit someone or maimed a child. Get help if you need it.

Psychotic Aggression

It's very rare that I come across a psychotic dog or puppy, but they do exist and it would be irresponsible if I didn't address this issue. Most, though not all, dogs with this problem are the result of poor puppy-mill type breeding. This problem is identified by erratic or fearful aggression responses in very atypical situations, which can often be traced back to early puppyhood. There are two categories:

➤ **Erratic Viciousness.** At unpredictable intervals, this dog/puppy will growl fiercely from his belly. It may happen when his owner passes his food bowl, approaches when he's chewing a toy, or even walks by him. At other times, the dog is perfectly sweet—a "Jekyll and Hyde" personality.

➤ **Fear Biters.** This puppy shows dramatic fear in or a startled bite response to non-threatening situations like turning a page of the newspaper or the movement of an arm. They can act extremely confused or threatened when strangers approach. Many well-educated dog people use this term incorrectly. There is a big difference in a dog/puppy that bites out of fear and a fear biter. Don't automatically assume the worst if someone labels your dog with this term.

Please don't panic if your dog occasionally growls at you or barks at the mailman. A lot of dogs/puppies growl when protecting a food dish or toy and the guarding instinct is strong in many breeds. These are behavioral problems that can be cured or controlled with proper training. Even many biters can be rehabilitated. The situations I'm speaking of involve *severe* aggression—bared teeth, hard eyes, a growl that begins in their belly and a bite response you'd expect from a trained police dog. These personality disturbances are seen very early, usually by four months of age.

It's both frightening and tragic because nothing can be done to alter their development. Their fate has been sealed by irresponsible, greedy people. If you suspect that your puppy might have either of these abnormalities, speak to your breeder and veterinarian immediately and call a specialist to analyze the situation. These puppies must be euthanized. In my career, I've seen only six cases and all were purchased from unknown or suspicious breeders.

The Least You Need To Know

➤ Aggression isn't black and white. It comes in various shades. To solve it, you must define it.

➤ With aggression, there are no guarantees. If you are afraid of your dog or your problem doesn't improve, seek professional help.

➤ To assert leadership, teach your dog a proper "Heel," insist that he follows you through doors and thresholds, say "Excuse me" when he's in your way, and keep him behind you when greeting company.

➤ Condition your dog to the shake cup or peanut butter jar. Use positive treating to help your dog adopt a more positive view on life.

Chapter 26

Other Socially Unacceptable Behaviors

Eating stool, ingesting socks, digging to China...there is a common theme. Dogs do these things when they're anxious. Some dogs have anxiety due to lack of structure and some are more on the obsessive-compulsive side of life. Read this chapter, identify these problems, and do your best to help.

Digging

Digging can be a favorite pastime when your dog gets bored. It can also be a cry for company. Dogs don't like being left alone. They fuss, and fussy dogs dig. Unfortunately, you cannot teach your dog not to dig. Instead, you must give him a place that's all his own. Here are some suggestions:

➤ Pick one area where your dog can dig to his heart's content.

➤ Go to the area ahead of time and hide some favorite biscuits/toys.

➤ Go to the area with your dog each day, instructing "Go dig!"

➤ Have a dig-fest. Dig with your dog and cheer him on.

➤ If you catch your dog digging somewhere he shouldn't be, correct him with "No!" then tell him (escorting him to the right spot, if necessary), "Go dig!"

Spraying your dog with a hose or setting mouse traps is cruel and I don't encourage it. Putting the dirt back into the hole is confusing—now you're digging in the same spot too. Place your dog indoors when you garden. It's just too tempting after seeing you dig in one area all day!

Bet You Didn't Know

Most dogs dig when left outside while you're home. They love to dig while you watch; it's a sure-fire attention-getter. Try to structure the environment so that he can be in the house when you're around.

Garbage Grabbing

Garbage grabbing is the perfect eye catcher. It's very rewarding, and very annoying. To solve this problem, keep a lid on it. Keep your garbage locked away under the cabinets. Prevention is the best solution. No table treats before or after your meal. I know, the eyes are pleading and it'll go to waste, but if your dog can have it in his bowl, he'll want it in the trash.

If your dog is still rummaging around, try practicing one of the following set-ups:

Ten-Foot Line. Place your dog on a ten-foot-long line (see Chapter 14) and toss something irresistible into the trash. The second he starts to show interest, step on the line and shout "No!" Rush up to the garbage can and kick and scream at it. Do not yell or look at your dog. Go back to whatever you were pretending to do and repeat the process from the top. If your dog ignores the temptation, give him a hug.

Sound Off. If your dog is sound-sensitive, construct a *pyramid of penny cans*. Place ten pennies each in six cans and arrange the cans with three on the bottom, two in the middle, and one on top. Tie a string to the middle can on the bottom row and either attach it to the can or hold it. When your dog shows interest, pull the string and shout "No!" at the can.

Balloon Pop. The last thing to try is the *balloon stay away*. Blow up a few balloons and pop them one at a time with a pin with your dog present. As each one pops, act afraid yourself. Don't pay any attention to your dog. Just act it out and trust me, he'll be watching. Next tape the balloons to the edge of the garbage can and leave them there a couple of weeks.

Is your dog an angel when you're in the room, but crafty when you leave? Smart dog. Your timing is probably off. Are you correcting after he's stolen something? He considers your correction as prize envy and figures he'll take it when you're not around to challenge him for it. There are several approaches you can try:

➤ Set up a bitter-tasting lure by soaking a paper towel in Tabasco sauce. Repeat this until he loses interest in the trash.

➤ Set up the penny can pyramid and booby trap him when you've left the room.

➤ Set up a mirror so that you can keep your eye on the garbage can even when you're not physically present. When you see your dog approaching the can, storm in and correct his thought process.

Inedible Ingestion (Pica)

Chewing sticks, rocks, slippers is perfectly normal. Eating them, however, isn't. If your dog is into swallowing everything in sight or has a hard time passing up the kid's underwear or socks, you are dealing with an obsessive-compulsive behavior.

I call it *prize envy*. When your dog grabs something he shouldn't, you think, "Bad dog, give it back!" Your dog, however, sees your body language from a dog's perspective. He thinks you're racing forward to steal what he's found. If he wants to keep it, he better split or gulp it. Some split. Others gulp it, whatever "it" is.

Sarah Says

If you own a dog with this problem, you'll have to keep a close eye on him. If you think your dog has eaten something non-digestible, call your veterinarian immediately. These items can block the intestine and, if left untreated, kill your dog.

To stop this behavior permanently, you may need to seek professional help. Until then, follow these guidelines:

➤ Do not chase after your dog angrily for anything.

➤ Place favorite treats in small party cups and distribute them around the house.

➤ If your dog picks up something he shouldn't, grab a party cup and encourage him to come to you and exchange the object for a treat.

➤ If you notice something tempting on the ground, don't dive for it. Remember, you're setting the example. Try to distract your dog and remove it calmly.

Separation Anxiety

Separation. Dogs hate it. If they had their way, they'd follow you to the ends of the earth. But alas, they can't. Dogs suffering from this condition may chew destructively, soil the house, bark excessively, or act out other destructive behaviors. It's not spite. Dogs can't think that way. It's anxiety, canine style. If you're experiencing this problem, your dog will fall into one of two categories:

> **The Passive Dog.** This dog clings to his owners when they are home, often soliciting attention and getting it. He interprets this love on demand for a desire to be led. This leads to over-identification, not too unlike a child who clings to his mother's leg. This dog is confused about himself and depends on people to reassure him. When they go, so does his identity.

> **The Dominant Dog.** This fellow thinks he is king of his castle, ruler of the roost. When his owners, whom he considers his subordinates, leave, his anxiety is in their best interest. "How will they survive without their great leader there to protect them?"

This problem must be resolved with training. For the passive dog, training will give him a sense of identity and the reassurance that a competent leader is on the job. For the dominant dog, training will place him in a subordinate, carefree pack-position. If you need help training, get it. In the meantime, follow these ground rules:

➤ Never correct your dog after the fact. Never. Corrections are not connected to the destruction; they're connected to your arrival. This makes your dog more anxious the next time you leave.

➤ Avoid theatrical hellos and good-byes. Lavishing your dog with kisses, biscuits, and drawn-out declarations of devotion do not reassure him. They stress him out.

➤ Leave a radio playing classical music to cover unfamiliar sounds.

➤ Place your dog in a dimly lit area to encourage sleep.

➤ Leave a favorite chew toy. Rub it between your palms for scent.

If you're leaving for over six hours, try to find someone to walk your dog. Otherwise, proof the house from her destruction; buy an indoor pen. They fold nicely to store when you're home and can be expanded before you leave to give your dog space when you're gone for extended periods. Dogs get cramped if left in small kennels for longer than six hours and can develop Hyper Isolation Anxiety (see Appendix A).

When home, temporarily decrease the attention you give your dog by 50 percent. Do not give in to solicitations. Although it relieves your feelings of guilt, it is too sharp a contrast from leaving your dog alone all day. When alone, your dog longs for companionship. Since chewing fingernails or watching the soaps isn't an option, he may settle for your couch.

If possible, buy a kitten for your dog. Kittens are super companions and they are great company for dogs if raised with them. Getting another dog is also an option, though it's better to wait until you've resolved this problem.

Sarah Says
Once he's comfortable at 30 minutes, go back to short separations, but this time, leave the house. Gradually work your way up to 30 minutes out of the house. Start over, this time getting into and starting your car. With patience, you'll be able to build his confidence and leave him for longer and longer periods of time.

Grrr
If you seek help, make sure you avoid trainers who encourage discipline.

Kittens and dogs make great companions, and a kitten can reduce your pup's separation anxiety.

Next, you'll need to set up practice departures. Station your dog in a familiar spot. Instruct "Wait" and leave the room for 15 seconds. Return and ignore him until he's calm, and then praise him lovingly. Repeat this ten times or until he stays calm.

Continue these short separations until he shows no anxiety. Double the separation time and repeat the procedure. Continue doubling the departure time until you're able to leave the room for 30 minutes.

Stimulated Sprinkling

Do you have a tinkler? The most frequent question I've been asked is, "Do they grow out of it?" Well, yes and no. Yes, if you handle yourself properly, and no if you don't. Tinkling isn't a conscious thing. Dogs do it because they are over-excited or anxious. Discipline your dog for doing it and you'll make it worse.

When you come in, ignore your dog until she's completely calm. Extend a jar of peanut butter or a cup of biscuits as you pet her. Divert her mind. Kneel down to pet her rather than leaning over.

If your dog is timid around certain people, have everyone (including yourself) ignore her. When you soothe her, it reinforces the fear. When your dog approaches the person, offer her treats. Use a shake cup or peanut butter jar. When she is calm, have guests kneel and pet her chest.

If your dog piddles during greetings or play sessions, ignore her or stop the play until she has better bladder control.

Stool Swallowing (Corprophagia)

This delightful habit comes in two varieties: other creatures' stool and their own stool. Believe it or not, they're both fairly common behaviors.

Other Creatures' Stool

Stool from other creatures is actually quite a delicacy to your dog. Deer duds, litter logs, goose goblets, they're all candies to suit your dog's delight. Corrections will make it worse. Your dog will think you want it too and will gulp faster. Most dogs outgrow this behavior if you feed them a balanced meal twice a day and ignore their stool fetish. Try to refocus your dog on a favorite activity. If you're suffering from litterbox blues, put the litter box in an inaccessible area, get a litter box with a lid, or correct the box as outlined in the chewing section of this chapter. There's only one thing to be happy about in this situation—be happy you're not a dog!

Own Stool

Though this is probably the most grotesque thing you could ever imagine, in dogland it's just a handy way to keep the den clean. When your dog was a puppy, he watched his mother do it, and when he sees you cleaning up after him, he thinks...well, you get the picture. To halt this habit:

➤ Never clean up messes in front of your dog.

➤ Don't correct your dog when he shows interest in his stool. If you fuss, he'll gulp.

➤ If your dog's showing interest, refocus him on a favorite game. "Get your ball!"

➤ Ask your veterinarian to give you a food additive that will make his feces distasteful. I know, what could be more distasteful than dog poop? But such things do exist.

➤ After your dog is finished eliminating, spray the pile with something distasteful, like Bitter Apple®, Tabasco sauce, or vinegar.

Timidity

Timid dogs look so pitiful. Like kids, you want to soothe them. But dogs are not kids; they'll think your soothing is a sign of your fear. Now you're both afraid. That's a big problem.

To help your dog, you must act confident when she is afraid. You're the leader. Stand up straight. Relax your shoulders. Breathe deep. Smile. Whether it's a bag blowing in the wind, a sharp noise (like thunder), or an uncommon face, act calm, face the feared object, and ignore your dog until she starts to act more like you.

If your dog is showing aggression when she's fearful, call a professional. Do not knowingly put her in "threatening situations."

Thunder!

Speaking of thunder phobias, there are ways to handle it. Let me start with the don'ts. Don't coddle your dog. Don't permit him to hide between the sheets or climb onto the couch. Don't isolate him. These make the fear worse. Depending on how bad your situation is, try one or all of these approaches:

➤ Turn on some classical music and play it loud.

➤ Lead your dog on his Teaching Lead® while you act completely calm. Set the example. Show him how to cope with the situation. Let your dog have his fears, just don't respond to them. When he calms down, pet him lovingly.

➤ Find (or make) a thunderstorm tape recording. Play it on low volume while you play your dog's favorite game with him. Slowly increase the volume.

➤ Ask your veterinarian for tranquilizers to soothe your dog before a storm.

The Least You Need To Know

➤ Certain behaviors fall in the normal range, others don't. If your dog is doing anything to the extreme, he may be over-anxious. You'll need to work on that together.

➤ If you overreact every time your dog puts something in his mouth, your dog will think that whatever he has must be good.

➤ If your dog tinkles when nervous, try to calm her or distract her with a shake cup or peanut butter jar.

➤ Yes, stool swallowing is gross, but to your dog, it's normal. Don't overreact, try to provide a balanced diet, and, if needed, get a food supplement from the vet that will make stool distasteful.

➤ If your dog's afraid of thunder, play classical music, keep him on the Teaching Lead®, and stay calm to set the right example.

Traveling with Your Pet

Everybody likes a vacation. The most depressing part, however, is parting with your beloved pal. His soulful stare can stay with you for hours. So why not take him along? Well, it can be great fun, but there are also some risks. In this chapter, I'll go over some hard and fast traveling rules, so you can make your own decision.

Planes

I myself am leery of planes, so you can imagine how neurotic I get thinking of a dog in the belly of one of those steel babies. Personally, I'd avoid taking any pet on a plane if I didn't have to. Even if only one dog in ninety dies, I don't want to be the one holding the empty leash. Sometimes air travel is unavoidable, however, so here are some hard and fast rules.

Pre-flight Preparations

➤ The cargo areas where pets are held before and after the flight are neither heated nor cooled. Thus, you want to minimize the amount of time your dog spends in "hold." Stay with him until just before flight and pick him up directly after. Avoid all extremes.

➤ Make reservations together. Planes only accept so many four-legged passengers.

➤ Book a direct flight in a large plane.

Sarah Says
If you can't fly direct, book a flight with a long enough lay over to reunite with your dog. Take him out for a stretch, drink, bathroom break, and a hug.

➤ If you're heading for warmer waters, book a night or early morning flight. Heat is often the culprit in airline tragedies.

➤ If you're planning to take your dog with you overseas, check ahead of time to see what quarantine rules apply.

➤ Health certificates and proof of vaccination are required by airlines. Get them from your veterinarian and forward a copy to the airline immediately. Carry one with you the day of the flight.

Canine Accommodations

➤ Purchase a sturdy USDA-approved travel kennel custom fit to your dog's size. It should only be large enough for your dog to stand up and turn around in.

➤ Get your dog comfortable with his kennel quarters a few days before departure.

➤ If you have a teenie-weenie dog who can come on board, buy a crate that will fit under the seat.

➤ Write LIVE ANIMAL in one-inch letters on top of the crate and on each side. Tape on some huge arrows to indicate the crate's upright position.

Grrr
Don't feed your dog within six hours of the trip.

➤ On the top of the crate, in 1/2-inch letters, write the flight's destination, including the name, address, and phone number of the person/place you're visiting.

➤ Remove all training collars. Your dog should wear a well-fitting buckle collar with identification tags.

➤ Prep the crate for take-off with light bedding and paper (taped down) in one end to absorb mistakes. Affix two bowls inside the crate. Freeze water in one so your dog can have a beverage while in flight!

➤ The last thing you should do before loading your dog? Let him go to the bathroom!

➤ If the flight is longer than 12 hours, tape a bag of food to the outside of the crate with feeding instructions.

➤ Never padlock your crate! You don't want your pet trapped in case of an emergency.

Upon arrival, go immediately to the baggage area and insist on seeing your dog. Kick and fuss if you must. This is another tricky time for your pet, especially if he turns out to be an escape artist. Imagine watching your dog tearing down the runway trying to herd a leer jet! That's one time "Fido, come!" just isn't going to work...

Trains

Though I looked high and low, I couldn't find a rail service that was dog friendly. Of course, they all allow service dogs on board. My local metro north allows dogs under 20 pounds to travel on off-peak hours. Pretty limiting.

Automobiles

I've never owned a dog who didn't love a road trip. I know some dogs have less than enjoyable experiences, but even they can be transformed with some patient car conditioning. (See Chapter 4, "Rolling Out Your Welcome Mat.")

Cars can be a dangerous place for dogs, however, so there are precautions you must take:

➤ Don't leave your dog in the car on a warm day. Even with the windows down, your car will bake like an oven, leaving your dog uncomfortable or dead. Nothing is worth that.

➤ Got a pick-up truck? Let your dog ride up in the cab. On a leash or off, the flat bed is no place for a dog.

➤ Keep the windows cracked, but not wide open. Some people think it's cool to let a dog hang his head out the window. Personally, it looks dumb and it's dangerous. Dogs can get hurled from the car in an accident or have debris fly into their eyes, causing permanent damage.

Sarah Says
You really want to take your dog with you while you do errands? Make an extra set of keys and leave the air conditioner running in hot weather and the heat in cold weather.

➤ Another crazy habit—the dog who rides in the driver's seat. Give me a break. Not only are the dog and the driver in jeopardy, but so is everyone passing them on the street. You can't drive and bond simultaneously.

Car Rules

Your dog must have structure in the car. If he doesn't, he'll think he owns it. That can lead to a cascade of problems, the least of which is barking at everything that moves. You have some options.

Crates are cumbersome and can be a little big, but they will keep your dog still while you drive. Buy a strong, wire mesh type (for good air circulation) sized for your dog's weight and breed. Line the bottom with something your dog can sink his paws into.

Barriers enclose your dog in the back compartment of a wagon or sports utility vehicle. Aesthetically, they're not too appealing and the cheaper models collapse easily, but if you buy a good one, it will effectively keep your dog safe and still.

Harness gadgets secure around your dog's body and will effectively keep him buckled in. The only drawback is that they're tough to put on and dogs are often less than thrilled.

The Seat Belt Safety Lead (SBSL)™ is my little invention. It hooks into a seat belt permanently and attaches to your dog's buckle collar while you drive. It's handy, it takes second to attach, and it keeps your dog safe while you take care of the driving.

Road Trips

Are you planning a long journey? Dogs make excellent traveling companions. Here are some guidelines to ensure that you both get there safe and sound.

➤ Check your dog's buckle collar to ensure that all identification tags have been updated.

➤ Avoid traveling in extreme heat unless you have a good AC system. Plan to travel at night or early in the morning.

➤ Never leave your dog unattended in an unlocked car. If the weather's extreme (either hot or freezing), make an extra set of keys so you can leave the climate control on while you lock the car and take care of your business.

➤ Keep your dog on a leash at every pit stop. This is a must, no matter how idiot-proof you think you are.

➤ Give your dog water and exercise at every rest area. Feeding should take place before a walk. Allow your dog half an hour to digest.

➤ If you're planning a hotel stay, call ahead and ask about their "welcome dog" policy when you make your reservations.

➤ Use your Teaching Lead® to help your dog adjust to his new surroundings. Station him at night on a familiar blanket with a trusty ol' bone.

Boats

Your dog's not a land lover, is he? Does he love the water? Well, perhaps you should take him boating. No regulations exist, so you'll have to use some good old-fashioned common sense. First, no beast, four-legged or two, can last 15 minutes in frigid waters. Second, if you're wearing a life vest, your dog should be also. You can buy a lifejacket for your dog in any pet specialty store. Make sure if fits right! Third, don't forget about dehydration. If it's hot and sunny, provide your dog with a bucket of water from which to sip! Have fun and think safe.

Grrr
Keep in mind that certain breeds of dogs don't swim well.

The Least You Need To Know

➤ If you're planning to fly with your pet, plan ahead. Book direct flights and avoid traveling in extreme weather conditions. Purchase a USDA-approved travel kennel to fit your dog's size.

➤ Find your dog immediately after arrival. He'll probably have to go bad, so make a beeline for the first blade of grass.

➤ The car exaggerates any weather condition, becoming like an oven in the summer and a refrigerator in the winter. If you must take your dog, make an extra set of keys so you can leave the climate control on while you run an errand.

➤ Planning a cross-country trip? Make sure you make all hotel reservations early to ensure that they're "dog friendly" and pack plenty of frozen water (it will thaw!). Never, never let your dog off lead in an unconfined space.

Saying Good-Bye

I have a good friend who, when I told her about this chapter, told me her dogs have promised her they'll live forever. No, she's not crazy, but she loves her dogs tremendously, as we all do. The thought of not having them as we travel through life is unimaginable. It is an inescapable truth, however, that people most often outlive their dogs. It is the pain of this loss and the decisions leading up to it that we'll face in this chapter.

When Euthanasia Isn't a Dirty Word

I've never been one for major decisions, and I can't think of a decision more major than that to put your dog to sleep. It's very…final. Euthanasia is a serious and sober topic, one that brings tears to my eyes just thinking about it. But it's important to realize that there are certain situations that call for it—even cry for it.

Severe Behavior Problems

The ugliest thing I'm forced to do in my profession is decide when a dog is too unsafe to be rehabilitated. The only responsible alternative in the cases of psychotic aggression is to have the dog put to sleep. It's mind boggling and angering because it is usually the result of irresponsible, greedy people who bred the dog for financial gain and did not support the puppy's emotional development. Often, these dogs as pups were stressed or separated from their "dog family" before seven weeks. (Please refer to Chapter 25 for more information on psychotic aggression.)

Please don't panic if your dog occasionally growls at you or barks at the mailman. A lot of puppies/dogs growl when protecting a food dish or toy; the guarding instinct is strong in many breeds. The behavioral problems that can't be cured or controlled with training must be labeled by a reputable professional. Most biters can be rehabilitated.

In Sickness and in Health

Sickness can strike your dog at any time. Cancer is not limited to the human race. Accidents happen. Should these fates reach your doorstep, you might face questions that seem larger than life: What risks should I take? How much pain will my dog have to bear? In the end, it is your personal decision. Everybody who has ever loved a dog knows how tragedy can catch us so unprepared. But if you find yourself in this situation, please don't think of yourself. Listen to your dog. Put yourself in his paws.

Why Can't They Go on Forever?

It's funny that dogs who share as much space in our hearts as some people live such a short time. In dogs, old age can come on rapidly. Suddenly, we are left with an old friend whose bodily capabilities deteriorate before our eyes. I remember the dog I grew up with for fifteen years, Shawbee. She was a gray husky-mix, so there were no colored hairs to mark the passage of time. Within the space of a year, when she was older, her eyes clouded and she went blind. She stopped responding to my voice because her hearing was failing. She needed help to get up and down stairs. It broke my heart because as she was growing old, I was growing up.

It's very hard for me to think about euthanasia, the decision to take your dog's life into your own hands. I'm crying as I write this because I still miss my childhood friend. There were so many lessons she taught me. So many that I pass on to my pupils. But there comes a time when something tells you that your dog's not happy, that the pain overrides the joy. And in your heart, you know your dog can't live forever.

It's All Right to Grieve

People grieve differently. The most unhealthy form of grieving is no grieving. The day you lose a companion you've shared days upon years with, your life will be changed in ways you'll be completely unprepared for. Things you never thought you'd miss—the interruptions at the dinner table, the embarrassing sounds made at all the wrong times, the muddy paws on a rainy day—will bring tears to your eyes. Your dog, your friend, is gone.

Finding Support

I think the hardest thing when you're grieving is to talk about it. People who have never had pets or who aren't attached to their own look at you as if you're crazy. "It was just a dog." Please don't take this personally. They just don't understand. Choose people to share your feelings with carefully. You need the support of someone who will listen.

Right now, you need to take care of yourself. Take some time off work. Talk to people who knew your dog. Surround yourself with people who will understand. Talk about your feelings. It may be weeks, perhaps months, before your world rights itself. Take all the time you need. In the end, that gaping hole in your heart will fill with happy memories that will last your lifetime.

Your Children

Do you have kids? Listen to them. The death of a dog affects children differently. Perhaps they'll want a memorial. They may write a poem or a song. They may construct a grave marker. Encourage these expressions of grief. Let your children hear your feelings too. Together, you loved your dog. Together, you should grieve her.

Your Part of a Circle

It's hard to imagine when you're in the middle of a loss, that other people have felt the same. But they have. Shared emotions and similar experiences is what ties us together as a human race. If you know people or can get into contact with people who have lost a dog recently, talk to them. Ask them how long it took for the pain to go away. Talk to them about their dog and tell them stories about yours. If you can't find anyone, locate a book I've read called *The Loss of a Pet*, by Wallace Sife (Howell Book House, 1993). You might find it helpful. I did.

Sarah Says
You can also locate a PLGSG by contacting the ASPCA in New York city at (212) 876-7700 (ext. 4355).

317

Guilt

Grief sometimes mixes with guilt, especially if your dog dies in an accident or must be euthanized. This is tough, because only you can set yourself free. Guilt must be vented. You need to hear yourself talk, so pick an understanding friend. It's normal to feel guilty; it's abnormal to hold on to it too long. If you can't let go of the guilty feelings, talk to a bereavement counselor.

Fresh Paws

Some people want to get another dog. Some don't. Some change their mind with time. It's your personal decision. But when you are ready for a new dog, do him a big favor. Don't compare. Puppies are puppies; they'll never act like your old faithful. Give yourself time to grieve your old dog, until only the good memories remain. Then you're ready to start again.

Burying Your Dog

You can bury your dog in several places. You can dig a grave beneath her favorite spot in the yard or under a tree. You can buy a plot at a pet cemetery. You can have your dog cremated and spread her ashes on a sunny day or keep the urn in your home. But the one place you must bury your dog is in your heart.

Doglish Glossary

About Face   A 180-degree turn to face the opposite direction. This is one of the moves practiced while heeling.

Agility   An obstacle course for dogs! This sport has its roots in horse shows.

AKC Obedience Trial   A competition of obedience. There are three different levels of competition: novice, open, and utility.

Allergies   Canine allergies include wool, dust, cedar chips, propylene glycol (a rawhide treat preservative), garden plants, and food products.

American Kennel Club (AKC)   A club that registers pure breeds and licenses dog shows, obedience trials, and other competitive events.

Anchoring   A position to put your dog in to calm him down using the Teaching Lead®.

Artificial Respiration (a.k.a. Mouth-to-Muzzle Respiration)   A method to restore and maintain respiration for a dog who has a heartbeat, but is not breathing.

Association of American Feed Control Officials (AAFCO)   Company that researches and controls what goes into dog food.

Bitter Apple®   A bitter-tasting spray that can be used to deter dogs from chewing on things such as leashes and furniture.

Body Language   Dogs have different postures for different modes—play, tension, and relaxation. Knowing how to interpret each will allow you to become a better teacher.

Buckle Collar   Adjustable collar made of cotton, nylon, or leather for your dog's tags. They do not slide or choke.

Canine Good Citizenship Test   A test used by the AKC to evaluate how well a dog fits into society. The dog must pass tasks such as allowing a stranger to groom him and keeping quiet when left alone.

Car Station   A special area in the car for your dog. You should secure him here for his own safety and your own peace of mind.

Chin Lead (a.k.a. Halti, Promise Collar, or Gentle Leader)   A collar that helps control rowdy, mouthing dogs in the most humane and natural way.

Come Front   The first step in teaching the command "Come." The dog is seated facing his owner and looking up.

Conjunctivitis   Infection of the third eyelid; similar to human "pink-eye."

CPR (Cardiopulmonary Resuscitation)   A life-saving technique involving keeping your dog's heart beating and breathing for him.

Cushing's Disease   A disease of hyperactive adrenal glands. It can be caused by drinking too much chlorinated water.

Delighted Tone   A praising tone to soothe your dog and make him feel proud.

Directive Tone   A tone in which you command your dog, clearly and directly, while standing in the peacock position.

Discipline Tone   A shameful or disapproving tone used with a constant expression, such as "Ep-Ep."

Down   This command requires a dog to lie down.

Earth Dog Trial   Working trials to test a terrier's natural instincts.

Electrical Fence   An invisible barrier around your yard; an underground wire that creates a shock in the dog's collar when he approaches the edge.

Emergency Down   This command is a fast "down" and is used in case of an emergency.

Erratic Viciousness   Unpredictable intervals of growling in an otherwise sweet dog; somewhat of a "Jekyll and Hyde" personality.

Excuse Me   A command to use if your dog crosses in front of or behind you, presses against you, or blocks your path. It communicates hierarchy.

Eye Contact   Eye contact is a key part of your dog's language, Doglish. The main principle behind eye contact is that you reinforce whatever you look at.

Fear Biters   Dogs that show dramatic fear in or a startled bite response to non-threatening situations.

Fear-Induced Aggression   A naturally timid dog reacting aggressively in a new situation.

Field Trial   Working trials for sporting breeds.

Flexi-Leash®   A retractable lead (16–26 ft.) that allows extended freedom *with* control.

Flyball®   An athletic sporting event involving speed-chasing a ball for accuracy and time.

Four Paw Rule   The technique of training a dog not to jump when greeted. This is accomplished by not petting your dog until *all four paws* are planted on the floor.

Frustrated Territorial Aggression   When a dog is put in isolation and cannot give his normal greeting response, he becomes even more assertive than he normally would be.

Group Training   Training your dog with a group of other dogs in an obedience class.

Habituation   The process in which a behavior becomes a habit because the dog is rewarded with attention (negative or positive).

Heartworm   A parasitic worm that infects the heart and lungs in its adult stages and can fatally clog arteries if not prevented with specialized medication. See your veterinarian.

Heel   In Heel position, a dog is aligned with the owner's left side; the dog's paws should always be behind his owner's ankles.

Herding Trial   Working trials for herding dogs.

Hierarchy   A system of submission and dominance that dogs establish among one another. This is pack behavior that stems from their ancestors, the wolves.

Hip Dysplasia   An abnormal development of the hip. It is a genetic disorder that can be frustrated by environmental factors, such as excessive exercise in young pups and poor nutrition.

Hookworm (Ancylostoma caninum)   An intestinal parasite. In addition to sharing the host's food, these parasites suck blood, which often causes anemia.

Housebreaking   The process of training a dog to eliminate outside or on paper.

Hybrid Vigor   A theory that due to the larger genetic pools, mixed breeds are superior in health and temperament than purebred dogs.

Hyper Isolation Anxiety (HIA)   Dogs who are over-isolated suffer from lack of stimulation and direction. This creates anxiety, canine style, which results in hyper behaviors, such as destructive chewing, excessive elimination, barking, or digging.

Kick Back   A step back taken by the owner to force the dog into a good heel position.

Leading   A technique used with the Teaching Lead® to establish control and dominance over your dog.

Let's Go   A command used whenever you start walking (casually, not heel) or changing direction.

Long Lines   Long leashes for gradual off-leash training. There are three different kinds: the tree line, drag line, and house line.

Look for Rain   A technique of folding your arms under your chin and ignoring your dog until he calms down.

Lure Coursing   Working trials for sight hounds.

Lyme Disease   A tick-transported disease affecting the joint and neurological processes.

Maternal Immunity   A puppy has maternal immunity, via nursing, from the same diseases as his mother for a short time.

National Research Council (NRC)   Company that researches ingredients before they are allowed in dog food.

Negative Attention   The principal that even if you give your dog negative attention, such as "No!" for an unwanted behavior, it is still attention and the dog will learn to repeat this behavior.

Neuter/Spay   To neuter/spay a dog is to remove his/her reproductive organs so he/she cannot have puppies.

No Pull Harness   A harness that tightens around your dog's underarms when he pulls. It is an effective way to curb pulling on leash, although it's not an effective training tool.

Nylon Training Collar   An "original" training collar made of nylon; these collars work best on fine-haired dogs with sensitive necks.

Original Training Collar (a.k.a. the "choke chain")   A chain-linked collar that tightens around your dog's neck when pulled. It is the sound of the collar, not the restraint, that teaches.

Parasite   An organism that depends on another organism (its host) for everything—food, shelter, and so on.

Peacock Position   The position from which to give your dog commands; stand tall like a peacock with your shoulders back.

Penny Can   An empty can filled with ten pennies that's used to startle a dog when he's doing something inappropriate.

Predatory Aggression   An instinctive behavior to prey on and/or kill another animal.

Prize Envy   Confrontation, canine style. If your dog is holding something and you approach threateningly, he assumes that whatever he has in his mouth must be valuable because you are challenging him for the prize.

Psychotic Aggression   Erratic or fearful aggression responses in very atypical situations; resulting from early stress, this is often seen in puppy mill puppies.

Restraining Technique   In accidents, a dog might bite out of fear or pain. To prevent that, restraining techniques are used. The most common is to wrap a piece of fabric around the dog's muzzle and then neck. Other restraining techniques are designed to prevent the dog from self-injury. For example, when the dog has broken a bone, you are going to want to transport him on a flat board.

Rocky Mountain Spotted Fever   A tick-transported disease.

Seat Belt Safety Lead (SBSL)™   An eight-inch lead. The buckle attaches to your dog's collar and the handle to a car's seat belt. Now you can set up a car station with blankets and toys. This is a safe way to transport your dog.

"Self-Correcting" Collar (a.k.a. the "Prong Collar")   This collar is for dogs who are insensitive to pain. It is ideal for dogs who continually choke themselves on the original training collar.

Settle Down   This command is used when instructing your dog to calm down at your side or go to his designated station.

Shelter Shock   The traumatizing effect of being in a shelter can leave some dogs low-spirited and problematic.

Shock   A life-threatening state resulting from loss of blood, sudden trauma, or drop in blood pressure.

Short Lead   A short (eight-inch) lead that can double as a car lead. It is a great way to control your dog around the house when he's running free.

Sit   A command used to make your dog sit.

Spatial Aggression   A dog who shows aggression while eating, sleeping, grooming, or being medicated by a family member or stranger.

Stationing   A special area in each room that is your dog's designated space. He is told to "Settle down" and secured with the Teaching Lead®.

Stay   The command that requires a dog to stay in the same position for a certain amount of time.

Stimulated Sprinkling   A subconscious release of urine; stimulated when excited or afraid.

Stool Swallowing (Corprophagia)   Dogs who swallow stool—both their own and other creatures'.

Teaching Lead®   A leather leash patented by the author. It is specially designed to attach around your waist or to a stationary object. It helps keep your dog with you when you're home so you can train him passively.

Therapy Dogs   Dogs that are specially trained to visit and provide loving companionship for the elderly or people with certain disabilities or diseases.

Tone   There are three types of tones that your dog understands: Delighted, Directive, and Discipline.

Tourniquet   A device used when a major artery has been cut that stops the loss of blood.

Tracking   Working trials testing a dog's ability to track a human or lost article. These trials are open to dogs of any breed.

Treat Cup   A cup with treats in it. This method is an effective way to get your dog to give you what he is chewing or biting on.

USDA Approved Travel Kennel   A kennel approved for air travel.

U.S. Dog Agility Association   A club that sets the guidelines for agility events and runs agility matches.

Vaccination   Injections of small amounts of a specified disease to build a dog's immunity to that disease.

Wait and OK   A command used to control your dog in doorways, on curbs, or on stairs.

Zipper Snap   The sound of the original training collar (choke chain) when used correctly. It is this sound that teaches the dog, not the restraint.

Index

Use these tools and you'll have a perfect dog in no time ...it's as easy as ONE, TWO, THREE!

① THE TEACHING LEAD® VIDEO

Sarah Hodgson teaches the most up-to-date and humane training techniques using The Teaching Lead® and this entertaining and informative three-part video.

② THE TEACHING LEAD®

The durable Teaching Lead® and its accompanying booklet train your dog to follow your lead - not vice versa.

③ THE SEAT BELT SAFETY LEAD (SBSL)/SHORT LEAD

Finally, a way to calm your dog in the car and gain quick control around you home.

ORDER NOW!

Available exclusively from:
**Sarah Hodgson
The Cooperative Canine
Corporation
P.O. Box 420
Bedford Village, NY 10506**

The Teaching Lead® Video $24.95
The Teaching Lead®...$19.95
The Seat Belt Safety Lead (SBSL)/Short Lead ....$ 9.95
Order all three items for only $49.95

Please add:
  Shipping and Handling $3.95
  6.75% New York Sales Tax .... $_____

My check for $_____ is enclosed.

NAME AND BREED OF DOG_____

ADDRESS _____

CITY _____ STATE _____ ZIP CODE _____

SIGNATURE

When You're Smart Enough to Know
That You Don't Know It All

For all the ups and downs you're sure to encounter in life, The Complete Idiot's Guides give you down-to-earth answers and practical solutions.

Lifestyle

The Complete Idiot's Guide to Learning French on Your Own
ISBN: 0-02-861043-1 ▪ $16.95

The Complete Idiot's Guide to Learning Spanish on Your Own
ISBN: 0-02-861040-7 ▪ $16.95

The Complete Idiot's Guide to Successful Gambling
ISBN: 0-02-861102-0 ▪ $16.95

The Complete Idiot's Guide to Hiking and Camping
ISBN: 0-02-861100-4 ▪ $16.95

The Complete Idiot's Guide to Choosing, Training, and Raising a Dog
ISBN: 0-02-861098-9 ▪ $16.95

The Complete Idiot's Guide to Trouble-Free Car Care
ISBN: 0-02-861041-5 ▪ $16.95

The Complete Idiot's Guide to Trouble-Free Home Repair
ISBN: 0-02-861042-3 ▪ $16.95

The Complete Idiot's Guide to Dating
ISBN: 0-02-861052-0 ▪ $14.95

The Complete Idiot's Guide to Cooking Basics
ISBN: 1-56761-523-6 ▪ $16.99

The Complete Idiot's Guide to the Perfect Wedding
ISBN: 1-56761-532-5 ▪ $16.99

The Complete Idiot's Guide to the Perfect Vacation
ISBN: 1-56761-531-7 ▪ $14.99

The Complete Idiot's Guide to Getting and Keeping Your Perfect Body
ISBN: 0-02-861051-2 ▪ $14.95

The Complete Idiot's Guide to First Aid Basics
ISBN: 0-02-861099-7 ▪ $16.95

Personal Business

The Complete Idiot's Guide to Getting Into College
ISBN: 1-56761-508-2 ▪ $14.95

The Complete Idiot's Guide to Terrific Business Writing
ISBN: 0-02-861097-0 ▪ $16.95

The Complete Idiot's Guide to Surviving Divorce
ISBN: 0-02-861101-2 ▪ $16.95

The Complete Idiot's Guide to Managing Your Time
ISBN: 0-02-861039-3 ▪ $14.95

The Complete Idiot's Guide to Speaking in Public with Confidence
ISBN: 0-02-861038-5 ▪ $16.95

The Complete Idiot's Guide to Winning Through Negotiation
ISBN: 0-02-861037-7 ▪ $16.95

The Complete Idiot's Guide to Managing People
ISBN: 0-02-861036-9 ▪ $18.95

The Complete Idiot's Guide to Starting Your Own Business
ISBN: 1-56761-529-5 ▪ $16.99

The Complete Idiot's Guide to a Great Retirement
ISBN: 1-56761-601-1 ▪ $16.95

The Complete Idiot's Guide to Protecting Yourself From Everyday Legal Hassles
ISBN: 1-56761-602-X ▪ $16.99

The Complete Idiot's Guide to Getting the Job You Want
ISBN: 1-56761-608-9 ▪ $24.95

Personal Finance

The Complete Idiot's Guide to Buying Insurance and Annuities
ISBN: 0-02-861113-6 ▪ $16.95

The Complete Idiot's Guide to Doing Your Income Taxes 1996
ISBN: 1-56761-586-4 ▪ $14.99

The Complete Idiot's Guide to Getting Rich
ISBN: 1-56761-509-0 ▪ S16.95

The Complete Idiot's Guide to Making Money with Mutual Funds
ISBN: 1-56761-637-2 ▪ $16.95

The Complete Idiot's Guide to Managing Your Money
ISBN: 1-56761-530-9 ▪ $16.95

The Complete Idiot's Guide to Buying and Selling a Home
ISBN: 1-56761-510-4 ▪ $16.95

You can handle it!
Look for The Complete Idiot's Guides at your favorite bookstore, or call 1-800-428-5331 for more information.